PREFACE

The present volume of translations of Dutch records in the Albany county clerk's office consists of two parts: (1) a miscellaneous record of deeds, mortgages, bonds, powers of attorney and depositions running from January 10, 1658, to November 4, 1660; (2) a series of wills, inventories and settlements of estates ranging in date from January 5, 168$\frac{0}{1}$, to October 30, 1765. The record of deeds, etc., covers the last 221 pages of a folio volume of 447 pages, of which the first 211 pages consist of minutes of the court of Fort Orange and the village of Beverwyck from January 8, 1658, to December 31, 1659, and the intervening 15 pages are blank. The front cover of this volume bears the title *Fort Orange Proceedings. Deeds. Indian Treaties. Bills of Sale &c. Bonds &c. Powers of Attorney. Jan. 1652 to Nov. 1660*, whereas the back is lettered at the top *Court Minutes 2, 1658-1660*, and below it, in larger type, *Mortgage No. 1, 1652-1660*. The latter title, by which the volume is generally cited, is a misnomer, based on an inscription in an early hand on the last page, which reads: "Mortages A." The date 1652, which appears both on the back and on the front cover of the volume, is a mistake, due to the appearance of the date April 10, 1652, at the top of the first page of the court minutes, which refers to the time when the court was established. The deeds and other instruments are all acknowledged before Johannes La Montagne, commissary of Fort Orange, and like the court minutes they are in the handwriting of the clerk, Johannes Provoost. The two records are closely related, the information in the court minutes being supplemented by that in the depositions and many of the bonds and mortgages being executed in pursuance of judgments of the court, so that for a complete understanding of the text the two records should be consulted together. Nevertheless, although a full translation of the court minutes for 1658-59 is among Professor Pearson's writings, only the record of deeds, etc., has been printed herewith, it having been thought best to reserve the court minutes till some future time when it may be possible to publish the entire series of minutes from 1652 to 1686 in regular order. Meanwhile, an abstract of the minutes of 1658-59, which appears between similar abstracts of Fort Orange records for 1656-57 and 1660 in the *Calendar of Historical Manuscripts, Dutch*, edited by E. B. O'Callaghan, Albany 1865, pages 317-22, will be found helpful.

As to the record of deeds, etc., an examination of the dates of the documents will show that it consists in reality of a consecutive register running from January 10, 1658, to July 15, 1659, to which have been added three documents dated respectively October 31, 1659, April 10, 1660, and November 4, 1660. The consecutive portion of the record forms the connecting link between two similar records kept by Johannes Provoost that are included in volumes 1 and 2 of *Deeds,* one ending on December 17, 1657, and the other beginning on July 16, 1659, (see *Early Records of Albany,* 1:63 and 248), a fact that appears to have been overlooked by Professor Pearson, who in the preface to the volume just mentioned speaks of this portion of the record as being " unfortunately missing."

Like the other records of earlier and later date, the present record has a practical as well as a historical and genealogical value in that it contains documents needed to complete the chain of title to various pieces of real estate. An interesting feature which distinguishes this record from similar ones of a later period is the large number of public sales of houses and lots. This method of disposing of real estate, which was very common up to about 1664, suggests that there was considerable speculation in such property, but also that among the population of Beverwyck there were many traders who secured only a temporary residence there in order to obtain the right to trade.

As to the wills and inventories and settlements of estates which constitute the second part of this volume, these are taken from a manuscript volume which on the back is labeled *Wills, Part 1 & 2, 1691–1835.* As the title indicates, this volume is made up of two parts, the first of which consists of an index and 370 pages and is entitled " Record of Letters of Administration &^{a}. Begunn y^e. 6th. of Octob^r. 1691," and the second contains 145 pages and is entitled " Book of Wills N°. 2. Began the 8th..day of June 1773. By: Step De Lancey Clerk." Though the first entry in the record is dated October 8, 1691, a few of the documents recorded are of earlier date, the earliest one being a will executed on January 5, 168$\frac{4}{5}$, before Notary Adriaen van Ilpendam. Most of the documents are in English, but some are recorded in the Dutch language, the original text being in one or two cases accompanied by an English translation. Some of the wills are followed by letters of administration issued by the court of common pleas of Albany county, others have at the end a statement that the will was proved before the court by the witnesses, and still others have appended to them a certificate of probate granted by the court, all in accordance with the act entitled "An act for the superviseing Intestates Estates, and Regulateing the Probate of Wills and granting of Letters of Administracon," passed November 11, 1692, which provides in part as follows:

And be it further Enacted by the authority aforesaid that the Probate of all Wills and Letters of Administration shall be from hence forth granted by the Governour or Such Person as he shall Delegate under the seal of the Prerogative Office for that purpose appointed and that all Wills relating to any Estate within the severall County's of Orange and Richmond West Chester Kings County, shall be proved at New-York before the Governr or such Person, as he shall delegate as aforsayd, but in reguard of the remoteness of the other County's from New York, and to Prevent the great charge and Inconveniency's of bringing witnesses so far, the court of Common Ples in each of these remote Countys, are hereby impowred and authorised to take the examination of Witnesses to any will within their respective County's, upon Oath, and the same, with the will to certifye to the secret'ry's Office at New-York, with all Convenient Speed under the hand of the Judge and Clerk of the said Court that the Probate thereof may be granted accordingly. . . .

AND IT IS FURTHER ENACTED by the authority aforesaid that the severall Judges of the Respective Courts within the said Remote County's in Open Court and on Extraordinary occasions or necessity out of Court assisted with two Justices of the Peac aforesaid may and are hereby authorized and impowered to grant Probates, of any will or Letters of Administration to any Person or Psons where the Estate of the Person makeing such will or of the Intestate on which Letters of Administration is desired doth not exceed the value of fifty pounds any thing herein contained to the contrary hereof in any ways notwithstanding PROVIDED alwayes that any Person or Persons concerned in the Probate of Such Wills' or Letters of Administration to be granted by the Judge of the said Courts as aforesd may within three Months after the granting thereof bring his or their Appeale or apeales there in before the Governour, or such Person Delegated as aforesaid.

The present volume contains translations of all the documents in the above-mentioned volume of *Wills* that are recorded in the Dutch language, to which, for the sake of greater completeness, have been added copies of the accompanying affidavits of witnesses and certificates of probate, which are invariably written in English. For abstracts of the remaining documents in the volume, which are entirely in English, the reader is referred to the *Calendar of Wills*, compiled by Berthold Fernow, New York 1896.

In the preparation of this volume, which brings to a close the publication of Professor Pearson's translations, the same method has been followed that was employed in the preceding volumes of the series. All translations have been carefully revised by comparison with the originals, the spelling of proper names has been brought into accord with that used in the Dutch text and headings and explanatory footnotes have been added.

A. J. F. VAN LAER

March 1916

Part 1

DEEDS, MORTGAGES, CONTRACTS OF SALE, BONDS POWERS OF ATTORNEY AND DEPOSITIONS
JANUARY 10, 1658 — NOVEMBER 4, 1660

RECORDED IN

MORTGAGE NO. 1, 1652–1660

Conditions of public sale of a house and lot of Dirck Jansen Croon

[227][1] Terms and conditions on which Dirck Janssen Croon proposes to sell at public sale his house wherein Master Jacob[2] dwells.

First, there shall be delivered to the buyer the house and lot, the house standing at the outer [end] of his ground, with a leaden gutter fastened to both houses, and the lot extending to the kill,[3] with a small house behind, the house being bounded on the east side by Cornelis de Vos and on the west side by the seller's house and lot.

Delivery shall be made on the first of May 1658.

Payment shall be made in good, whole, merchantable beavers in two terms, the first on the first day of July of this year 1658, being the just half, and the second on the first day of July 1659, being the balance of the same.

The buyer shall be holden to furnish two sufficient sureties, jointly and severally [bound] as principals, to the satisfaction of the seller, within 24 hours. If the buyer is not able to furnish sufficient sureties within said time, then the premises shall be offered for sale again at his expense and charge and whatever less they shall bring

---

[1] Pages 1–211 contain the Proceedings of the Court of Fort Orange, village of Beverwyck and the dependencies thereof, from January 8, 1658, to December 10, 1659, and pages 212–26 are blank, page 225 being marked: "Records of Transports, &c., from 1658 to 1659."
[2] Jacob de Hinse, one of the early surgeons at Beverwyck.
[3] The Fuyck or Rutten kill, now Norton street. The house offered for sale stood on the lot now occupied by the National Commercial Bank on the south side of State street, the property of Cornelis de Vos, which adjoined it on the east, being situated west of Green street and not, as shown in the Diagrams of Lots in Beverwyck, in Munsell's *Collections*, 4:187, on the east side of that street.

he shall be holden to make good and whatever more they shall bring shall not inure to his benefit.

The auction fees shall be charged to the buyer.[4]

Conditions of public sale of a house and lot of Stoffel Jansen Abeel

[228 blank; 229] Terms and conditions on which Stoffel Janssen proposes to sell at public sale to the highest bidder his house and lot lying in the village of Beverwyck.

First, the house and lot shall be delivered to the buyer as it stands and is inclosed, east, west and north a street and to the south Gillis Pietersen,[5] excepting a hogpen.

Delivery shall be made on the first of May A°. 1658.

Payment shall be made in two instalments, the first on the first of July of this year A°. 1658, and the second on the first of July A°. 1659, in good, merchantable beavers.

The buyer shall be holden to give two sufficient sureties jointly and severally [bound] as principals to the satisfaction of the seller, within 24 hours. If the seller can not give sufficient sureties within the aforesaid time, then the premises shall again be sold at his expense and charge, and whatever less they shall bring he shall be holden to make good, and whatever more they shall bring, he shall not profit thereby.

The auction fees shall be charged to the buyer.[6]

Conditions of public sale of the house and lot of Gillis Pietersen

[230 blank; 231] Terms and conditions on which Gillis Pietersen proposes to sell at public sale to the highest bidder his house and lot lying in the village of Beverwyck.

First, the house with all that is fast by nail and earth shall be delivered to the buyer as it is now occupied by the seller, lying next to Stoffel Janssen Abeel, with the lot extending from one road to the other, in breadth thirty-five wood feet, leaving an alley of five feet on the south side.

Delivery shall be made on the last of May 1658.

---

[4] Canceled in the record, indicating that there was no sale.
[5] Compare deed from Jochem Wesselsen, the baker, to François Boon, August 8, 1665, old style, in *Early Records of Albany*, 1:78, where apparently the same property is described as "bounded on the east, west and south by the king's highway, and on the north the house of Gillis Pieterse."
[6] Canceled in the record.

Payments shall be made in two instalments, the first on delivery, the half in good, merchantable seawan, the other in good, deliverable beavers; the second payment on the last of May A°. 1659 also one-half in good, merchantable seawan and the other half in good, whole, deliverable beavers.

The buyer shall be holden to give two sufficient sureties jointly and severally [bound] as principals, to the satisfaction of the seller, within 24 hours.

If so be the buyer can not give sufficient sureties in the aforesaid time, then the premises shall be again sold at his expense and charge and whatever less they shall bring he shall make good, and whatever more they shall bring he shall not profit thereby.

The auction fees shall be charged to the buyer.[7]

Conditions of public sale of the house and lot of Jurriaen Teunissen Tappen

[232 blank; 233] Terms and conditions on which Jurriaen Teunissen Glasemaecker[8] proposes to sell at public sale to the highest bidder his house and lot lying in the village of Beverwyck.

First, there shall be delivered to the buyer the house with all that is fast by earth and nail (save his tools), lying on the third kill,[9] where he now dwells, with a lot along the wagon road, in length nine rods, breadth on the end of Jan de wever's[10] lot thirteen rods, breadth on the river side seven rods.

Delivery shall be made on the last of May 1658.

Payment shall be made in two instalments, the first on the last of June of this year A°. 1658, the second on the last of June A°. 1659, all in good, whole, deliverable beavers.

The buyer shall be holden to furnish two sufficient sureties within 24 hours to the satisfaction of the seller.

If the buyer can not furnish sufficient sureties within said time, the premises shall be again sold at his expense and charge and whatever less they shall bring he shall be holden to make good and whatever more they shall bring he shall receive no profit therefrom. The auction fees shall be charged to the buyer.

[234] After much bidding, [the bids being run] first up and

---
[7] Canceled in the record.
[8] Jurriaen Teunissen Tappen, the glazier.
[9] Vossen, or Fox, kill.
[10] Jan Martensen, the weaver.

then down, Jan Roeloffsen[11] remained the last bidder on the house of Jurriaen Teunissen according to the aforesaid conditions for the sum of one thousand nine hundred and ten guilders and Gillis Pietersz and Philip Gietersz became sureties for said sum, binding thereto their persons and estates, personal and real. Done in the village of Beverwyck on the 10th of January A°. 1658, in presence of Lowies Cobus and Johannes Provoost.

JAN ROELOFSEN
JELIS PIETERSE
PHILIP PIETERSEN

Ludouicus Cobes, witness

Conditions of public sale of the house and lot of Cornelis Wyncoop

[235] Terms and conditions on which Cornelis Wyncoop proposes to sell at public sale to the highest bidder his house and lot lying in the village of Beverwyck.

First, the house shall be delivered to the buyer, with all that is fast by earth and nail, with the lot behind it, entire length nine rods and breadth thirty feet.

Delivery shall be made on the first of May A°. 1658.

Payment shall be made ir good, whole, deliverable beavers in two instalments, the first on the first of July A°. 1658 and the other half or second payment on the first of July A°. 1659.

The buyer shall be holden to furnish within 24 hours two sufficient sureties jointly and severally bound as principals, to the satisfaction of the seller.

If the buyer can not furnish sufficient sureties within the aforesaid time, then the premises shall again be sold at the expense and charge of the buyer and whatever less they shall bring he shall be holden to make good and whatever more they shall bring shall not redound to his profit.

The auction fees shall be charged to the buyer.

[236] After much bidding Claes Ripsen remained the last bidder on the house of Cornelis Wyncoop on the aforesaid conditions for the sum of seven hundred and ninety guilders and Rutger Jacobsen

---

[11] Jan Roelofsen conveyed this house and lot to Pieter Hartgers on August 12, 1659; see *Early Records of Albany,* 1:269–70; also incomplete conditions of sale on page 267. Jan Roelofsen was the son of Anneke Jans by her first husband Roelof Jansen van Masterlant. The name "De Goyer," supplied by Professor Pearson, is a mistake.

and Teunis Jacobsz became sureties for said sum, binding thereto their persons and estates, personal and real. Done in the village of Beverwyck on the 10th of January A°. 1658, in presence of Lowies Cobussen and Johannes Provoost.

CAELS [12] RIPSEN VAN DAM
RUTGER JACOBSZ
TUENES JACOBSEN

Ludouicus Cobes, witness [13]

Contract of sale of a house and lot on the hill in Beverwyck from Willem Fredericksen to Goosen Gerritsen

[237] Appeared before me, Johannes de la Montagne, in the service of the Chartered West India Company, commissary [14] at Fort Orange, village of Beverwyck, etc., Willem Fredericksen, burgher and inhabitant here, who declared, as he hereby does declare, that he has transferred to the Honorable Goose Gerrits, burgher and inhabitant of this village, his heirs and assigns, a certain house lying in this village of Beverwyck on the hill, together with the lot, in length and breadth according to the patent, adjoining to the south Pieter Bronck, to the north Hendrick Andriesen, with all his right and title in and to said house and lot as he received the same from Lourens Lourensen by contract dated the 6th of October A°. 1657, for the sum of seven hundred and eight guilders, to be paid in two instalments in good, whole, salable beavers, to wit, on the first of June A°. 1658 the first payment and on the first of June A°. 1659 the second payment, renouncing all the right and interest therein which he may have by virtue of the above-mentioned contract. For the performance of this contract the grantor [238] and the grantee bind their persons and estates, personal and real, present and future, submitting the same to all courts and judges. Done in

---

[12] Thus in the original, intended for Claes.
[13] Cornelis Wyncoop gave a formal deed for the property on August $\frac{11}{21}$, 1666; see *Early Records of Albany,* 1:404 and 261. Cornelis Wyncoop was the ancestor of the Wyncoop family of America. He applied on November 25, 1659, for the appointment of administrators of the estate of his *neeve* (nephew, or cousin?) Gysbert Philipsen van Velthuysen, who had been killed by the Indians at the Esopus. A few years later he moved with his family to the Esopus. See Court Minutes, 1658-59, in *Mortgage No.* 1, p. 202 (Alb. co. cl. off.); *Early Records of Albany,* 1:46, 190; and *Doc. Rel. to Col. Hist. N. Y.,* 13:117.
[14] *Commies,* meaning the official in charge of a fort or trading post. Professor Pearson has variously translated this term as "clerk," and "deputy." See *Early Records of Albany,* v. 1, preface p. III, note; p. 2, 3, 6 etc.; also *Van Rensselaer Bowier Mss,* p. 27-28.

Fort Orange, the 11th of January A°. 1658, in presence of Philip Pietersz Schuyler, magistrate, and Dirck Jansen Croon, ex-magistrate.

This is the X mark of WILLEM FRERICKSEN
This is the X mark of GOOSEN GERRITS

Philip Pietersen Schuyler
Dirck Jansen Croon

Conditions of public sale of the house and lot of Pieter Bronck

[239] Terms and conditions on which Pieter Bronck proposes to sell at public sale to the highest bidder his house and lot lying in the village of Beverwyck on the hill.

First, the house shall be delivered to the buyer with all that is fast by earth and nail, together with the lot, in length twenty rods and in breadth five rods, according to the patent, with an Indian house, excepting a shed which is behind the house.

Delivery shall be made on the first of May 1658.

Payment shall be made in two instalments, the first in the middle of June A°. 1658, the second in the middle of September 1658, in good, whole, salable beavers.

The buyer shall be holden to furnish two sufficient sureties, jointly and severally liable as principals, to the satisfaction of the seller, within 24 hours.

If the buyer can not furnish sufficient sureties within said time, then the premises shall be sold again at his expense and charge and whatever less they shall bring, he shall make good and whatever more they shall bring shall not redound to his profit.

The auction fees shall be charged to the buyer.[15]

Conditions of public sale of the house and lot of Reyer Elbertson

[240 blank; 241] Terms and conditions on which Reyer Elbertsz proposes to sell at public sale to the highest bidder his house and lot lying in the village of Beverwyck.

First, the house with all that is fast by earth and nail shall be delivered to the buyer together with the lot, six rods in length and four rods in breadth.

Delivery of the aforesaid house and lot shall be made on the first of May of this year A°. 1658.

---

[15] Canceled in the record. The property was again offered for sale at the end of July, 1659; see *Early Records of Albany;* 1:266.

Payment shall be made in three instalments, the first on delivery in good, merchantable seawan; the second on the first of July next coming in good, whole, deliverable beavers; the third one year therefrom, on the first of July 1659, in good, deliverable beavers. The buyer shall be holden to furnish two sufficient sureties within 24 hours to the satisfaction of the seller.

If the buyer can not furnish sufficient sureties in said time, then the premises shall be sold again at his expense and charge and whatever less they shall bring he shall be holden to make good, and whatever more they shall bring he shall not profit thereby.

The auction fees shall be charged to the buyer.

After much bidding Johan Baptist van Rencelaer remained the last bidder for the house of Reyer Albertsen [242] for the sum of eight hundred and fifty-six guilders, according to the aforesaid conditions, for which sum Goossen Gerritsen and Cornelis Teunissen, as sureties and principals, bind their persons and estates, real and personal. Done in the village of Beverwyck, this 17th of January A°. 1658, in presence of Lowies Cobussen and Johannes Provoost.

JAN BAPTIST VAN RENSSELAER
CORNELUS THONISEN [16]
This is the X mark of GOOSEN GERRITSEN

Ludouicus Cobes, witness
Johannes Provoost

Conditions of public sale of the house and lot of Cornelis Segersen van Voorhout

[245][17] Terms and conditions on which Cornelis Segersen proposes to sell at public sale to the highest bidder his house and lot lying in the village of Beverwyck, on the hill.

First, the house with all that is fast by earth and nail shall be delivered to the buyer, with the lot, nine rods long along the road, in breadth to the west on the hill six rods and three feet, to the east five rods, one or two feet more or less, to the north nine rods.

Delivery of the aforesaid house and lot shall be made on the first of May 1658.

Payment shall be made in two instalments, the first on the first

---

[16] Cornelis Teunissen Bos, from Westbroeck.
[17] Page 243 contains a canceled draft of the same terms and conditions and page 244 is blank.

of July A°. 1658 and the second on the first of July A°. 1659, in good, whole, deliverable beavers.

The buyer shall be holden to furnish two sufficient sureties, jointly and severally [liable] as principals to the satisfaction of the seller within 24 hours.

If the buyer can not furnish sufficient sureties within said time the premises shall be sold again at his expense and charge and whatever less they shall bring he shall be holden to make good and whatever more they shall bring he shall profit nothing thereby.

The auction fees shall be charged to the buyer.

After much bidding, Gerrit Slechtenhorst remained the last bidder for the sum of one thousand four hundred and ten guilders on the aforesaid conditions and Mr Johan Baptist van Rencelaer [and Cornelis Thonissen] became sureties for said sum, binding thereto their persons and estates, real and personal. Done in the village of Beverwyck, on the 17th of January 1658, in presence of Lowies Cobussen and J. Provoost.[18]

       GERRIT VAN SLICHTENHORST
       JAN BAPTIST VAN RENSSELAER
       CORNELUS THONISEN

Ludouicus Cobes, witness
Johannes Provoost

Conditions of public sale of a lot on the hill owned by Cornelis Segersen van Voorhout

[246] Conditions on which Cornelis Segersen proposes to sell his lot lying on the hill to the north of Anderies Herbertsen.

First, there shall be delivered to the buyer the lot lying northerly of Anderies Herbertsz, along the road eight rods in length, to the west three rods and a half (two or three feet more or less) broad, to the east three rods broad.

Delivery shall be made at once.

Payment shall be made in two instalments, the first the middle of June of this year 1658 and the second on the first of June 1659, one year thereafter, in good, whole, deliverable beavers.

The buyer shall be holden to furnish two sufficient sureties within 24 hours to the satisfaction of the seller.

---

[18] Cf. deed from Cornelis Segersen to Gerrit van Slichtenhorst, December 10, 1660, in *Early Records of Albany,* 1:288.

If the buyer can not furnish sufficient sureties in said time then the premises shall be sold again at his expense and charge and whatever less they shall bring he shall be holden to make good and whatever more they shall bring he shall profit nothing thereby. The auction fees shall be charged to the buyer.[19]

Conditions of public sale of a lot of Cornelis Wyncoop

[247] Terms and conditions on which Cornelis Wyncoop proposes to sell at public sale to the highest bidder his lot lying next to Marcelis, to wit, to the north.

First, there shall be delivered to the buyer, the lot lying northerly of Marcelus Janssen, length nine and a half rods, breadth thirty feet, as the seller bought the same.

Delivery shall be made on the first of May A°. 1658.

Payment shall be made on the first of July of this year A°. 1658, in good, whole, deliverable beavers.

The buyer shall be holden to furnish two sufficient sureties within 24 hours to the satisfaction of the seller.

If the buyer can not furnish sufficient sureties in said time then the premises shall be sold again at his charge and expense and whatever less they shall bring he shall be holden to make good and whatever more they shall bring he shall profit nothing thereby.

The auction fees shall be charged to the buyer.

After much bidding Claes Ripsen remained the last bidder for the sum of one hundred and sixty-three guilders according to the above conditions and Philip Pietersen and Cornelis Woutersen[20] became sureties for said sum, binding thereto their persons and estates, real and personal. Done in the village of Beverwyck on the 17th of January 1658, in presence of Lowies Cobussen and J. Provoost.[21]

CLAES RIPSEN VAN DAM
COERNELIS COERNELISSEN
PHILIP PIETERSEN

Ludouicus Cobes
Johannes Provoost

---

[19] Canceled in the record.
[20] See signature, which is that of Cornelis Cornelissen van Sterrenvelt.
[21] See also public sale of January 10, 1658, in this volume and *Early Records of Albany*, 1:404 and 261.

Conditions of public sale of the house and lot of Pieter Meessen Vrooman

[248] Terms and conditions on which Pieter Meessen proposes to sell at public sale to the highest bidder his house and lot lying in the village of Beverwyck.

First, the house as it stands with all that is fast by earth and nail shall be delivered to the buyer with the lot, seven rods and some feet in length and four rods in breadth.

Delivery shall be made on the first of May next coming.

Payment shall be made in two instalments, the first on the first of June of this year 1658, the second on the first of June 1659; each payment, one-half in good, merchantable seawan and the other half in good, whole, deliverable beavers.

The buyer shall be holden to furnish two sufficient sureties, jointly and severally [liable] as principals, to the satisfaction of the seller, within 24 hours.

If the buyer can not furnish sufficient sureties within said time then the premises shall be sold again at his expense and charge and whatever less they shall bring, he shall be holden to make good and whatever more they shall come to, he shall profit nothing thereby.

The auction fees shall be charged to the buyer.

Conditions of public sale of the house and lot of Teunis Dircksen van Vechten

[249 blank; 250] Terms and conditions on which Teunis Dircksz proposes to sell at public sale to the highest bidder his house and lot lying to the south of Fort Orange, wherein Arent van [den]Berch lives.

First, the house with all that is fast by earth and nail shall be delivered to the buyer with the lot, twenty rods in length and eighteen rods in breadth, according to the patent thereof.

Delivery shall be made in the middle of May or on the 16th day of said month next ensuing.

Payment shall be made in three instalments, the first on the first of July of this year 1658, the second on the first of July 1659, the third on the first of July 1660, all in good, whole, deliverable beavers.

The buyer shall be holden to furnish two sufficient sureties, jointly and severally [liable] as principals, to the satisfaction of the seller, within 24 hours.

If the buyer can not furnish sufficient sureties within said time then the premises shall be sold again at his expense and charge, and whatever less they shall bring, he shall be holden to make good and whatever more they shall bring, he shall profit nothing thereby. The auction fees shall be charged to the buyer.

Conditions of public sale of the house of Hendrick Jochemsen

[251 blank; 252] Terms and conditions on which Henderick Jochimsen proposes to sell at public sale his house wherein Jan Cloet dwells, lying to the south of his house wherein he dwells.

First, the house with all that is fast by earth and nail shall be delivered to the buyer with the lot, as broad as the house and the lot south of the house are and in length to the Mr Rencelaer's fence, with a garden five rods long and four rods wide.

Delivery shall be made on the first of May 1658.

Payment shall be made in two instalments; the first on the first of July of this year 1658, in good, whole, deliverable beavers; the second on the first of October A°. 1658 in the same year, in good, merchantable seawan.

The buyer shall be holden to furnish two sufficient sureties within 24 hours. If the buyer can not furnish sufficient sureties within said time, then the premises shall be sold again at his expense and charge and whatever less they shall bring, he shall be holden to make good and whatever more they shall bring, he shall profit nothing thereby.

The auction fee shall be charged to the buyer.

Power of attorney from Teunis Jacobsen to Cornelis Teunissen Bosch

[253] Appeared before me, Johannes La Montagne, commissary at Fort Orange and the village of Beverwyck, Teunis Jacobsen, who declared that he had given power of attorney, as he does give hereby, to Cornelis Teunissen Bosch,[22] in the name of Willem Kock and of himself, by virtue of the assignment given by said Willem Kock, dated the 9th of February A°. 1653, to claim of the honorable West India Company at the office in Amsterdam in New Netherland the sum of one hundred and sixty-seven guilders and eight

---

[22] Cornelis Teunissen Bos, from Westbroeck, see *Van Rensselaer Bowier Mss*, p. 181, 814.

stivers, which to said Willem Kock is due by settlement of accounts signed by P. Stuyvesant and Carel van Bruggen, promising to hold good and valid all that shall be done in this matter. Done the 23d of February A°. 1658, in presence of Johannes Provoost and Jan Eerraers.

TUENES JACOBSEN

Johannes Provoost, witness
Johannes Eerraets[23]

Acknowledged before me,

LA MONTAGNE, *Commissary at Fort Orange*

Deed from Willem Hofmeyer to Jochem Wesselsen, the baker, of a lot and garden at Beverwyck

[254] Appeared before me, Johannes La Montagne, commissary at Fort Orange and the village of Beverwyck in the service of the General Chartered West India Company, in presence[24] of the Honorable Jacob Schermerhorn and Philip Pietersen, magistrates of the said jurisdiction, Willem Hofmeyer, who declared that he had conveyed, as he hereby does convey, in real and actual possession to and for the behoof of Jochim Wesselsen, his heirs and assigns, a certain lot lying in the village of Beverwyck, adjoining to the north Jochim Keteluyn, to the south and east a road, to the west a plain, breadth 4 rods, length 9 rods; together with a lot behind Fort Orange for a garden, bounded on the east side by Pieter Jacobsen,[25] on the north side by Lambert van Valckenborch, on the south and west sides by a road, almost triangular, seven rods long and three rods broad, according to the patent to the grantor given by the honorable director general and council of New Netherland, of date the 25th of October 1653,[26] for the sum of thirteen hundred guilders, of which sum the grantor acknowledges the

---

[23] Johannes Eerraets (Eerrats, Eerraerts, or Eeraerts) was a soldier from Wesel, on the Rhine, in Germany.

[24] In the Dutch documents a distinction is made between the expressions *ten overstaen van* and *ter presentie van,* the first being used in all formal transfers of land which had to be executed before two magistrates and the second being used in contracts of sale, powers of attorney and other instruments which were attested by ordinary witnesses. In Professor Pearson's translations both expressions have been rendered by the phrase " in the presence of."

[25] Pieter Jacobsen Bosboom.

[26] This patent, like all others of the same date, is lost. Cf. description of the same property in the patent to Adriaen van Ilpendam, May 21, 1667, cited in a note to the deed from Jochem Wesselsen to Van Ilpendam, March 14, 1658, printed on one of the following pages.

receipt of eight hundred guilders, for which he acquits the said Jochim Wesselsen; and as respects the remaining five hundred guilders, the said Wesselsen promises to pay the same in July 1658, with which the grantor is content; the parties binding their persons and estates, real and personal, submitting the same to all courts and judges. Done in Fort Orange, the 7th October [27] 1658.

WILLEM HOFFMEYER
JOCH BACKER[28]

Acknowledged before me,

LA MONTAGNE, *Commissary at Fort Orange*

Power of attorney from Jan Bembo to Philip Pietersen Schuyler

[255] Appeared before me, Johannes La Montagne, in the service of the General Chartered West India Company commissary at Fort Orange, village of Beverwyck, etc., Jan Bemboo,[29] a soldier of the honorable West India Company, who declared that he had empowered, as he hereby does empower, the Honorable Philip Pietersen Schuyler to claim, demand and receive in the principal's name from the honorable director general or his commissary the sum of four hundred and fifty-four guilders and five stivers, for service rendered by said Bembo to the honorable directors in New Netherland, as appears by the accounting under date of A°. 1656, signed on the credit side P. Stuyvesant and on the debit side Carel van Bruggen; [the principal] promising to hold good and valid all that the attorney shall do in the matter, binding thereto his person and estate, real and personal, under submission to all courts and judges. Done in Fort Orange, the 8th of March A°. 1658, in presence of Gerrit Willemsen and Jan Eeraerts.

JAN BEMBO

Johannes Eerrats

This is the X mark of *Gerrit Willemsen*

Acknowledged before me,

LA MONTAGNE, *Commissary at Fort Orange*

Power of attorney from Arent van den Berch to Jan Thomassen

[256] Appeared before me, J. La Montagne, commissary at Fort Orange and the village of Beverwyck in the service of the General

---

[27] Thus in the original; probably a mistake for the 7th of March.
[28] Jochem Wesselsen, the baker.
[29] Jan Bembo van Lingen; see *Early Records of Albany*, 1:10. Lingen is a town in Hanover.

Chartered West India Company, Arent vanden Berch, who declared that he had empowered, as he hereby does empower, the Honorable Jan Tomassen in the name and on behalf of the principal to demand and receive from the honorable director general or his commissary at Amsterdam in New Netherland an account and payment thereof amounting to the sum of six hundred and sixty-eight guilders and nine stivers, earned by the principal of the honorable West India Company at Amsterdam in New Netherland; [the principal] promising to hold good and valid whatever the attorney shall do in the matter, binding thereto his person and estate, real and personal, submitting the same to all courts and judges. Done in Fort Orange, this 14th of March A°. 1658, in presence of J. Provoost and Jan Eerraerts.

This is the mark AB of ARENT VANDEN BERCH

Johannes Provoost, witness
Johannes Eerraets

Acknowledged before me,

LA MONTAGNE, *Commissary at Fort Orange*

Conditions of public sale of two sawmills belonging to Evert Pels

[257] Terms and conditions on which Evert Pels proposes to sell at public sale to the highest bidder his two sawmills lying in the colony of Rencelaerswyck.[80]

The two mills shall be delivered to the buyer with their appurtenances.

With the upper mill there shall be delivered an iron crank, an iron pinion, an iron rack and two marking irons.

With the lower mill there shall be delivered a wooden wheel, an iron rack and an iron crank.

For both mills shall be delivered 10 saws such as they are, sixteen iron bars, two peaveys, two cant hooks, three files, eight racks, a saw-set, a pair of iron sledge hammers, two axes.

The buyer shall be holden to carry out the contract made between the patroon and the seller.

The buyer shall have the right of the road from the upper mill as it has been used by the seller without damage to the farm.

---

[80] Situated on the Mill creek, behind the *greene bosch* (Greenbush), on the east side of the Hudson river. See deed from Willem Fredericksen Bout to Evert Pels, March 17, 1659, for a house, lot and garden in Beverwyck, in exchange for these two mills, on page 99 of this volume.

Delivery of the aforesaid mills shall be made tomorrow, being the 15th of March.

Payment shall be made in two instalments, the first on the 15th of June A°. 1658, in good, whole, merchantable beavers, the second on the 15th of June A°. 1659, in good, merchantable seawan at fl. 10 the beaver.

The buyer shall be holden to furnish two sufficient sureties within 24 hours to the satisfaction of the seller.

If the buyer does not furnish sufficient sureties within said time, then the mills shall be sold again at his charge and [258] expense and whatever less they shall bring he shall be holden to make good and whatever more they shall bring he shall not benefit by.

The auction fees shall be charged to the buyer.

Whoever shall be the buyer shall have the privilege of buying the seller's logs for so much as they cost him in cutting, drawing and other expenses, to be paid in boards.

Conditions of public sale of a house in Fort Orange belonging to Evert Pels

[259] Terms and conditions on which Evert Pels proposes to sell at public sale to the highest bidder his house situated in Fort Orange.

First, the house shall be delivered to the buyer as it stands, with all that is fast by earth and nail, about 39 or 40 feet in length, lying next the house of Jacob Schermerhoorn and J. van Twillert.

The delivery shall be made tomorrow, being the 15th of March.

The payment shall be made in two instalments, the first on the 15th of June A°. 1658, one-half in good, whole, deliverable beavers and the other half in good, merchantable seawan, and the second payment on the 15th of June A°. 1659, one-half also in good, whole, deliverable beavers and the other half in good, merchantable seawan at ten guilders a beaver.

The buyer shall be holden to furnish two sufficient sureties, jointly and severally [liable] as principals, to the satisfaction of the seller, within 24 hours. If the buyer can not furnish sufficient sureties within said time, then the premises shall be sold again at his expense and charge, and whatever less they shall bring, he shall be holden to make good and whatever more they shall bring shall not be to his profit.

The auction fees shall be charged to the buyer.[31]

---

[31] Apparently no sale. Cf. deed from Evert Pels to Jan Barentsen Wemp, February 4, 1661, in *Early Records of Albany*, 1:291.

Deed from Jochem Wesselsen, the baker, to Adriaen Jansen van Ilpendam of a lot and garden at Beverwyck (not executed)

[260] Appeared before me, J. La Montagne, in the service of the General Chartered West India Company vice director and commissary at Fort Orange and the village of Beverwyck, in the presence of the Honorable Philip Pietersen and Jacob Schermerhoorn, magistrates of said jurisdiction, Jochim Wesselsen, who declared that he had conveyed, as he hereby does convey and grant in real and actual possession, to the behoof of Adriaen Janssen van Ilpendam, his heirs and assigns, a certain lot lying in the village of Beverwyck adjoining to the north Jochim Kettelluyn, to the south and east a common highway, to the west a plain, breadth 4 rods, length 9 rods, together with a lot behind Fort Orange for a garden, bounded on the east side by Pieter Jacobsen, on the north side by Lambert van Valckenborch, on the south and west sides a road, almost triangular, length seven rods and breadth three rods,[32] by conveyance granted by William Hoffemeyer to said Jochim Wesselsen upon title given to said Hofmeyer by patent from the honorable director general and council of New Netherland dated the 25th of October 1653, for a certain sum the receipt of which Jochim Wesselsen acknowledges, promising to free the said lot and garden from all claims and demands which may be made thereon, for which he binds his person and estate, personal and real, submitting the same to all courts and judges. Done in Fort Orange, the 14th of March A°. 1658.[33]

---

[32] *belenden[de] ten noorden Jochem Kettelluyn ten suyden en[de] ten oosten een gemeene wech, ten westen een pleyn, breedt vier Roeden, lanck 9 roeden, mitsgaders een erff achter de fortress Orange tot een tuyn, bepalende aende oostsyde Pieter Jacobsen. aende Noordt syde Lambert van Valckenborch, aende suyt en[de] west syde een wech, meest driekant, lanck seven roeden, en[de] breedt drie Roeden.*" Cf. description in patent of May 21, 1667, cited in following note.

[33] Not executed. Cf. contract of sale between Jochem Wesselsen and Adriaen van Ilpendam, February 28, 1656, with receipts of Jochem Wesselsen, *Early Records of Albany*, 1:228–29. Van Ilpendam received a patent for this lot and garden on May 21, 1667, which refers to this deed of March 14, 1658, and in which the property is described as follows: "a certain Lott of Ground lying in Beverwyck at Albany having to the North Jochem Kettlehuyns, to the South & East the Common highway & to the West the plaine. To which sd Lott there being an addicon of Ground graunted by the Commissaryes to the sd Adriaen Jansen van Ilpendam, as it now lyes it abutteth to the North on Jacob Tyssen vander Heydens to the East on Jellis Pieters, & to the West & South the Common Highway, in all conteyning in length on the South side nine Rod & on the North side eight Rod, eight foot, & one Inch, in breadth on the East side four Rod tenn foot, & tenn Inches. Together W.th a Lott of Ground & Garden in the sd Transport menconed lying behind the Fort on the East side of Pieter Jacobs, on the North side of Lambert van Valchemburgh, on the South & West side of the Highway, allmost in a Triangle, being in length seaven Rod, & in breadth three Rod."

Bond of Cornelis Cornelissen Sterrenvelt and Pieter Meessen Vrooman as sureties for Jan Andriessen de Graeff and Pieter Jacobsen Bosboom

[261] Appeared before me, J. La Montagne, in the service of the General Chartered West India Company, commissary at Fort Orange and the village of Beverwyck, Cornelis Cornelissen wouters and Pieter Meessen, inhabitants of the aforesaid village of Beverwyck, who declared, as they hereby do declare, that they bind themselves as sureties and principals for the persons of Jan Anderiessen de Graeff and Pieter Jacobsen Bosboom in the sum of two hundred and fifty guilders and two beavers in specie or ten guilders in seawan for each beaver current payment, which sum they promise to pay on the 15th of July of this year 1658, submitting thereto their persons and estates, personal and real, to all courts and judges. Done in Fort Orange, the 16th of March 1658, in presence of Lowies Cobussen and Nataniel Pietersen.[34]

       PIETER MEESZ VROOMAN
       COERNELIS COERNELISSEN STERRENUELT

Ludouicus Cobes
Nataniel Pietersen

Acknowledged before me,

  LA MONTAGNE, *Commissary at Fort Orange*

Bond of Rem Jansen as surety for Michiel Poulussen

[262] Appeared before me, J. La Montagne, in the service of the General Chartered West India Company commissary at Fort Orange, Rem Yanssen, who binds himself as surety for Michiel Poulussen in the sum of one hundred and sixty-eight guilders, to be paid to Cornelis Cornelissen, submitting thereto his person and estate, personal and real. Done in Fort Orange, the 26th of March 1658, in presence of Barent Albertsz and Johannes Provoost.

       REM YANSZEN

This is the X mark of *Barent Allertsen*
Johannes Provoost, witness

Acknowledged before me,

  LA MONTAGNE, *Commissary at Fort Orange*

---

[34] This bond was for the payment of a fine imposed on March 11, 1658, on Jan Andriessen de Graeff and Pieter Jacobsen Bosboom for swindling an Indian; see *Calendar of Dutch Manuscripts*, p. 318.

Bill of sale of a sloop from Pieter Lourensen to Jan Martensen

[263] On this first day of May A°. 1658, appeared before me, Johannes La Montagne, commissary at Fort Orange and the village of Beverwyck, Pieter Lourensen, who declared that he had conveyed, as he hereby does convey, in full ownership to Jan Martensen his sloop with all its appurtenances, named *de Hoop* (the Hope), which sloop said Jan Martensen declares that he has accepted and received to his satisfaction for the number of five hundred and fifty merchantable pine boards, to be delivered in two parcels, to wit, three hundred in the month of May of this year A°. 1658, and the remainder of the same in the month of May A°. 1659, binding thereto his person and estate, personal and real, submitting the same to all courts and judges. Done in Fort Orange, this first of May A°. 1658, in presence of Johannes Provoost and Zacharias Sickels.[35]

This is the mark + of PIETER LOURENSEN
This is the mark + of IAN MARTENSEN

Johannes Provoost, witness
Sacharys Seckels

Acknowledged before me,

LA MONTAGNE, *Commissary at Fort Orange*

Power of attorney from Arent Jansen to Willem Jansen at Amsterdam

[264] Appeared before me, J. La Montagne, in the service of the General Chartered West India Company vice director and commissary at Fort Orange and the village of Beverwyck, in the presence of the hereinafter named witnesses, Arent Janssen, who declared that he had constituted, as he does hereby constitute, Willem Janssen, dwelling at Amsterdam, his attorney, in his, the principal's, name and in his behalf to collect and to receive all debts and all that is coming to the principal there, and for the receipts acquittance to give, promising to hold good and valid all that the attorney shall do in said matter, binding thereto his person and estate, personal and real, submitting the same to all courts and

---

[35] Zacharias Sickles was a corporal in the service of the West India Company. He came from Weenen, or Vienna, Austria. See *Early Records of Albany*, 1:8, 255–56, 259.

judges. Done in Fort Orange, the 11th of May A°. 1658, in presence of Jan Lambertsen and Johannes Provoost.

ARENT JANSEN

This is the mark of X *Ian Lambertsen*
Johannes Provoost, witness

Acknowledged before me,

LA MONTAGNE, *Commissary at Fort Orange*

Conditions of public sale of a sloop of Albert Andriessen and Willem Martensen

[265] Terms and conditions upon which Albert Anderiessen and Willem Martensen propose to sell at public sale to the highest bidder their sloop as it rides [at anchor] and sails.[36]

First, the sloop shall be delivered to the buyer with its appurtenances, including a mizzen sail, a foresail, a flag, a pennant and a *geusjen*,[37] a kedge and an anchor and two cables; in the caboose there shall be delivered a kettle, a pan, two wooden benches, a pewter platter, tongs, a brass candlestick, an axe, everything as it is.

In the presence of the sureties, the boat was delivered this date.[38] The payment shall be in two instalments; the first on the first of June next ensuing in good, merchantable seawan and the second in good, whole, deliverable beavers to be paid on the last of July next ensuing.

The buyer shall be holden to furnish two sufficient sureties, jointly and severally [liable] as principals, to the satisfaction of this seller, within 24 hours.

If the buyer can not furnish sufficient sureties in the aforesaid time, [the sloop] shall be offered again at his expense and charge and whatever less it shall bring, he shall be holden to make good and whatever more it shall bring, he shall receive no profit therefrom.

[266] The auction fees shall be charged to the buyer.

---

[36] *Soo als het reedt ende seylt;* the same as the modern phrase *zooals het reilt en zeilt*, meaning, just as it is, with all its appurtenances.
[37] A small bowsprit flag. The name is derived from the *geuzen*, or *gueux*, or sea-beggars, who first used a flag composed of orange, white and blue, the orange being after 1630 gradually replaced by the more distinct and durable red. See J. C. de Jonge, *Geschiedenis van het Nederlandsche Zeewezen*, 1:165–71.
[38] The last sentence is interlined.

After much bidding, Willem Martensen remained the last bidder on the above-written conditions for the sum of one thousand one hundred and thirty guilders, for which he binds his person and estate, real and personal, submitting the same to all courts and judges. Done in the village of Beverwyck, the 15th of May A°. 1658, in presence of Lowies Cobussen and J. Provoost.

WILLEM MARTENSZ HUES

Ludouicus Cobes
Johannes Provoost, witness

Bond of Cornelis Teunissen and Thomas Jansen Mingael as sureties for Willem Martensen

Appeared before me, J. La Montagne, in the service of the General Chartered West India Company commissary at Fort Orange and the village of Beverwyck, Cornelis Teunissen and Tomas Janssen Mingael, who bind themselves as sureties and principals in the sum of one thousand one hundred and thirty guilders which Willem Martensen owes to Albert Anderiessen for the purchase of his sloop at public sale, submitting thereto their persons and estates, real and personal, to all courts and judges. Done in the village of Beverwyck, the 16th of May A°. 1658, in presence of Henderick Jochimsen and J. Provoost.

CORNELUS THONISEN [39]
THOMES JANSEN MINGAEL

Hendrick Jochemsz
Johannes Provoost, witness

Acknowledged before me,

LA MONTAGNE, *Commissary at Fort Orange*

Deposition of Sander Leendertsen Glen regarding the delivery of beavers to the late Willem Thomassen

[267] Appeared before me, Johannes La Montagne, in the service of the General Chartered West India Company commissary at Fort Orange and the village of Beverwyck, in presence of the Honorable Abraham Staets and Jan Tommassen, the worthy Sander Leendersen Geleyn,[40] who declared under solemn oath taken in our presence that by the hands of Willem Teljer he had delivered to the late Willem Tomassen, skipper, twenty-one pounds of coat

---

[39] Cornelis Teunissen Bos, from Westbroeck.
[40] A mistake for "Glen."

beaver,[41] to bring from Holland merchandise or goods for the aforesaid Sander Leendersen and not in payment of any debt. Done in Fort Orange, the 17th of May A°. 1658.

SANDER LENRSEN

Abram Staas
Jan Thomasz
Acknowledged before me,
LA MONTAGNE, *Commissary at Fort Orange*

Power of attorney from Daniel Rinckhout (incomplete)

[268] Appeared before me, Johannes La Montagne, in the service of the General Chartered West India Company commissary at Fort Orange and the village of Beverwyck, Daniel Rinckhout, who declared that he constituted . . . [not finished and canceled]

Conditions upon which Thomas Jansen Mingael proposes to sell his house at public sale

[269] Conditions and terms on which Tomas Janssen Mingael proposes to sell at public sale to the highest bidder his house situated in the village of Beverwyck opposite Mr Boon.[42]

First, the house shall be delivered to the buyer with all that is fast by earth and nail; furthermore, there shall be delivered . . . [remainder of page blank]

[270] After much bidding Teunis Teunissen *metselaer* remained the highest bidder.

[271] Tomas Janssen Mingael proposes to sell at public sale to the highest bidder his house situated in the village of Beverwyck over against Mr Boonnus.[43]

First, the house shall be delivered to the buyer with all that is fast by earth and nail; furthermore, the seller shall deliver the gable built up, in [the house] a chimney and a partition wall, the tiles and ridge tiles laid and the window panes set; together with a lot four rods in breadth and in length from the street in front to the back street, according to the patent thereof.

---

[41] *Rockbever.*
[42] François Boon. He married in 1654 Elisabeth Cornelis, the widow of Gysbert Cornelissen, from Weesp, the tavernkeeper. See *Early Records of Albany,* 1:193, 202, 365.
[43] François Boon.

Delivery shall be made on the 4th of June next coming.

Payment shall be made in three instalments, to wit: on delivery the buyer shall pay four hundred guilders in seawan; the second payment on the 15th of July next coming in good, whole, merchantable beavers; and the third payment on the first of July 1659, also in good, whole, merchantable beavers.

The buyer shall be holden to furnish two sufficient sureties, jointly and severally liable as principals, to the satisfaction of the seller, within 24 hours, and if the buyer can not furnish sufficient sureties in the aforesaid time then [the house] shall be sold again at his charge and expense and whatever less it shall bring, he shall be holden to make good and whatever more it shall bring, he shall profit nothing thereby.

The auction fees shall be charged to the buyer.

[272] Teunis Teunissen *metselaers* after much bidding remained the last bidder for the house of Tomas Janssen Mingael for the sum of one thousand four hundred and seven guilders according to the aforesaid conditions and as sureties and principals for the aforesaid sum the worthy Anderies Herbertsen and Reyer Albertsz have bound their persons and estates, real and personal. Done in the village of Beverwyck, the 20th of May A°. 1658, in presence of Loduvicus Cobus and Johannes Provoost.

TEUNIS TEUNISZ
ANDRIES HERBERTS

This is the mark X of REYER ALBERTSEN

Ludouicus Cobes
Johannes Provoost, witness

Acknowledged before me,

LA MONTAGNE, *Commissary at Fort Orange*

Conditions of public sale of the sloop of Hendrick Hendricksen Obe

[273] Terms and conditions on which Pieter Pietersen van Neften,[44] as attorney for Henderick Hendericksz Obe,[45] proposes to sell to the highest bidder at public sale the sloop of the said principal.

First, the aforesaid sloop named *Jan and Mary* shall be delivered to the buyer with all her appurtenances, to wit: a boat, two new hawsers, an anchor and a kedge, two yard sails, a topsail, a

---

[44] Given in *Records of New Amsterdam*, 7:16, as Pieter Pietersen van Nesten.
[45] Hendrick Hendricksen Obe was a resident of New Amsterdam.

flag, a compass and a night glass, a sounding line with the lead. In the caboose there shall be delivered one pot, one pan, one platter and a wooden bowl, one ladle; furthermore the running and standing rigging as it appears,[46] all according to the conveyance made by the curators appointed to take charge of the estate of Jems Butt to Henderick Hendericksen Obe.

The delivery shall be made tomorrow the 21st of May.

Payment for the aforesaid sloop shall be made in two instalments; the first payment in the middle of July of this year 1658, in good, whole, merchantable beavers; the second payment on the first of April A°. 1659, in good, whole, merchantable beavers.

[274] The buyer shall be holden to furnish two sufficient sureties, jointly and severally liable as principals, to the satisfaction of the seller, within twenty-four hours.

If the buyer can not furnish sufficient sureties within said time, then the sloop shall be again offered for sale at his charge and expense and whatever less it shall bring he shall be holden to make good and whatever more it shall bring he shall receive no profit from.

Deed from Evert Jansen Wendel to Hendrick van Bommel of a house and a third part of a lot at New Amsterdam

[275] Appeared before me, Johannes La Montagne, in the service of the General Chartered West India Company commissary at Fort Orange and the village of Beverwyck, in the presence of Pieter Hartgers and Françoys Boon, magistrates, Evert Janssen Wendel, who declared that he had conveyed, as he hereby does grant and convey, to Henderick van Bommel, his heirs and assigns, his house and a third part of his whole lot according to the patent to him, the grantor, given by the honorable director general and council of New Netherland, dated the 8th of February A°. 1647;[47] which house and lot are situated in Amsterdam in New Netherland; for which aforesaid house and lot the said grantor, Evert Jansse Wendel, has received to his satisfaction the sum of four hundred guilders from the Honorable Isaack de Foreest on account of Henderick van Bommel, wherefore the grantor releases the said Henderick van Bommel from all further demands and claims which

---

[46] At this point the following words are crossed out: "It is hereby stipulated, inasmuch as the aforesaid sloop is taken over by execution, that the seller releases [the buyer] from all future claims as far as this jurisdiction is concerned."

[47] Recorded in *Land Patents*, GG, p. 168, the lot being described as being on the Graft on Manhattan island.

may hereafter arise, binding thereto his person and property, real and personal under submission to all courts and judges. Done in Fort Orange, the 3d of June A°. 1658.

EVERT JANSEN WENDEL

Pieter Hartgertsz
Françoys Boon

Acknowledged before me,

LA MONTAGNE, *Commissary at Fort Orange*

[276] Appeared before me, Johannes La Montagne, in the service . . . [remainder of page blank]

Deed from Willem Jansen Stol to Huybert Jansen of a lot in Beverwyck

[277] Appeared before me, Johannes La Montagne, in the service of the General Chartered West India Company commissary at Fort Orange, and the village of Beverwyck, in the presence of the Honorable Pieter Hartgers and Fransois Boon, magistrates of said jurisdiction, Willem Jansen Stoll, inhabitant of said village of Beverwyck, who declared, as he hereby does declare, that he had conveyed, as he hereby does grant and convey, to the behoof of Huybert Jansen, his heirs and assigns, the half of a lot lying in the village of Beverwyck, to him the grantor, given by the honorable director general and council of New Netherland as appears by the patent thereof dated the 25th of October of the year 1653, which conveyed half is the south part of the whole lot that was granted, in length ten rods and in breadth two rods, bounded east and west by a common highway, on the south side by Pieter Loockerm[ans] ;[48] for which lot the grantor acknowledges satisfaction and payment by said Huybert Jansen, relinquishing all right and title which he may have to the same and promising the same to warrant against all demands and claims, for which he binds his person and estate, real and personal, present and future, submitting the same to all courts and judges. Done in Fort Orange, the 4th of June A°. 1658.

WILLEM JANSEN STOL

Françoys Boon
Pieter Hartgerts

Acknowledged before me,

LA MONTAGNE, *Commissary at Fort Orange*

---

[48] See note to next deed.

Deed from Huybert Jansen to Thomas Jansen Mingael of a lot in Beverwyck

[278 blank; 279] Appeared before me, Johannes La Montagne, in the service of the General Chartered West India Company commissary at Fort Orange and the village of Beverwyck, in the presence of the Honorable Pieter Hartgers and Fransois Boon, magistrates of said jurisdiction, Huybert Jansen, inhabitant of said village of Beverwyck, who declared, as he hereby does declare, that he had conveyed, as he hereby does grant and convey, to the behoof of Tomas Jansen, his heirs and assigns, the half of a lot lying in the village of Beverwyck, to Willem Jansen Stol granted by the honorable director general and council of New Netherland by patent dated the 25th of October of the year 1653, which conveyed lot is the southerly half of the whole lot so granted, in length ten rods and in breadth two rods, bounded east and west by a common highway, south by Pieter Loockermans; for which lot the grantor acknowledges that he has had satisfaction and payment from said Tomas Jansen, relinquishing all right and title which he may have thereto and promising the same to warrant against claims and demands, for which he binds his person and estate, real and personal, present and future, submitting the same to all courts and judges. Done in Fort Orange, the 4th of June A°. 1658.

This is the X mark of HUYBERT JANSEN, made by himself

Françoys Boon
Pieter Hartgertsz

Acknowledged before me,

LA MONTAGNE, *Commissary at Fort Orange*[40]

---

[40] This deed is referred to in a confirmatory patent to Jacob Gevinck, or Hevick, the abstract of which reads as follows: "A Patent Graunted upon a Transport made by Hubert Jansen unto Thomas Jansen Mingael bearing date the 4th day of June 1658 for the moyety or one halfe of a certain Lott of Ground lying in Beverwick at Albany being in Length tenn Rod, & in breadth two Rod having to the East and West the common Highway & to the south Pieter Loockermans. And there being also a Transport made by Juriaen Jansen Groenewout who married Maritien the widdow of Thomas Mingael deceased unto Hendrick Hendrickse at pres^t. the wife of Jacob Gevinck of the moyety, or one halfe of another certain Lott of Ground lying in the place aforesd together with the Housing thereupon being bounded in length & breadth as in the Groundbriefe of the 4th of June 1658 is set forth. Now the right & Interest in both the sd Transports being devolv'd upon the

Conditions of public sale of a small house belonging to Dirck Bensem

[280 blank; 281] Terms and conditions on which Dirck Bensich [50] proposes to sell at public sale his small house [51] standing in the village of Beverwyck.

First, the small house standing by said D[r]. Bensich's large house shall be delivered to the buyer with all that therein is fast by earth and nail, together with a lot in breadth, front and rear, 15 feet and ten rods in length.

Delivery shall be made on the 11th of June of this year 1658.

Payment shall be made in two instalments, both in whole, merchantable beavers, the first on delivery, the second on the 11th of July of the coming year A°. 1659.

The buyer shall be holden to furnish two sufficient sureties to the satisfaction of the seller.

If the buyer can not furnish sufficient sureties immediately, then the house shall be offered again at his charge and expense and whatever less it shall bring, he shall be holden to make good and whatever more it shall bring, he shall receive no profit therefrom.

The auction fees shall be charged to the buyer.

[282] After much bidding Jacobes Jansen remained the buyer for the sum of twelve hundred and ten guilders according to the aforesaid conditions, for which sum as sureties the Honorable Rutger Jacobsen and Johannes Withart have bound their persons and estates, real and personal, present and future.

---

sd Jacob Gevinck, for a confirmacon &c. The Patent is dated the 27th day of Apr: 1667."

This abstract contains two mistakes. In the first place, Maritien was not the widow of Thomas Jansen Mingael, but probably his daughter, the widow having married in 1663, a year after Mingael's death, Evert Jansen Wendel, who was still living in 1672. See *Early Records of Albany*, 1:122 note, 419; 327–28, 496. In the second place, " Hendrick Hendrickse, at present the wife of Jacob Gevinck," should read: Hendrick Hendrickse van Harstenhorst, whose widow, Geertruy Barents van Dwingeloo, married in 1662 Jacob Gevick. See *Early Records of Albany*, 1:311. In a note on p. 327 of the same volume Professor Pearson says that Maria Abrahamse, the widow of Thomas Jansen Mingael, was a daughter of Abraham Pieterse Vosburgh. This is apparently also a mistake, as Vosburgh's daughter Maritie was not born till about 1656. See " The Vosburgh Family," by R. W. Vosburgh, in *The New Netherland Register*, 1:120.

[50] Written also Bensing and Bensingh, though he signs his name " Dirck Bensem."

[51] Probably the house which Rutger Jacobsen on December 21, 1654, contracted to build for Dirck Bensem and which was conveyed to Cobus Jansen on October 19/9, 1665, by Harmen Thomassen Hun, who married Dirck Bensem's widow. See *Early Records of Albany*, 1:215, 394.

Done in the village of Beverwyck, the 12th day of July A°. 1658, in presence of Lowyes Cobes and Aanderies Herperts.

This is the mark X of JACOBUS JANSEN, made with his own hand

RUTGER JACOBSZ
JOAN WITHART

Ludouicus Cobes
Andries Herberts
Quod attestor
LA MONTAGNE, *Commissary at Fort Orange*

Contract of sale between Jan Vinhaeghen and Barent Meyndersen of one-half of a house in Beverwyck

[283] Appeared before me, Johannes La Montagne, in the service of the General Chartered West India Company commissary of Fort Orange and the village of Beverwyck, Jan Vinhagel, inhabitant and burgher of said village of Beverwyck, who declared that he had conveyed, as he hereby does grant and convey, in real and actual possession, to Barent Meynders, his heirs and assigns, the just half of his house standing in the village of Beverwyck, bounded on the west side by the house of Rut Jacobsen and on the east side by Gerrit Bancker, with the half of the rights which the grantor has in said house and lot according to the contract of sale to him executed by Claes Hendricksen under date of the 28th of March A°. 1657;[52] for the number of 100 merchantable beavers, the same to be paid on the first of July A°. 1659, delivery to be made in May A°. 1659. Said grantor relinquishes all right and title which he may have to said half of the house and lot and promises to warrant the same against claims and demands, the respective parties binding hereto their persons and estates, real and personal, present and future, submitting the same to all courts and judges. Done in Fort Orange, the 12th of June A°. 1658,[53] in presence of Nataniel Pietersen and Jan Pietersen.

JAN VINHAEGHEN
BAERENT MEYNDERS

Jan Pieters
Nattanyel Pieterse

Acknowledged before me,
LA MONTAGNE, *Commissary at Fort Orange*

---

[52] See *Early Records of Albany*, 1:61.
[53] Cf. deed from Barent Meyndersen to Barent Reyndersen, July 17, 1659, in *Early Records of Albany*, 1:250, which refers to conveyance of July 12, 1658.

Power of attorney from Andries de Vos to Arent Andriessen

[284 blank; 285] Appeared before me, Johannes La Montagne, in the service of the General Chartered West India Company commissary at Fort Orange, the village of Beverwyck, etc., in the presence of the hereinafter named witnesses, Anderies de Vos, inhabitant of said village, who declared that he had constituted, as he hereby does constitute, Arent Anderiesen his attorney with power in his, the principal's, name to claim and demand of Jacob Coutillau,[54] in charge of the estate of the late Mr Cornelis Werckhooven[55] on Long Island, or others in possession of said estate, the payment of a certain sum which the said Mr Werckhoven, deceased, owed to him, the principal, as appears by an obligation written and signed by the aforesaid gentleman, dated the 10th of September A°. 1652; also to cause the said Jakes Corteliou or others to be cited before the competent courts, to proceed against them to final judgment and to obtain execution thereof according to law; and furthermore in said matter to act as the said principal being present could do, provided that the attorney shall be bound to render an accounting and to turn over the balance to the principal, who hereby binds his person and estate, real and personal, present and future, submitting the same to all courts and judges. Done in Fort Orange the 13th of June A°. 1658, in presence of Sacharias Sickels and Jan Lambers.

ANDRYES DE VOS

Sacharys Seckelsz
This is the mark X of JAN LAMBERS

Acknowledged before me,

LA MONTAGNE, *Commissary at Fort Orange*

Deed from Albert Gerritsen to Cornelis Jansen Clopper of a lot in New Amsterdam

[286 blank; 287] Appeared before me, Johannes La Montagne, in the service of the General Chartered West India Company commissary at Fort Orange and the village of Beverwyck, Albert Gerrits, inhabitant of R[ensselaers]wyck, who declared, as he hereby does declare, that he has granted and conveyed in real and actual possession to Cornelis Jansen Clopper, inhabitant of the city of

---

[54] Jacques Cortelyou, the founder of New Utrecht, L. I.
[55] Cornelis van Werckhoven; about his purchases of land on Long Island and in New Jersey, see Brodhead, *History of the State of New York*, 1:537.

Amsterdam in New Netherland, his heirs and assigns, a certain lot, lying in said city of Amsterdam, next the house of Adriaen Vincent, in length and breadth as in the patent, dated the first of June A°. 1654, and the conveyance thereafter given,[56] for the sum of *fl.* 250 in good strung seawan; which sum the grantor is to receive on the date hereof, promising said lot to warrant against all claims and demands, for which he binds his person and estate, real and personal, present and future, submitting the same to all courts and judges. Done in Fort Orange, the 26th of June A°. 1658, in presence of Michiel Tates and Jan Roelofsen, as witnesses.

in the service of the General Chartered West India Company com-
AALBERT GERRETSEN

Michgil Tadens
Jan Roelofsen

Acknowledged before me,

LA MONTAGNE, *Commissary at Fort Orange*

Mortgage of Jacques Teyssen's house in Beverwyck to secure the payment of money due to the estate of the late Jan Hardenberg

[288 blank; 289] Appeared before me, Johannes La Montagne, missary at Fort Orange, etc., in presence of Abraham Staes and Adriaen Gerits, magistrates of said jurisdiction, Jacob Tysen,[57] who declared, as he hereby does declare, that he has mortgaged and pledged his house lying in the village of Beverwyck to Mr Govert Loockermans, as attorney for the curators of the estate of the late Jan Hardenbers, for the sum of *fl.* 100 in beavers and *fl.* 150 in seawan, which sums he promises to pay on the first of June 1659 and which the said Jake Tysen owes to said estate; promising to hold this bond good and valid, without any exception, under submission of his person and estate, real and personal, present and

---

[56] See deed of September 4, 1654, from Symon Volckertsen to Albert Gerritsen, carpenter, in *Early Records of Albany*, 1:202-3. In a power of attorney from Albert Gerritsen to Symon Jansen, April 18, 1657, printed in *Early Records of Albany*, 1:27, the date of the patent is given as the first of June 1644.
[57] Apparently not Jacob Tyssen van der Heyden, as suggested in *Early Records of Albany*, 1:66-67, 264-65, as Jacques Teyssen was dead in 1665 and Van der Heyden was still living in 1676; see same volume, page 126.

future, to all courts and judges. Done this first of July A°. 1658, in Fort Orange.

JACQUE TEYSE

Abram Staas
Adriaen Gerretsen

Acknowledged before me,

LA MONTAGNE, *Commissary at Fort Orange*

Conditions of public sale of the house, blacksmith's shop and horse stable of Rem Jansen

[290 blank; 291] Terms and conditions on which Rem Jansen proposes to sell at public sale his house and smithy lying in the village of Beverwyck, with the lot.

First, there shall be delivered to the buyer a house, earth and nail fast, with a bake oven in the house, a smith's shop and the lot whereon stands a stable, one board long.

Delivery shall be made on the 15th of September 1658.

Payment shall be made in two terms in good, whole, merchantable beavers, to wit, the half on the delivery and the other half in June of the coming year 1659.

The buyer shall be holden to furnish two sufficient sureties, jointly and severally [liable] as principals to the satisfaction of the seller, within twenty-four hours.

If the buyer can not furnish sufficient sureties, the premises shall be offered for sale again at his charge and expense and [292] whatever less they shall bring, he must make good and whatever more they shall bring, he shall profit nothing thereby.

The auction fees shall be charged to the buyer.[58]

Conditions of public sale of the new house and lot of Cornelis Vos

[293] Terms and conditions on which Cornelis Vos proposes to sell at public sale his new house and lot lying in the village of Beverwyck.

First, the house with all that is therein fast by nail and earth shall be delivered to the buyer, in breadth in front on the street nineteen feet and four inches and behind eighteen feet, length twenty-

---

[58] No sale. The premises were again offered for sale on June 16, 1659, and bought by Jan Thomassen van Witbeck. See also deed from Rem Jansen to Jan Thomassen, August 3, 1660, in *Early Records of Albany*, 1:283–84.

five feet, with a lot behind the same 65 feet long and fourteen feet broad and extending from the kill to the breadth of the house, so that the lot in front on the street is nineteen feet and four inches wide and behind on the kill side 14 feet.

Delivery shall be made on the first of July of this year 1658.

Payment shall be made in whole, merchantable beavers in two instalments, the first on delivery of the house, the second or last payment on the first of August A°. 1659.

The buyer shall be holden to furnish two sufficient sureties, jointly and severally [liable] as principals to the satisfaction of the seller, within 24 hours.

[294] If the buyer can not furnish sufficient sureties in the aforesaid time, then the premises shall be offered for sale again at his charge and expense and whatever less they shall bring he shall be bound to make good and whatever more they shall bring shall not inure to his benefit.

The auction fees shall be charged to the buyer.

After much bidding, Carel Jansen remained the last bidder for the sum of *fl.* 1400.[59]

CAREL JANSEN
PIETER DE MAKER, as surety for the above

Acknowledged before me,

LA MONTAGNE, *Commissary at Fort Orange*[60]

Conditions of public sale of a sloop of Rutger Jacobsen

[295] Terms and conditions on which Rut Jacobsen proposes to sell at public sale his sloop named *den Eycken Boom* (the Oak Tree)[61]

First, said sloop shall be delivered to the buyer as she rides and sails, according to the inventory thereof.

Delivery shall be made at once.

Payment shall be made in merchantable seawan, to wit, in two terms, the first term or payment on delivery, the last payment in the coming year on the first of July 1659.

The buyer shall be holden to furnish two sufficient sureties, each

---
[59] See deed from Cornelis Vos to Pieter de Maecker and Carel Jansen, July 16, 1658, in this volume.
[60] The last part of the document is canceled.
[61] This sloop had been conveyed to Harmen Jacobsen and on account of failure of payment by him reconveyed to Rutger Jacobsen on August 10, 1657; see *Early Records of Albany*, 1:49.

[liable] as principal, to the satisfaction of the seller, and if the buyer does not furnish sufficient sureties within twenty-four hours, then [the sloop] shall be offered for sale again at his expense and charge and whatever less it shall bring, he shall make good and [296] whatever more it shall bring shall not inure to his profit.

The auction fees shall be charged to the buyer.

After much bidding Rut Jacobsen remained the buyer for the sum of *fl.* 779 on the aforesaid conditions the 1st of July A°. 1659, in the village of Beverwyck.

Conditions of public sale of a garden belonging to Roelof Swartwout

[297] Terms and conditions on which Roelof Swartwout proposes to sell at public sale a garden lying by the garden of D° Scaets.

First, said garden shall be delivered to the buyer in length on the east side seven and one-half rods, length on the west side six and a half rods, breadth on the south side six rods four feet, on the north side four rods and two feet.

Delivery shall be made on the first of November of the year 1658.

Payment shall be made in merchantable beavers on the 15th of August of this year 1658.

The buyer shall be holden to furnish two sufficient sureties to the satisfaction of the seller.

If the buyer can not at once furnish sufficient sureties then [the garden] shall be sold again at his expense and charge and whatever less it shall bring, he shall make good and whatever more it shall bring shall not inure to his profit.

The auction fees shall be charged to the buyer.

Conditions of public sale of two lots belonging to Roelof Swartwout

[298 blank; 299] Terms and conditions on which Roelof Swartwout proposes to sell at public sale two lots lying in the village of Beverwyck, to the west his house, to the east Volckert Jansen, length 50 feet and breadth 30 feet.

First, said lots shall be delivered to the buyer with the exception of the buildings.

Payment shall be made the first of August in good, merchantable beavers.

The buyer shall be holden to furnish two sufficient sureties, each [liable] as principal, within 24 hours, to the satisfaction of the seller. If the buyer can not furnish sufficient sureties [the lots] shall be offered for sale again at his charge and expense and whatever less they come to be worth, he shall make good and whatever more they shall be worth shall not inure to his profit.

The auction fees shall be charged to the buyer.

[300] After much bidding, Jan Dareth became the buyer at the sum of *fl.* 129 of one of the two lots, lying to the south on the road. Done in the village of Beverwyck, this 1st of July A°. 1658.

JAN BARETH

Acknowledged before me,

LA MONTAGNE, *Commissary at Fort Orange*

Bond and mortgage of Cornelis Vos to Barent van Marlen

[301] Appeared before me, Johannes La Montagne, in the service of the General Chartered West India Company commissary of Fort Orange and the village of Beverwyck, etc., in presence of François Boon and Pieter Hartg[ers], Cornelis de Vos, who declared, as he hereby does declare, that he is truly indebted to Baerent van Marlen, in the sum of *fl.* 624 in good, merchantable beavers, to be paid on the first of July 1659, for which he, C: Vos, specially mortgages his house wherein he now dwells, and furthermore binds his person and estate, real and personal, present and future, submitting the same to all courts and judges. Done in Fort Orange, the 2d of July A°. 1658.

CORNELIS VOS

Françoys Boon
Pieter Hartgerts

Acknowledged before me,

LA MONTAGNE, *Commissary at Fort Orange*

Bond and mortgage of Femmetie Alberts to Govert Loockermans

[302 blank; 303] Appeared before me, Johannes La Montagne, in the service of the General Chartered West India Company commissary at Fort Orange and the village of Beverwyck, in the presence of Abraham Staets and Jan Tomassen, magistrates of said village of Beverwyck, Femmetie A[l]bers,[62] who declared, as she

---

[62] Femmetje Albers was the widow of Hendrick Jansen Westerkamp, the baker, who died before January 17, 1655. She is also referred to as Femmetje de Baxter, meaning *de backster,* the bakeress. See *Early Records of Albany,* 1:3, 218, 399, 417; and *Dutch Records of Kingston,* revised translation by Samuel Oppenheim, p. 3, 8, 9, 20.

hereby does declare, that she is truly indebted to the curators of the estate of Jan van Hardenberch in the sum of fl. 166, as appears by obligation executed in the year 1655, which sum she promises to pay to Mr Govert Loockermans, as attorney for the estate of the late Hardenberch, on the first of July of the coming year 1659, with interest thereon at 10 per cent, amounting for three years to the sum of fl. 48, in good, merchantable beavers, for which she binds her person and estate, real and personal, present and future, and especially mortgages her house standing in the village of Beverwyck; for the greater security and payment of said sum and interest, the said Femmetie Albers waiving all rights which she may have under laws and customs made for the benefit of the wife. Done in Fort Orange, the 3d of July A°. 1658.

This is the X mark of FEMMETIE ALBERSEN
Abram Staas
Jan Thomasz

Acknowledged before me,

LA MONTAGNE, *Commissary at Fort Orange*

Deed of a house and lot in Beverwyck from Pieter Hartgers to Johannes Withart

[304] Appeared before me, Johannes La Montagne, in the service of the General Chartered West India Company commissary at Fort Orange and the village of Beverwyck, etc., in the presence of Jan Thom[a]ssen and Adriaen Gerrits, magistrates of said jurisdiction, the Honorable Pieter Hartgers, who declared, as he hereby does declare, that he has conveyed, as he hereby does grant and convey, in real and actual possession, to the behoof of Mr Johannes Withart, trader, his house lying in the village of Beverwyck, which, he, the grantor, built upon a part of the lot to him granted by the director general and council of New Netherland by patent dated the 23d of April 1652, which house and lot are in length and breadth as [follows]: on the street before the house two rods, nine feet, nine inches; length from the [front of the] house to the kill[63] seven rods; breadth in the rear on the kill two rods, three feet, ten inches; behind, measured from the house to the kill, length five rods, nine feet, six inches, all Rhineland measure, and six inches free on both sides of the lot for drip; for the sum

---

[63] Rutten Kill, now Norton street. The house stood on Joncker, now State street; see *Early Records of Albany*, 1:125.

of twenty-seven hundred guilders, of which the grantor acknowledges the receipt of so much as appears by settlement of accounts made between both parties, and the remainder of said sum [305] the grantee promises to pay on the 15th of July 1659, in merchantable beavers, the grantor promising the said house and lot to warrant against claims and demands, for which he binds his person and estate, real and personal, present and future, submitting the same to all courts and judges, as the grantee in like manner submits himself for the satisfaction of the above-promised sum. Done in Fort Orange, the 4th of July A°. 1658..

PIETER HARTGERTS

Jan Thomasz
Adriaen Gerretsen
   Acknowledged before me,
     LA MONTAGNE, *Commissary at Fort Orange*

Deed of a garden in the village of Beverwyck from Albert Gerritsen to Jan Roelofsen

[306] Appeared before me, Johannes La Montagne, in the service of the General Chartered West India Company commissary at Fort Orange and the village of Beverwyck, in the presence of François Boon and Jan Tomassen, magistrates of said jurisdiction, Albert Gerrits, inhabitant of the colony of Renselaerswyck, who declared, as he hereby does declare, that he has conveyed, as he hereby does grant and convey, in real and actual possession, to Jan Roelofsen, inhabitant of the village of Beverwyck, his heirs and assigns, a garden lying in the village of Beverwyck, in length seven rods, in breadth five rods, according to the patent granted to Albert Gerrits dated [blank][64] by the director general and council, for the sum of *fl.* 120 in beavers, which sum the grantee promises to pay on the last of August A°. 1658, the grantor promising said garden to warrant against all claims and demands, for which he binds his person and estate, real and personal, present and future, submitting the same to all courts and judges. Done in Fort Orange, the 4th of July A°. 1658.

ALBERT GERRETSEN

Françoys Boon
Jan Thomasz
   Acknowledged before me,
     LA MONTAGNE, *Commissary at Fort Orange*

---

[64] October 25, 1653; see deed for same garden from Jan Roelofsen to Willem Brouwer, July 24, 1664, in *Early Records of Albany*, 1:356–57.

Power of attorney from Carel Jansen to Pieter de Maecker

[307] Appeared before me, Johannes La Montagne, in the service of the General Chartered West India Company commissary at Fort Orange and the village of Beverwyck, Carel Jansen, who declared, as he hereby does declare, that he has constituted, as he hereby does, Pieter de Maecker his attorney, with full power in the principal's name to take possession of the new house of Cornelis de Vos, which the principal bought at public sale on the first of July of this year 1658, and in the matter all things to do as if the principal himself were present, promising to hold and to cause to be held as good, valid and binding whatever [the attorney] may do in the matter aforesaid, binding thereto his person and estate, movable and immovable, present and future, submitting the same to all courts and judges. Done in Fort Orange, the 4th of July 1658, in the presence of Sacharias Sickels and Jan Pieterse as witnesses.

CAREL JANSEN

Sacharys Seckels
Jan Pieters

Acknowledged before me,

LA MONTAGNE, *Commissary at Fort Orange*

Bond and mortgage of Femmetie Albers to Pieter Hartgers

[308] Appeared before me, Johannes La Montagne, in the service of the General Chartered West India Company commissary at Fort Orange and the village of Beverwyck, in the presence of Abraham Staets and Jan Tomassen, magistrates of said jurisdiction, Femmetie Albers, who acknowledged that she was well and truly indebted to the Honorable Pieter Hartgers, burgher and inhabitant of said place, in the sum of two hundred and twenty-four guilders and ten stivers, which sum she promises to pay in the month of August of the year 1659, in good, merchantable beavers, for which she binds her estate, real and personal, present and future, submitting the same to all courts and judges, and specially mortgages and pledges her small house wherein at present Daniel Rinckhout resides, waiving all exceptions which may be taken by law or cus-

tom for the benefit of the wife. Done in Fort Orange, the 5th of July A°. 1658.

This is the mark X of FEMMETIE ALBERSEN

Abram Staas
Jan Thomasz

Acknowledged before me,

LA MONTAGNE, *Commissary at Fort Orange*

Deed of a lot in Beverwyck from Jacob Jansen van Noortstrant to Hendrick Gerritsen

[309] Appeared before me, Johannes La Montagne, in the service of the General Chartered West India Company commissary at Fort Orange and the village of Beverwyck, in the presence of the Honorable Jan Tomassen and Pieter Hartgers, magistrates of said jurisdiction, Jacob Janssen van Noortstrant, who declared that he had conveyed, as he hereby does grant and convey in actual possession to the behoof of Henderick Gerritsen,[65] his heirs and assigns, a lot bounded on the east by the grantor's house, on the west by the street, on the north by the kill, on the south by a road, 9 rods in length and thirty feet in breadth, being part of a patent to the grantor given by the honorable director general and council of New Netherland dated the 23d of April A°. 1652, for which the aforesaid grantor acknowledges that he has been fully satisfied, promising to hold this deed good and valid and to warrant the aforesaid Henderick Gerritsen against all claims and demands which may arise, for which he binds his person and estate, real and personal, submitting the same to all courts and judges. Done in Fort Orange, the 12th of July A°. 1658.

JACOB JANESN[66]

Jan Thomasz
Pieter Hartgerts

Acknowledged before me,

LA MONTAGNE, *Commissary at Fort Orange*

Deed from Hendrick Gerritsen Vermeulen to Teunis Slingerlant of a house and lot in Beverwyck

[310] Appeared before me, Johannes La Montagne, in the service of the General Chartered West India Company commissary

---

[65] Hendrick Gerritsen Vermeulen? See next deed and *Early Records of Albany*, 1:419–20; also p. 6, note.
[66] Thus in the original; intended for Jacob Jansen.

at Fort Orange and the village of Beverwyck, in presence of the Honorable Jan Tomassen and Adriaen Gerritsen, magistrates of said jurisdiction, the worthy Henderick Gerrits, who declared that he had conveyed, as he hereby does grant and convey, in real and actual possession, to the behoof of Teunis Slingerlant, his heirs and assigns, a house and lot lying in the village of Beverwyck, over against the widow of Antony de Hoges,[67] in length five rods and four feet, in breadth thirty feet, for which the grantor acknowledges that he has received satisfaction and for security the aforesaid Henderick Gerritsen warrants the said Slingerlant against claims and demands, binding thereto his person and estate, real and personal, submitting the same to all courts and judges. Done in Fort Orange, the 12th of July A°. 1658.

HYNDRICK GEIRES[68]

Jan Thomasz
Adriaen Gerretsen

Acknowledged before me,

LA MONTAGNE, *Commissary of Fort Orange*

Conditions of public sale of the house of Teunis Slingerlant

[311] Terms and conditions on which Teunis Slingerlant proposes to sell at public sale to the highest bidder his house lying in the village of Beverwyck, wherein he now lives.

First, the house shall be delivered to the buyer as it stands with all that is fast by earth and nail, in length 30 feet, in breadth 22 feet, with a lot on the side of the house, in length 40 wood feet, in breadth 32 wood feet.

Delivery shall be made on the 22d of this month of July A°. 1658.

Payment shall be made in two terms, one payment on delivery and the second payment on the first of July A°. 1659, all in good, whole, merchantable beavers.

The buyer shall be holden to furnish two sufficient sureties, jointly and severally [liable] as principals, to the satisfaction of the seller, within 24 hours.

If the buyer can not furnish sufficient sureties in said time, then the premises shall be offered again at his charge and expense, and

---

[67] Eva Alberts, a daughter of Albert Andriessen Brat. On August 13, 1657, she married Roelof Swartwout, so that at the time of this deed she was no longer a widow.

[68] This signature is identical with that of Hendrick Gerritsen Vermeulen in *Deeds,* 2:664–65.

whatever less they shall bring, he shall be holden to make good and whatever more they shall bring, he shall profit nothing thereby. The auction fees shall be charged to the buyer.

Deed from Jochem Wesselsen to Wouter Albertsen of a house and lot in Beverwyck

[312] Appeared before me, Johannes La Montagne, in the service of the General Chartered West India Company commissary at Fort Orange and the village of Beverwyck, in presence of the Honorable Jan Tomassen and Pieter Hartgers, magistrates of said jurisdiction, Jochim Wesselsen, who declared that he had conveyed, as he hereby does grant and convey, in real and actual possession, to the behoof of Woutert Albertsen (inhabitant of this village of Beverwyck), his heirs and assigns, a house and lot, in length seven rods and ten feet, in breadth four rods and eight feet, with a garden, in breadth five rods, nine feet on the east end and on the west end four rods, seven feet, in length seven rods and four feet, which was granted to the grantor by patent given him by the director general and council of New Netherland of date the 25th of October A°. 1653, for the sum of nineteen hundred and fifty guilders in whole, merchantable beavers and a red scarlet coat bordered with gold and silver lace, of which sum the grantor acknowledges that he has received the half to his content, and the remainder [the grantee] promises to pay this day, promising said house, lot and garden to warrant against all claims and demands, binding thereto his person and estate, real and personal, submitting the same to all courts and judges. Done in Fort Orange, the 16th of July A°. 1658.[69]

JOCHEM BACKER

Jan Thomasz
Pieter Hartgerts

Acknowledged before me,

LA MONTAGNE, *Commissary at Fort Orange*

Power of attorney from Barent Albertsen Bratt to his mother-in-law Maritien Jans

[313] Appeared before me, Johannes La Montagne, in the service of the General Chartered West India Company commissary

---

[69] Cf. contract of sale of May 30, 1657, in *Early Records of Albany*, 1:28.

of Fort Orange and the village of Beverwyck, Barent Albertsen,[70] husband of Susanna Dirckx, who in the presence of the hereinafter named witnesses declared that he had constituted, as he hereby does constitute and appoint Maritien Jans, his wife's mother, his attorney, with full power in the principal's name and on behalf of himself and his wife to demand and receive in Norway,[71] from the estate of Dirck Dircksz, father of the principal's wife, and of the parents of the said Dirck Dircksz, such share and portion of the estates of the same as the principal's wife is entitled to; also in said matter to plead in due course of law as shall be needful to be done, the case to prosecute to final judgment, to cause the same to be executed or to appeal therefrom, or to compound, as she may deem best, promising to hold valid whatever the attorney shall do in the matter, for which he binds his person and estate, real and personal, submitting the same to all courts and judges. Done in Fort Orange, the 16th of July A°. 1658, in presence of Albert Gerritsen and Adriaen Symonsen.

This is the X mark of BARENT ALBERTSEN
This is the S mark of SUSANNA DIRCKX

Albert Gerretsen
Aryiana S[y]mensen

Acknowledged before me,

LA MONTAGNE, *Commissary at Fort Orange*

Bond of Albert Gerritsen to Adriaen Symonsen

[314] Appeared before me, J. La Montagne, in the service of the General Chartered West India Company commissary at Fort Orange and the village of Beverwyck, in the presence of the Honorable Françoys Boon and Pieter Hartgers, magistrates of said jurisdiction, Albert Gerritsen, who acknowledged that he was well and truly indebted to Adriaen Symensen in the sum of two hundred and four guilders, which sum he promises to pay on the last of August next ensuing in good, whole, merchantable beavers, for which he specially pledges the second payment on his house sold at public sale for which Jan van Eeckelen remained the highest bidder on the 17th of December A°. 1657[72] for the sum of fourteen

---

[70] Barent Albertsen Bratt.
[71] *Uyt Noorweegen.*
[72] Cf. *Early Records of Albany,* 1:60–61, 418.

hundred and seven guilders, binding furthermore his person and estate, real and personal, submitting the same to all courts and judges. Done in Fort Orange, the 16th of July A°. 1658.

ALBE[R]T GERRETSEN

Françoys Boon
Pieter Hartgertsz

Acknowledged before me,

LA MONTAGNE, *Commissary at Fort Orange*

Deed from Cornelis Vos to Pieter de Maecker and Carel Jansen of a house and lot in Beverwyck

[315] Appeared before me, Johannes La Montagne, in the service of the General Chartered West India Company commissary at Fort Orange and the village of Beverwyck, in the presence of the Honorable Jan Tomassen and Adriaen Gerritsen, magistrates of said jurisdiction, Cornelis Vosch, who declared that he had conveyed, as he does grant and convey hereby, in real and actual possession, to the behoof of Pieter de Maecker and Carel Janssen, their heirs and assigns, his house as broad as it stands under its roof, in length twenty-five feet, with a lot in the rear from the house to the kill, at the house or at the north end of the same breadth as the front of the house, in length from the rear wall of the house to the kill sixty-five feet, in the rear on the kill from the division fence of Dirck Janssen to the end of a straight line drawn from the first post set on the east side to the rear of said place, which place is about eighteen feet in width;[73] with the stipulation that in case the grantor pull down his old house, he shall be holden to leave a proper drip according to the custom of the fatherland; agreeing also that the grantee shall have the water running from the gutter; for the sum of fourteen hundred guilders in merchantable beavers, of which sum the grantor acknowledges he has received the half and Pieter Maecker and Carel Janssen promise to pay the other half on the first of August A°. 1659; wherefore the grantor promises to warrant the said house and lot against all claims and demands, binding thereto his person and estate, real and

---

[73] *Achter aende kil vande heyninge van Dirck Janssen gemeen tot het ende van een rechte lynie vande eerste styl getrocken aende oost syde gestelt tot de achter breete vande selve plaets welcke plaets is ontrent achter breedt achtien voeten.*

personal, submitting the same to all courts and judges. Done in Fort Orange, the 16th of July A°. 1658.

CORNELIS VOS

Jan Thomasz
Adriaen Gerretsen

Acknowledged before me,

LA MONTAGNE, *Commissary at Fort Orange*

Mr Jrermias[74] van Renselaer acknowledges that in satisfaction of the second payment on the new house he has received the sum of five hundred and ten guilders. Done in Fort Orange, the 8th of August A°. 1659.

JEREMIAS VAN RENSSELAER

Power of attorney from Dirck Dircksen to his mother Maritien Jans

[316] Appeared before me, Johannes La Montagne, in the service of the General Chartered West India Company commissary at Fort Orange and the village of Beverwyck, Dirck Dircksen (in the presence of Barent Albertsen,[75] his brother-in-law and guardian), who declared in presence of the hereinafter named witnesses, that he had constituted, as he hereby does constitute and appoint, Maritien Jans, his mother, his attorney, with full power in the principal's name and on his behalf to demand and receive from their honors the directors of the General Chartered East India Company, at the chamber in Amsterdam, all such moneys as to the aforesaid Dirck Dircksz' father are due for service rendered to said company in the East Indies, promising to hold as valid all that shall be done in said matter by the attorney, for which he binds his person and estate, real and personal, submitting the same to all courts and judges. Done in Fort Orange, the 17th of July A°. 1658, in presence of Arent Janssen and Egbert Sandersen, witnesses.

DIERCK DIERCKSEN
This is the mark X of BARENT ALBERTSEN

Arent Jansen
This is the mark X of *Egbert Sandersen*

Acknowledged before me,

LA MONTAGNE, *Commissary at Fort Orange*

---

[74] Thus in the original.
[75] Barent Albertsen Bratt.

Bond of Cornelis Vos to Johanna de Hulter

[317] Appeared before me, Johannes La Montagne, in the service of the General Chartered West India Company commissary at Fort Orange and the village of Beverwyck, in presence of Abram Staets and Adriaen Gerritsen, magistrates of said jurisdiction, Cornelis Vosch, who acknowledges that he was well and truly indebted to Madam Johanna de Hulter in the sum of one hundred and ninety Carolus guilders in good, whole beavers, which he promises to pay on the first of August A°. 1659; as security[70] and special pledge for which sum he, Cornelis Vosch, offers the last payment on his new, sold house, which payment is due on the date above named; binding furthermore his person and estate, real and personal, under submission to all courts and judges. Done in Fort Orange, the 18th of July A°. 1658.

Abram Staas CORNELIS VOS
Adriaen Gerretsen

Acknowledged before me,

LA MONTAGNE, *Commissary at Fort Orange*

Satisfaction of above bond

Appeared before me, Johannes La Montagne, commissary of Fort Orange and the village of Beverwyck, Madam Johanna Ebbinghs,[77] who declared that the above bond was fully satisfied and paid. Done in Fort Orange, the 8th of August A°. 1659.

JOHANNA EBBINCK

Acknowledged before me,

LA MONTAGNE, *Commissary at Fort Orange*

Bond and mortgage of Teunis Slingerlant to Johanna de Hulter

[318] Appeared before me, J. La Montagne, in the service of the General Chartered West India Company commissary at Fort Orange and the village of Beverwyck, in presence of the Honorable Jan Tomassen and Françoys Boon, magistrates of said jurisdiction, Teunis Slingerlant, who acknowledged that he was well and truly indebted to Madam Johanna de Hulter in the sum of thirteen

---

[70] *Hypoteeq*, usually translated "mortgage."
[77] Johanna Ebbingh was the daughter of Johannes de Laet. Her first husband was Johannes de Hulter, with whom she came to New Netherland in 1653.

good, whole beavers, which beavers he promises to pay in the middle of July A°. 1659. As security for the payment and satisfaction of said thirteen beavers the aforenamed Teunis Slingerlant especially mortgages his house, promising to satisfy said mortgage, for which he binds his person and estate, real and personal, submitting the same to all courts and judges. Done in Fort Orange, the 19th of July, A°. 1658.

         TUENYS CORNELIS SLYNGHERLANT
Jan Thomasz
Françoys Boon

Satisfaction of the mortgage

On the 28th of July A°. 1659, appeared before me, Johannes La Montagne, Madam Ebbingh, widow of the late Johannes de Hulter, who declared that she had received satisfaction for the above-written bond or mortgage.[78] Done as above.

         JOHANNA EBBINCK
Acknowledged before me,

 LA MONTAGNE, *Commissary at Fort Orange*

Power of attorney from Carsten Carstensen to Pieter Hartgers

[319] Appeared before me, Johannes La Montagne, in the service of the General Chartered West India Company commissary at Fort Orange and the village of Beverwyck, in presence of the hereinafter named witnesses, Karsten Karstensen from Norway,[79] who declared that he had constituted, as he hereby does constitute and appoint, the Honorable Pieter Hartgers his attorney, in the principal's name and on his behalf to demand and receive from the honorable director general of New Netherland or his commissary (*Commies*) the sum of two hundred and eighty guilders, as appears by the account in the custody of the commissary (*Commissaris*) on account of wages earned by the principal here at Fort Orange in the time of Mr Kieft, deceased, and of the receipt acquittance to give, if necessary; promising to hold good all that the attorney shall do in the said matter, for which he binds his person and estate, real and personal, submitting the same to all courts and judges.

---

[78] The banns of marriage of Hieronymus Ebb'ng and Johanna de Laet, widow of the late Johannes de Hulter, were registered at New Amsterdam on February 22, 1659.

[79] Usually referred to as Carsten Carstensen Noorman; he arrived in the colony of Rensselaerswyck in 1637. See *Van Rensselaer Bowier Mss*, p. 810.

Done in Fort Orange, the 20th of July A°. 1658, in presence of Sacharias Sickels and Daniel [80] Pietersen.

This is the mark X of CARSTEN CARSTENSEN

Sacharyes Seeckels
Nattaniel Pieterse

Acknowledged before me,

LA MONTAGNE, *Commissary at Fort Orange*

Conditions of public sale of the house and lot of Ulderick Klein

[320] Terms and conditions on which Ulderick Kleyn proposes to sell at public sale to the highest bidder his house and lot lying in the village of Beverwyck.

First, the house, 16 feet or one board long and 20 feet broad, shall be delivered to the buyer with a lot 8 rods long and four rods broad according to patent.

Delivery shall be made on the first of May A°. 1659.

Payment shall be made in two terms; the first payment shall be on delivery of the house, in good, merchantable seawan at 10 guilders to the beaver; the second payment on the first of August A°. 1659, in good, whole, merchantable beavers.

The buyer shall be holden to give two sufficient sureties, jointly and severally [liable] as principals, to the satisfaction of the seller, within 24 hours.

If the buyer does not furnish sufficient sureties within said time, the premises shall be offered for sale again at his expense and charge and whatever less they shall bring, he shall be holden to make good, and whatever more they shall bring, shall not inure to his profit.

The auction fees shall be charged to the buyer.[81]

On the aforesaid conditions, by decreasing bids, Jan Hendricksz van Bael remained the last bidder on the house of Ulderick Kleyn for the sum of seven hundred and nine guilders, for which, in accordance with the above conditions, he binds his person and

---

[80] Thus in the original.
[81] The following part of the document is recorded on page 322. See deed from Ulderick Klein to Jan Hendricksen van Bael, August 2, 1659, in *Early Records of Albany*, 1:268–69.

estate, real and personal. Done in the village of Beverwyck, the 22d of July 1658, in presence of J. Provoost and Lowies Cobussen.

JAN HENDERICKSEN VAN BAELEN

Ludouicus Cobes
Johannes Provoost

For the payment of the said sum of seven hundred and nine guilders, the following persons as sureties and principals, to wit, Philip Hendericksz and Jan van Aecken, bind their persons and estates. Done in Beverwyck, the 22d of July A°. 1658, present J: Provoost and L: Cobus.

PHLIP HENRICKSEN

This is the X mark of JAN VAN AECKEN

J: Provoost

Acknowledged before me,

LA MONTAGNE, *Commissary at Fort Orange*

Conditions of public sale of the house and lot of Pieter de Maecker and Carel Jansen

[321][82] Terms and conditions on which Pieter Maecker and Carel Janssen propose to sell at public sale to the highest bidder their house and lot lying in the village of Beverwyck.

First, the aforesaid house and lot shall be delivered to the buyer as it adjoins to the west Dirck Janssen Croon with a common fence, to the east Cornelis Vosch, to the north the street and to the south the kill, extending from the front on the street to the rear on the kill; breadth in front on the street 24½ feet, breadth in the rear on the kill eighteen feet or thereabouts, length throughout in a straight line 90 feet; it is specified that the house of Cornelis Vosch may remain standing as it now stands, but in case of its removal or rebuilding, he, said Vosch, shall be holden to leave a proper drip for both houses, and the water which now comes from both roofs is for the benefit of the buyer;— further everything as it stands.

Delivery shall be made on the twenty-third day of this month of July.

Payment shall be made in whole, deliverable beavers in two instalments; the first payment on the last of July of this year A°. 1658, and the second payment on the first of August A°. 1659.

---

[82] Between pages 320 and 321 a leaf has been cut out and on the remaining stub is written: "This leaf was gone July 3, 1874."

The buyer shall be holden to furnish two sufficient sureties, jointly and severally [liable] as principals, to the satisfaction of the seller, at once.

[322] If the buyer can not furnish sufficient sureties in the aforesaid time, the premises shall be offered for sale again at his expense and charge, and whatever less they shall bring, he shall be holden to make good, and whatever more they shall bring, shall not inure to his profit.

The auction fees shall be charged to the buyer.[83]

Account of auction sales

[323] The 22d July 1658

Conditions [of sale] of the goods of Jan de Groot. Payment shall be made within 8 days, in beavers. Everything less than 8 guilders shall be counted as one beaver and all that amounts to less than 4 guilders shall be counted as one-half beaver.

Pieter Gemackelyck, 16½ ells of duffel	fl. 38: —
Henderick Jochimsen, a straw mattress and a pillow	16: —
Reyer Albertsen, 2 coverlets	14: —
Adriaen Symonsen, a bear skin	9: —
Jan van Aecken, a bear skin	11: —
Abraham de Lanoy, an elk skin	11:15
Henderick Jochimsen, a shovel	7: —
C[l]aes Bever, a spade	7:15
Teunis de metselaer, a box of sugar	33: —
Symon Groodt, a little box	6: —
Harmen Janssen Scheel,[84] a pair of stockings and a frock	10: —
Cors Bouts, 3 pairs of stockings and a pair of breeches	9: —
Teunis Jacobsen, a hat and an ax	5: —
Mayken van Nes, a piece of duffel	7: —
Tomas Janssen Mingael, ditto	6:10
Reyerroom,[85] an old suit of clothes	13: —
Willem Moer,[86] a little coat	4:10

---

[83] Canceled in the record.
[84] *Scheel* means cross-eyed. It may have been a nickname of either Harmen Jansen van Salsbergen, or Harmen Jansen Knickerbacker.
[85] Uncle Reyer, perhaps referring to Reyer Jacobsen Schermerhorn.
[86] Willem Martensen Moer; see *Early Records of Albany*, 1:76. He was not a negro, as suggested by Professor Pearson, but probably an English sailor, or skipper, by the name of William Martin Moor, or More. See *Records of New Amsterdam*, 2:306; 3:279; 6:104, 107.

Pieter Tymonsen, a pair of white breeches and a cap....	5: 5
Poulus Dircksz, an *innocent*[87]........................	23:10
Pieter Bosboom, a lot of miscellany..................	6:15
Claes van Bockhoven, two books.....................	7:—
Reyer Albertsen, thread and a fur cap...............	4: 5
Ren Janssen, two pairs of woman's stockings...........	6:15
Tomas Janssen Mingael, 2 pairs of stockings..........	8:—
Claes van Bockhoven, ditto..........................	6:10
Harmen Janssen Scheel, two old shirts...............	4:—
Reyeroom, 2 new shirts.............................	9:15
Toomas Poulussen, 2 ditto..........................	13:—
Robbert Engel, 2 ditto..............................	14: 9
Reyeroom, 2 ditto...................................	12: 2
Willem Bout, 7 cravats and a band...................	6:10
Henderick Claessen, 2 jugs and a cravat..............	5:10
J. Provoost, a lot of miscellany......................	4: 5
Reyer Albertsen, a chest............................	18:—
	fl. 364: 1

[324] A coat of Jan Hendericksen van Bael on the above conditions

Anderies Herbertsen, a black coat.................... *fl.*	35:—
Barent de molenaer,[88] a black ditto...................	31:—
Adriaen Symonsen, one ditto.......................	35:—

A gun of Jurriaen de glaesemaker[89] [to be paid] in beavers within a month. This 22d of July.

Adriaen van Ilpendam, a gun....................... *fl.*	20:—

A parcel of tobacco of Barent van Marle, which Michiel de karman[90] bought at 3 stivers a pound, in beavers, to be paid in the time of 8 days..................................... *fl.* 5: 8^{m}

Cobus Janssen, two rolls of the same tobacco, in seawan.. *fl.*	7: 5
Gerrit Bancker, two rolls for seawan.................	6:—
Jan van Aecken, 3 rolls of tobacco...................	6:—

---

[87] A loose-fitting garment for house wear, much worn in the 17th century.
[88] Barent Coeymans, the miller.
[89] Jurriaen Teunissen Tappen, the glazier.
[90] Michiel [Paulussen?], the carter.
[91] In the margin is written: "Paid by de karman *fl.* 7:15." This means that he paid in seawan, 10 guilders of which equaled 8 guilders in beavers.

Of Mr Poulus,[92] 6 knives and a pistol, bought by Kit
Davids, in beavers... *fl.* 12: 5

Of the hoedemaker Samuel,[93] goods to be paid for in beavers
within 8 days.

Jan v: Eeckelen, 2 pairs of stockings.................. *fl.* 10: —
Jan van Aecken, a ring for............................ 22: —

Bond and mortgage of Cornelis Vos to Jeremias van Rensselaer

[325] Appeared before me, Johannes La Montagne, in the service of the General Chartered West India Company commissary at Fort Orange and the village of Beverwyck, in the presence of the Honorable Jan Tomassen and Adriaen Gerritsen, magistrates of said jurisdiction, Cornelis Vosch, who acknowledged that he was well and truly indebted to Jeremias van Rencelaer in the sum of fourteen hundred and eighty-eight guilders, which sum he, Vosch, promises to pay on the first of July A°. 1659, in good, whole, merchantable beavers. As special security for said sum, the aforesaid Cornelis Vosch pledges the second payment on his new house, [now] sold, which was bought at public sale by Carel Janssen and Pieter Maecker, on which aforesaid payment this is the second lien; furthermore he mortgages the house wherein he now dwells with the lot in the rear thereof, this being the second mortgage on said property, hereby binding all this for the satisfaction of the said sum [and furthermore] binding his person and estate, real and personal, submitting the same to all courts and judges. Done in Fort Orange, the 23d of July A°. 1658.

CORNELIS VOS

Jan Thomasz
Adriaen Gerretsen

Acknowledged before me,
LA MONTAGNE, *Commissary at Fort Orange*

Bond of Ulderick Klein to Reynier Rycken

[326] Appeared before me, Johannes La Montagne, in the service of the General Chartered West India Company commissary at Fort Orange and the village of Beverwyck, in the presence of

---
[92] Poulus Cornelissen?
[93] Samuel ?, the hatter.

the Honorable Jan Tomassen and Adriaen Gerritsen, magistrates of said jurisdiction, Ulderick Cleyn, who acknowledged that he was well and truly indebted to Reynier Rycken [94] in the sum of two hundred and sixty-four guilders in good, whole, merchantable beavers, which said sum the aforenamed Ulderick Cleyn promises to pay on the first of August A°. 1659 to the said Reynier Rycken, or his attorney. As security and special pledge for the payment of the said sum he, Ulderick Kleyn, by order and judgment of the Court, offers the last payment on his house bought at public sale by Jan Hendericksz van Bael, under submission of his person and estate, real and personal, to all courts and judges. Done in Fort Orange, the 23d of July A°. 1658.

ULDERYCK KLEIN

Jan Thomasz
Adriaen Gerretsen

Acknowledged before me,

LA MONTAGNE, *Commissary at Fort Orange*

Deed from Cornelis Cornelissen and Thomas Powell to Jan Barentsen Wemp of two lots in the village of Beverwyck

[327] Appeared before me, Johannes La Montagne, in the service of the General Chartered West India Company commissary at Fort Orange and the village of Beverwyck, in the presence of Jan Tomassen and Adriaen Gerritsen, magistrates of said jurisdiction, Cornelis Cornelissen and Tomas Poulussen, who declared that they had conveyed, as they hereby do convey and grant, in real and actual possession, to the behoof of Jan Barentsen Wemp, his heirs and assigns, their lots lying next to each other in the village of Beverwyck, adjoining easterly a road, westerly the other road, southerly Wouter de Ramaecker [95] and northerly the grantee and Rademaecker together, in length nine rods and in breadth four rods; for which lots the grantors acknowledge that they have had satisfaction; the aforesaid grantors promise that they will warrant the grantee against all persons claiming any right or interest in the aforesaid lots, for which they bind their persons and estates, real

---

[94] Reynier Rycken was a resident of New Amsterdam.
[95] Wouter Aertsen van Nieukerck, the wheelwright.

and personal, submitting the same to all courts and judges. Done in Fort Orange, the 24th of July A°. 1658.[96]

       This is the X mark of CORNELIS CORNELISSEN
Jan Thomasz   THOMAS POWELL
Adriaen Gerretsen

Acknowledged before me,

  LA MONTAGNE, *Commissary at Fort Orange*

[328] Inventory of the property of Jan Teunissen, the 25th of July A°. 1658

One blue and one red jug of large size
Nine earthen mugs and small jugs
A pewter pint
A copper kettle and an iron pan
Eleven wine glasses, a ½ *mutsjen*,[97] and a pewter plate
A wooden bowl and a pewter platter
Two earthen dishes, 3 chairs
The remainder of a box of sugar, about 50 lb
Two round boxes, a gun, a horn, a rapier
Five blue earthen saucers and one white one
In the cellar were found a remnant of mead, a remnant of *alsemwijn*,[98] four half aams of Spanish wine and a small keg of pipes.

Deed of a house and lot in Beverwyck from Goosen Gerritsen to Marcelis Jansen

[329] Appeared before me, Johannes La Montagne, in the service of the General Chartered West India Company commissary of Fort Orange and the village of Beverwyck, in presence of the Honorable Abraham Staets and Pieter Hartgers, magistrates of said jurisdiction, Goossen Gerritsen, burgher and inhabitant of said village, who declared that he had conveyed, as hereby he does grant and convey, in real and actual possession, to the behoof of Marcelus Janssen, his heirs and assigns, a house and lot lying in the village of Beverwyck, adjoining northerly Pieter Bronck and southerly

---

[96] Cf. public sale of a house and lot from Cornelis Cornelissen to Thomas Powell, December 18, 1657, in *Early Records of Albany*, 1:61. The name De Vos, supplied by Professor Pearson, is apparently a mistake and should be Van Voorhout; see signatures in *Early Records of Albany*, 1:46, 499; also note on p. 42 of same volume and signatures of Cornelis Cornelissen Sterrenvelt and Cornelis Cornelissen de Boer in this volume.

[97] A small gin measure, containing about 1/16 of a pint.

[98] Either absinth or vermuth.

Jan Roeloffsen, according to the patent, excepting a garden to him, the grantor, given under date of the 25th of October 1653 by the honorable director general and council of New Netherland, which [house and lot] the aforesaid Marcelus Janssen bought of the aforesaid Goossen Gerritsen on the 2d of September A°. 1654 [99] and for which the grantor acknowledges that he had satisfaction, promising to warrant the aforesaid Marcelus Janssen against all claims and demands which may arise, for which he binds his person and estate, real and personal, under submission to all courts and judges. Done at Fort Orange, the 26th of July 1658.

This is the mark X of GOOSSEN GERRITSEN, made with his own hand

Abram Staas
Pieter Hartgerts

Acknowledged before me,

LA MONTAGNE, *Commissary at Fort Orange*

Power of attorney from Lambert van Valckenborch to Govert Loockermans

[330] Appeared before me, Johannes La Montagne in the service of the General Chartered West India Company commissary at Fort Orange and the village of Beverwyck, in presence of the hereinafter named witnesses, Lambert van Valckenborgh, who declares that he hereby constitutes and appoints the Honorable Govert Loockermans his attorney in the principal's name and on his behalf to demand and receive of Jan Dircksen *alias* de Schreder, a certain three and a half beavers due to him, the principal, from the aforesaid Jan Dircksz for house rent, promising to hold good whatever the attorney shall do in this matter, for which he binds his person and estate, real and personal, submitting the same to all courts and judges. Done in Fort Orange, the 28th of July A°. 1658, in presence of Fredrick Harmsen and J. Provoost, witnesses.

This is the X mark of LAMBERT VAN VALCKENBORCH, made by himself

This is the S E mark of *Fredrick Harmsen*
Johannes Provoost, witness

Acknowledged before me,

LA MONTAGNE, *Commissary at Fort Orange*

---

[99] See contract of sale printed in *Early Records of Albany*, 1:200-1, in which Professor Pearson has by mistake supplied the name "De Goyer" after that of Jan Roeloffse.

Conditions of public sale of the house and lot of Jan Harmensen

[331] Terms and conditions on which Jan Harmsen, senior, proposes to sell at public sale to the highest bidder his house and lot lying in the village of Beverwyck.

First, the house with all that is fast by earth and nail shall be delivered to the buyer, in length 15 feet, in breadth 18 feet, with a hog pen, an oven, a third interest in a well, and the lot behind the aforesaid house; length 43 wood feet with the house and all, and in breadth 22 wood feet, front and rear.

Delivery of the aforesaid house and lot shall be made on the 20th of August next coming.

The payment shall be made in two terms or payments; the first payment on delivery of the aforesaid house and lot, the second payment on the 15th of July A°. 1659, all in good, whole, deliverable beavers.

The buyer shall be holden to furnish two sufficient sureties, jointly and severally [liable] as principals, to the satisfaction of the seller, within 24 hours.

If the buyer can not furnish sufficient sureties within the aforesaid time, then the premises shall be offered again at his expense and charge and whatever less they shall bring, he shall be holden to make good and whatever more they shall bring shall not inure to his profit.

[332] The auction fees shall be charged to the buyer.

On the above-written conditions, at public sale, the bids being run first up and then down, Stoffel Janssen remained the buyer of the house of Jan Harmsen for the sum of one thousand one hundred guilders, for which he has bound his person and estate, real and personal. Done in Beverwyck the 29th of July 1658.

Stoffel Jansz refusing to subscribe, although he remained the last bidder, therefore I subscribe the same as a witness.

Ludouicus Cobes, Court Messenger

Bond of Jan van Aecken and Pieter de Maecker as sureties for Stoffel Jansen Abeel

Appeared before me, Johannes La Montagne, in the service of the General Chartered West India Company commissary at Fort Orange and the village of Beverwyck, Jan van Aecken and Pieter Maecker, who offered themselves as bondsmen for Stoffel Janssen in the action instituted by the [prosecuting] officer in the matter of the sale of the house of Jan Harmssen, the said bondsmen to be liable as sureties and principals for the payment of the purchased house in case the court decides that the aforesaid Stoffel Janssen must keep the house, for which they bind their persons and estates, real and personal. Done in Fort Orange, the 29th of July 1658, in presence of Lowies Cobus and J. Provoost.

This is the X mark of JAN VAN AECKEN
PIETER DE MAKER

Ludouicus Cobes
Johannes Provoost

Acknowledged before me,

LA MONTAGNE, *Commissary at Fort Orange*

Agreement of Jan Roelofsen to pay for a garden bought by him at public sale of Jacob Loockermans

[333] Jan Roeloffsen was the last bidder on the garden of Jacob Loockermans, which garden shall be delivered to the buyer in tight fence as it now lies inclosed, for the sum of eighty-one guilders, on condition that the payment be made within three weeks, the auction fees to be charged to the buyer. For the full payment of which sum Tomas Janssen offers himself as surety. Done in Beverwyck, the 29th of July 1658, in presence of Lowies Cobussen and J. Provoost.

JAN ROELOFSEN
THOMES JANSEN MINGAEL

Ludouicus Cobes
Johannes Provoost

Acknowledged before me,

LA MONTAGNE, *Commissary at Fort Orange*

Conditions of public sale of the house and lot of Jan Teunissen

[334] Terms and conditions on which the honorable prosecuting officer proposes to sell at public sale to the highest bidder the house and lot of Jan Teunissen *alias* de paep.[1]

First, the house with all that is fast by earth and nail shall be delivered to the buyer together with the lot, in breadth in front on the road 34 feet, in length according to the bill of sale of Cornelis Teunissen, such as it is now occupied by the aforesaid Jan Teunissen.

---

[1] Jan Teunissen, *alias* "the papist," not "the priest," as translated in *Early Records of Albany,* 1:288.

Delivery shall be made within 24 hours.

Payment shall be made in two terms; the first payment on the first of September of this year 1658, the half in good, whole, deliverable beavers and the other half in good, merchantable seawan; the second payment shall be on the first of July A°. 1659, the half also in good, whole, deliverable beavers and the other half in good, merchantable seawan.

The buyer shall be holden to furnish two sufficient sureties, jointly and severally [liable] as principals, to the satisfaction of the seller, within 24 hours.

If the buyer can not furnish sufficient sureties within the aforesaid time, then the premises shall be offered for sale again at his expense and charge and whatever less they shall bring, he shall be holden to make good and whatever more they shall bring shall not inure to his profit.

[335] On this date, the 30th of July 1658, at the aforesaid sale of the house of Jan Teunissen, the last bidder on the aforesaid conditions was the Honorable Cornelis Teunissen, and that for the sum of one thousand one hundred and twenty guilders, for the full payment of which the Honorable Anderies Herbertsen and Stoffel Janssen as sureties and principals bind their persons and estates, real and personal, submitting the same to all courts and judges. Done in the village of Beverwyck as above, in presence of Lowies Cobussen and J. Provoost.

    CORNELUS THONISEN BOS
    STOFFEL JANSZ
    ANDRIES HERBERTS

Ludouicus Cobes
Johannes Provoost, witness

Acknowledged before me,

 LA MONTAGNE, *Commissary at Fort Orange*

Conditions of public sale of the house and lot of Willem Fredericksen Bout and Harmen Bastiaensen

[336] Terms and conditions on which Willem Fredericksz Bout and Harmen Bastiaensen propose to sell at public sale to the highest bidder their house and lot on the north side of Fort Orange.

First, the house and lot with all that is fast by earth and nail shall be delivered to the buyer, in breadth on the road four rods and a half, on the west three rods and five feet, length eight rods, according to the patent thereof.

Delivery shall be made on the first of October of this year A°. 1658, and on delivery as aforesaid, payment, all in good, merchantable seawan.

The buyer shall be holden to furnish two sufficient sureties within 24 hours.

If the buyer can not furnish sureties in the aforesaid time, then [the house and lot] shall be offered for sale again at his expense and charge, and whatever less they shall bring, he shall be holden to make good and whatever more they shall fetch shall not inure to his profit.

The auction fees shall be charged to the buyer.

After many offers Jacob Adriaensz Neus[2] remained the last bidder on the aforesaid conditions for the sum of four hundred and four guilders, for [the payment of] which he binds his person and estate, real and personal.

Done in the village of Beverwyck, the 30th of July 1658, in presence of Loweis Cobussen and J. Provoost.

JACOB ADRYAEN

Ludouicus Cobes
J: Provoost, witness

Acknowledged before me,

LA MONTAGNE, *Commissary at Fort Orange*

Bond and mortgage of Roelof Swartwout to Govert Loockermans as attorney for the administrators of the estate of Jan van Hardenbergh

[337] Appeared before me, Johannes La Montagne, in the service of the General Chartered West India Company commissary at Fort Orange and the village of Beverwyck, in the presence of the Honorable Jan Tomassen and Pieter Hartgers, magistrates of said jurisdiction, Roeloff Swartwout, who acknowledges himself to be well and truly indebted to Mr Govert Loockerm[ans], attorney for the administrators of the estate of Jan van Hardenbargh, in the sum of one hundred and ninety-seven guilders and ten stivers, in good, whole, deliverable beavers, which sum the said

---

[2] *Neus* means Nose and may have been a nickname of Jacob Adriaensen from Hilversum, the wheelwright. See *Van Rensselaer Bowier Mss,* p. 820–21, 831.

Swartwout owes to the estate of the aforesaid Jan van Hardenbargh and which he promises to pay in the middle of July A°. 1659. As special security for the aforesaid sum the said Swartwout mortgages his house situated in the village of Beverwyck, promising to hold this bond good and valid, without any exception, for which he binds his person and property, movable and immovable, submitting the same to all courts and judges. Done in the village of Beverwyck on the first of August 1658.

Roelof Swartwout

Jan Thomasz
Pieter Hartgerts
    Acknowledged before me,
    La Montagne, *Commissary at Fort Orange*

Power of attorney from Poulus Martensen to Johanna de Hulter

[338] Appeared before me, Johannes La Montagne, in the service of the General Chartered West India Company commissary at Fort Orange and the village of Beverwyck, Poulus Martensen, who declared that he had constituted, as he hereby does constitute and appoint Madam Johanna de Hulter his attorney in the principal's name and on his behalf to demand and receive from Jacob Janssen Stol the sum of three beavers, which beavers will serve as a payment to the aforenamed Madam Johanna de Hulter by the principal, who promises to hold good whatever the attorney shall do in said matter, for which he binds his person and estate, real and personal, submitting the same to all courts and judges. Done in Fort Orange, the first of August A°. 1658, in presence of Diderick van Hamel and J. Provoost.

Pouls Marten

D: V: Hamel, as witness
Johannes Provoost, witness
    Acknowledged before me,
    La Montagne, *Commissary at Fort Orange*

Bond and mortgage of Femmetie Alberts to Teunis Cornelissen Slingerlant with assignment from Slingerlant to Daniel Rinckhout

[339] Appeared before me, Johannes La Montagne, in the service of the General Chartered West India Company commissary at Fort Orange and the village of Beverwyck, in the presence of the Honorable Françoys Boon and Pieter Hartgers, magistrates of said

jurisdiction, Femmetie Albertsen, who acknowledged that she was well and truly indebted to Teunis Cornelissen Slingerlant in the sum of four hundred and forty-five guilders,[3] which she promises to pay to said Slingerlant in the month of June A°. 1659, mortgaging as special security for the payment of said sum her house where Daniel Rinckhout dwells. Also, Teunis, Cornelissen Slingerlant assigns the aforesaid sum to Daniel Rinckhout for the sum of two hundred and seventy-five guilders, the receipt of which the said Slingerlant acknowledges, the parties binding thereto their persons and estates, real and personal. Done in Fort Orange, the 3d of August A°. 1658.

This is the X mark of FEMMETIE ALBERTS
TUENYS CORNELIS SLYNGHERLANT

Françoys Boon
Pieter Hartgertsz

Acknowledged before me,

LA MONTAGNE, *Commissary at Fort Orange*

Deed of one-half of a house and lot in Beverwyck from Carel Jansen to Pieter de Maecker

[340] Appeared before me, J: La Montagne, in the service of the General Chartered West India Company commissary at Fort Orange and the village of Beverwyck, in the presence of Pieter Hartgers and Jan Tomassen, magistrates of said jurisdiction, Carel Janssen, who declared that he had conveyed, as he hereby does grant and convey, in real and actual possession, to the behoof of Pieter de Maecker, his heirs and assigns, his half of the house and lot lying in the village of Beverwyck which he, the grantor, received from Cornelis Vosch by conveyance dated the 16th of July of this year 1658; for which half house and lot the grantor acknowledges that he has had satisfaction, wherefore the grantor promises to warrant the grantee against all [persons] claiming any right or interest in the aforesaid house and lot, binding thereto his person and estate, real and personal, under submission to all courts and judges. Done in Fort Orange, the 12th of August A°. 1658.

CAREL JANSEN

Pieter Hartgerts
Jan Thomasz

LA MONTAGNE, *Commissary at Fort Orange*

---

[3] Judgment for this amount was given against Femmetje Albers on July 9, 1658, the court ordering her to pay in proportion to the amounts due to her other creditors.

Contract of sale of a house and lot in Beverwyck between Jan Baptist van Rensselaer as attorney for Jan Labatie and Jacob de Hinse

[341] Appeared before me, Johannes La Montagne, in the service of the General Chartered West India Company commissary at Fort Orange and the village of Beverwyck, the Honorable Johannes Baptist van Rencelaer, attorney of the worthy Jan Labitie, who declared in the presence of the hereinafter named witnesses that by his order he had sold, as he hereby does sell, to the worthy Jacob de Hince, the house and lot lying in the village of Beverwyck, adjoining northerly the kill, southerly Sander Leendersen, except a lot forty feet in breadth on the street, beside Sander Leendertsen, and in the rear twenty feet broad, and a garden behind Fort Orange, which the aforenamed Labitie reserves; and that in full possession and ownership, with all the right, title and interest which the aforenamed Labitie has therein, for the sum of two thousand three hundred and fifty guilders in good, whole, deliverable beavers (with so much scarlet cloth as is required for a waistcoat for said Labitie's wife), in three payments, the first payment in the month of August A°. 1659, the second payment in the month of August A°. 1660, and the third payment also in the aforesaid month A°. 1661: The seller shall deliver the aforesaid house and lot on the first of May A°. 1659, the parties mutually binding their respective persons and estates, real and personal, subject to the control of all courts and judges. Done in the village of Beverwyck, the 12th of August A°. 1658.

JAN BAPTIST VAN RENSSELAER
J. DE HINSSE

Hendrick Jochemsz, witness
Johannes Provoost, witness

LA MONTAGNE, *Commissary at Fort Orange*

Bond of Hendrick Jochemsen to Jacob Visch

[342] I, the undersigned, Henderick Jochimsen, acknowledge that I am well and truly indebted to Mr Jacob Visch[4] in the sum of forty-three beavers and a half, growing out of the purchase of three hogsheads of French wine, the receipt of which wine from the hands of said Jacob Visch's servant I acknowledge. Which aforesaid sum of forty-three and one-half beavers I promise to pay in the month of July A°. 1659 to the aforenamed Visch, or his attorney,

---
[4] Jacob Visch, or Vis, was a trader at New Amsterdam.

for which I bind my person and estate, real and personal, submitting the same to all courts and judges. In witness whereof I have subscribed this with my usual hand. Done in the village of Beverwyck, the 14th of August A°. 1658.

HENDRICK JOCHEMSZ

Bond and mortgage from Teunis Cornelissen Slingerlant to Carsten Claessen with satisfaction of the same

[343] Appeared before me, Johannes La Montagne, in the service of the General Chartered West India Company commissary at Fort Orange and the village of Beverwyck, in the presence of the Honorable Françoys Boon and Dirrick Janssen Croon, magistrates of said jurisdiction, Teunis Cornelissen Slingerlant, who acknowledged that he was well and truly indebted to Carsten Claessen, carpenter, in the sum of twenty-two good beavers, which the aforesaid Slingerlant promises to pay in the month of June A°. 1659 and as special security for the payment of said sum he mortgages his house standing in the village of Beverwyck, binding for the satisfaction of said mortgage his person and estate, real and personal, under submission to all courts and judges. Done in Fort Orange, the 14th of August A°. 1658.

TUENIS CORNELIS SLYNGHERL[A]NT

On this 28th of July A°. 1659 appeared before me, Johannes La Montagne, Carsten Claessen, who declared that the above-written bond or mortgage had been fully satisfied. Dated as above.

This is the X mark of CARSTEN CLAESSEN

Acknowledged before me,

LA MONTAGNE, *Commissary at Fort Orange*

Bond and mortgage from Teunis Cornelissen Slingerlant to Bastiaen Jansen van Gudsenhoven

[344] Appeared before me, Johannes La Montagne, in the service of the General Chartered West India Company commissary at Fort Orange and the village of Beverwyck, in the presence of the Honorable Pieter Hartgers and Jan Tomassen, magistrates of said jurisdiction, Teunis Cornelisz Slingerlant, who acknowledged that he was well and truly indebted to Jan Bastiaensz van Gudsenhooven in the sum of three hundred and thirteen guilders, four stivers and eight pence, in good, whole, deliverable beavers, with

interest on the same at ten per cent, and promises the same to pay in the month of June A°. 1659; as special security for which sum the said Slingerlant gives a mortgage on his house and lot lying in the village of Beverwyck, whereof the said Gudsenhooven shall have the preference excepting Madam De Hulter, and for the satisfaction of the same he binds his person and estate, real and personal, submitting the same to all courts and judges. Done in Fort Orange, the 14th of August A°. 1658.

TUENYS CORNELIS SLYNGHERLANT

Pieter Hartg[erts]
Jan Thomasz

LA MONTAGNE, *Commissary at Fort Orange*

Deposition of Jan Joosten and Adriaen Symonsen respecting the purchase of two iron cannon from Jan Dareth

[345] Appeared before me, Johannes La Montagne, in the service of the General Chartered West India Company commissary at Fort Orange and the village of Beverwyck, in the presence of the Honorable Abraham Staets and Pieter Hartgers, magistrates of said jurisdiction, Jan Joosten and Adriaen Symonsen, who declare and attest that in the year 1657 they bought and received from the worthy Jan Dareth two small iron pieces,[5] for which the deponents paid five beavers at eight guilders apiece, which they, the deponents, at the request of the said Dareth, declare in the presence of the aforesaid magistrates to be true and trustworthy, [in witness whereof] they have subscribed this in their usual hands. Done in Fort Orange, the 19th of August A°. 1658.

JAN JOOSTEN
ADRIAEN SYMENSEN

Pieter Hartgerts
Abram Staas

LA MONTAGNE, *Commissary at Fort Orange*

Deposition of Rem Jansen respecting the purchase of gun barrels from Jan Dareth

[346] Appeared before me, Johannes La Montagne, in the service of the General Chartered West India Company commissary at Fort Orange and the village of Beverwyck, in the presence of

---

[5] *Twee Issere stuckjens.*

the Honorable Abraham Staets and Pieter Hartgers, magistrates of said jurisdiction, Rem Janssen, who declared and attested that in the year 1657 he bought and received from the worthy Jan Dareth forty-five gun barrels, as well whole as half, which were burnt and damaged by the fire in the house of Mr Arent van Curler, so that I swear they were no more than old iron, for which barrels I paid ninety-five guilders in seawan reckoned at ten guilders a beaver, which I swear and declare in presence of the above-named magistrates and at the requisition of the aforenamed Dareth to be true and trustworthy, and have subscribed the same in my accustomed hand. Done in Fort Orange, the 19th of August A°. 1658.

REM YANSZEN

Pieter Hartgerts
Abram Staas

LA MONTAGNE, *Commissary at Fort Orange*

Conditions of public sale of the house and lot of Jacob Loockermans

[347] Terms and conditions on which Jacob Loockermans proposes to sell at public sale to the highest bidder his house and lot lying in the village of Beverwyck.

First, the house shall be delivered to the buyer with kitchen, cellar and a small chamber built up with brick; the seller shall [furthermore] deliver the house [as follows]: the garret floor and the main floor laid; the gable of matched boards; a stairway to the garret and a stairway to the cellar; a bedstead in the chamber; [the house] with the lot extending in length to Anderies Herbertsen's fence and in breadth thirty feet.

Delivery shall be made on the last day of September next ensuing.

Payment shall be made in good, whole, merchantable beavers in two instalments; the first payment shall be made on delivery of said house and lot and the second payment on the first of July A°. 1659.

The buyer shall be holden to furnish two sufficient sureties jointly and severally [liable] as principals, to the satisfaction of the seller, within the time of 24 hours.

If the buyer can not furnish sufficient sureties within said time, then [the house and lot] shall be again offered for sale at his expense and charge and whatever less they shall come to, he shall be holden to make good and whatever more they shall fetch shall not inure to his benefit.

The auction fees shall be charged to the buyer.

Deposition of Abraham Staets about the purchase of a small iron cannon from Jan Dareth

[348] Appeared before me, Johannes La Montagne, in the service of the General Chartered West India Company commissary at Fort Orange and the village of Beverwyck, in the presence of Jan Tomassen and Françoys Boon, magistrates of said jurisdiction, Abraham Staets, who declared and attested that in the year 1657 he bought and received from the worthy Jan Dareth a small iron piece, for which he paid four beavers at eight guilders apiece, which he declares in the presence of the aforesaid magistrates and at the request of the said Jan Dareth to be true and trustworthy and he has subscribed this in his usual hand. Done in Fort Orange, the 19th of August A°. 1658.

ABRAM STAAS

Jan Thomasz
Françoys Boon
LA MONTAGNE, *Commissary at Fort Orange*

Deposition of Rutger Jacobsen against Nicolaes Gregory Hillebrant, a soldier, accused of attempting to commit sodomy

[349] Appeared before me, Johannes Provoost, clerk of the court of Fort Orange and the village of Beverwyck, Rutger Jacobsen, who declared and attested at the requisition of the [prosecuting] officer, Johannes La Montagne, in presence of Jan Tomassen and Adriaen Gerritsen, magistrates of said jurisdiction, that this day, being the 20th of August, being come behind the fort near the garden of Jochim Ketluyn and hearing the shrieking or crying of the youngster named Pieter Adriaensen, the son of the wife of Henderick Jochimsen, he hastily walked to [the spot] and there saw a soldier named Nicolaes Gregory Hillebrandt[6] lying on his knees *met syn mannelyckheyt uyt syn broeck* and having before him the aforesaid youngster, which said Nicolaes Gregory Hillebrant forcibly wanted to undo the boy's breeches, who struggling and crying defended himself as best he could, saying "There is Rutt oom;" whereupon said Nicolaes Hillebrant looked around and

---

[6] August 26, 1658, Hillebrant stated before the court that he was 29 years of age and born at Prague.

this deponent said: "You rascal, what are you doing there?" Then said Nicolaes Hillebrant got up and went out of the garden, whereupon the deponent took the child and brought him to his mother's house, being followed by the aforesaid Nicolaes Gregory, who said: "If you tell anything, I will say you lie like a thief," and followed him to Henderick Jochimsen's house, where coming would perforce [350] drink with the deponent, which he refused to do, whereupon Nicolaes Gregory said: "Are you angry with me?" and was so importunate that the bystanders said: "What's the matter with you, Nicolaes; have you anything on your conscience that you want to force the man to drink with you?" All of which he attested under oath to be true and trustworthy. Done in Fort Orange, the 20th of August A°. 1658.

RUTGER JACOBSZ

Jan Thomasz
Adriaen Gerretsen

On the same date, in presence of the aforesaid magistrates, Pieter Adriaensen, aged about seven years, declared that this day the trumpeter wanted to undo his breeches and threatened to beat him with a stick and that the trumpeter had taken him out of his mother's yard and led him behind the gardens and said that he saw him pull his *mannelyckheyt uyt syn broeck*. All of which he declared, being assisted by his mother Elsjen, Henderick Jochimsen's wife.

Jan Thomasz
Adriaen Gerretsen

Power of attorney from Dirck Dircksen Keyser to Philip Pietersen Schuyler

[351] Appeared before me, Johannes La Montagne, in the service of the General Chartered West India Company commissary at Fort Orange and the village of Beverwyck, in presence of the hereinafter named witnesses, Dirrick Dircksz Keysser, who declared that he had constituted, as he hereby does constitute and appoint, the Honorable Philip Pietersen Schuyler his attorney, in the principal's name and on his behalf to collect and receive [the amount of] the following obligations: of Rutger Jacobsen, one of fifty-four and another of thirty-eight good, whole, merchantable beavers; of Jan V[er]beeck an obligation of twenty-seven good, whole beavers; and of Claes Hendericksz six whole beavers; and on receipt acquittance to give and to the said principal a proper accounting to make; promising to hold good whatever the attorney in said

matter shall do, binding thereto his person and estate, real and personal, under submission to all courts and judges. Done in Fort Orange, the 22d of August A°. 1658, in presence of Claes Pietersen and Johannes Provoost.

DIRCK DIRCKSEN KEYSER

Claesz Pierszen
Johannes Provoost

LA MONTAGNE, *Commissary at Fort Orange*

Receipt of Philip Pietersen Schuyler for the above obligations

[352] I, the undersigned, Philip Pietersen, acknowledge that I have received from Dirrick Dircksen Keysser four obligations, to wit: two of Rutger Jacobsen, amounting to the sum of ninety-two good, whole beavers; one of Jan Verbeeck for twenty-seven good beavers; and one of Claes Hendericksz, amounting to six beavers; which I promise to send off as soon as I have collected the same; and for the better satisfaction the said Dirck Keyser has delivered the aforesaid obligations to Philip Pietersen in presence of Johannes Provoost. Done in Fort Orange, this 22d of August A°. 1658.

PHILIP PIETERSEN

Johannes Provoost, present

Deposition of Asser Levi regarding the ownership of a brandy cask which an Indian took from the island opposite the fort

[353] Appeared before me, Johannes Provoost, clerk of the court of Fort Orange and the village of Beverwyck, Asser Levy, who attested and declared in presence of the Honorable Abraham Staets, at the requisition of the [prosecuting] officer, that the empty anker which the Indian [took?] from the island over against the fort was his and that he sold three of the same mark to Hans Vosch, one of which, containing brandy, was still lying in the cellar of the said Hans Vosch, marked I.H.; which he attests to be true and trustworthy. Done in Fort Orange, this 22d of August A°. 1658.

ASSER LEVI

Abram Staas

Power of attorney from Pieter Symonsen to Françoys Boon

[354] Appeared before me, Johannes La Montagne, in the service of the General Chartered West India Company commissary at Fort Orange and the village of Beverwyck, Pieter Symonsen, who

declared that he had constituted, as he hereby does constitute and appoint, the Honorable Françoys Boon his attorney, in the principal's name and on his behalf to collect and receive here in New Netherland such debts and moneys as are due to the principal according to obligations, writings and other proofs thereof; against the delinquent to proceed and all legal steps to observe; the attorney to have power to give acquittance for receipts and when requested to make a proper accounting of his transactions and receipts; [the principal] promising to hold good and valid whatever the attorney shall do in the matter, for which he binds his person and estate, real and personal, submitting the same to all courts and judges. Done in Fort Orange, this 30th of August 1658, in presence of Johannes Provoost and Jan Claessen.

PIETER SYMENSZ

Johannes Provoost, witness
Jan Claesz Backer

Acknowledged before me,

LA MONTAGNE, *Commissary at Fort Orange*

Contract of sale between Gerrit Bancker and Jan Dareth of a house and lot in Beverwyck

[355] Appeared before me, Johannes Provoost, clerk of the court of Fort Orange, in the presence of the hereinafter named [persons], the worthy Gerrit Bancker, who declared that he had sold and granted, as he hereby does [sell and grant], to the worthy Johan Dareth, his house and lot lying in the village of Beverwyck with all such right and title as the aforenamed Gerrit Bancker is possessed of according to the patent thereof, adjoining to the south Meyndert Fredricksz, to the north Jan van Eeckelen,[7] and that for the sum of one thousand eight hundred guilders in good, whole, deliverable beavers, which aforesaid sum the aforenamed Jan Dareth promises to pay in two payments, to wit, the first payment in the month of June A°. 1659 and the second payment in the month of June A°. 1660, wherefore the seller shall be holden to deliver the aforesaid house and lot on the first of May A°. 1659, free and unincumbered, and for the payment of said sum the worthy Philip Pietersen and Anderies Herbertsen offer themselves as sureties and principals to the content of the seller, which sale and bargain each

---

[7] Cf. deed for the same property from Jan Coster van Aecken to Gerrit Bancker, April $\frac{8}{18}$, 1667, in *Early Records of Albany,* 1:407.

for himself promises to carry out, therefor binding their persons and estates, real and personal, submitting the same to all courts and judges. Done in the village of Beverwyck, the last of August A°. 1658, in presence of Jacob Schermerhoorn and Cornelis Jacobsen.

JAN DARETH
PHILIP PIETÈRSE SCHUYLER
ANDRIES HERBERTS

Jacob Jansen Schermerhooren, witness
Cornelis Jacobsz, witness

Acknowledged before me,

JOHANNES PROVOOST, *Clerk*

Testimony of Jan Eeraerts and Tys Servaes regarding the killing of Claes Cornelissen

[356 blank; 357] Information given about the death of Claes Cornelissen, struck dead with a knife in the house of Henderick Jochimsen, innkeeper, on the 31st of August A°. 1658.

Jan Eeraerts, from Wesel, aged 23 years, testifies that Daniel Bonvou, a soldier, and Claes Cornelissen got into a fight about some words and threw each other down. Thereafter they again went at each other and Daniel Bonvoo tried to stab the aforesaid Claes Cornelissen with his rapier, whereupon the deponent took his rapier from him. For the third time Claes Cornelissen wanted to strike the said Daniel Bonvoo with his fists, whereupon Daniel Bonvou stabbed him in the breast with a knife and forthwith ran away. All of which he testifies to be true and trustworthy.

JOHANNES EERRAERTS

Which Jan Eraers attests having taken place in presence of Pieter Moree, Abraham Stevensen *alias* Crawaet[8] and Tys Servaes.

Tys Servaes, at the requisition of the prosecuting officer, testifies that the deposition of Jan Eerraets is true and trustworthy.

This is the O mark of TYS SERVAES

Bond of Aert Goosen van Twiller to Jacob Hendricksen

[358] Appeared before me, Johannes Le Montagne, in the service of the General Chartered West India Company commissary at Fort Orange, Arent Gosen van Twiller,[9] who acknowledged himself to

---

[8] Probably intended for "Crowaet," the Croatian; see *Van Rensselaer Bowier Mss*, p. 819.
[9] See about him *Van Rensselaer Bowier Mss*, p. 840.

be indebted to Jacob Hendericksse in the sum of four hundred
guilders, to be paid in Holland in current money, for which he binds
his person and estate, real and personal, present and future, submitting the same to all courts and judges. Done in Fort Orange, in
presence of Jan Eeraerts and Daniel Pietersse, witnesses, the 5th
of September 1658.

AERT GOOSEN

Johannes Eeraerts
Nattaneiel Pieterse

Acknowledged before me,

LA MONTAGNE, *Commissary at Fort Orange*

Power of attorney from Jan Dareth to Jan Baptist van Rensselaer

[359] Appeared before me, Johannes La Montagne, in the service
of the General Chartered West India Company commissary at
Fort Orange and the village of Beverwyck, Jan Dareth, who
declared that he had constituted, as he hereby does constitute and
appoint, the Honorable Johannes Baptist van Rencelaer his attorney,
in the principal's name and on his behalf to demand and receive
from the curators by the court appointed over the estate of the late
Joost Dareth, or of others in whose hands the said estate may be,
such portion as is coming to the principal on account of his mother,
the late Lysbet Rycken, late wife of said Joost Dareth, deceased;
also in said matter to sue, compound or proceed otherwise in due
course of law as if the principal were himself present; to obtain
judgment and in case of need to appeal therefrom, or to acquiesce
therein, as the attorney may think best, and for receipts acquittance
to give (provided the attorney be holden to render an accounting and
the balance to the principal); for which [the principal] binds his
person and estate, real and personal, present and future, submitting
the same to all courts and judges. Done in Fort Orange, the 13th
of September A°. 1658, [in presence of] Teunis Teunissen and
Johannes Provoost.

JAN DARETH

Teunis Teunisz
Johannes Provoost, witness

LA MONTAGNE, *Commissary at Fort Orange*

Deed from Rutger Jacobsen to Harmen Albertsen Vedder of a house and lot in Beverwyck

[360] Appeared before me, Johannes La Montagne, in the service of the Chartered West India Company commissary at Fort Orange and the village of Beverwyck, in presence of the honorable Françoys Boon and Adriaen Gerritsen, magistrates of said jurisdiction, Rutger Jacobsen, who declared that he had granted and conveyed, as he hereby does grant and convey, in real and actual possession, to the behoof of Harmen Albertsen Vedder, his heirs and assigns, his house and lot lying in the village of Beverwyck, adjoining to the east Goosen Gerritsen, to the west Jan Vinhagel, to the north the street, to the south the grantor; length sixty-four feet, breadth thirty-six feet, front and rear, with an alley of five feet in breadth extending to the kill, lying between Goossen Gerritsen and the aforesaid grantor; for which said house and lot the grantor acknowledges that he has been fully satisfied and he therefore warrants the grantee against all claims and demands, binding thereto his person and estate, movable and immovable, present and future, submitting the same to all courts and judges. Done in the village of Beverwyck, the 14th of September A°. 1658.

RUTGER JACOBSZ

Françoys Boon
Adriaen Gerretsen

LA MONTAGNE, *Commissary at Fort Orange*

Power of attorney from Cornelis Jacobsen to Pieter de Jongh

[361] Appeared before me, Johannes La Montagne, in the service of the General Chartered West India Company commissary at Fort Orange and the village of Beverwyck, the worthy Cornelis Jacobsen, who declares that he has constituted, as he hereby does constitute and appoint, the worthy Pieter de Jongh [10] his attorney, in the principal's name and on his behalf to demand and receive here in New Netherland such debts and moneys as are due here to the principal according to obligations, notes and other evidences thereof; against the delinquent to proceed, taking all necessary legal steps, and to cause execution to be made as the case may require; with power to give acquittance for receipts; provided that the attorney on request is to make a proper return of his transactions and

---

[10] Pieter Cornelissen de Jongh; see *Early Records of Albany*, 1:255.

receipts; [the principal] promising that he will hold good and valid whatever the attorney shall do in the matter, for which he binds his person and estate, real and personal, submitting the same to all courts and judges. Done in Fort Orange, the 16th of September A°. 1658, in presence of Gysbert van Inborch and Johannes Provoost.

CORNELIS JACOBSZ

Gysbert van Imborch
Johannes Provoost, witness

LA MONTAGNE, *Commissary at Fort Orange*

Power of attorney from Jan Claessen Backer to François Boon

[362] Appeared before me, Johannes La Montagne, in the service of the General Chartered West India Company commissary at Fort Orange and the village of Beverwyck, in presence of the hereinafter named witnesses, Jan Claessen Backer, who declared that he had constituted, as he hereby does constitute and appoint, the Honorable Françoys Boon his attorney, in the principal's name and on his behalf to collect and receive here in New Netherland all such debts and moneys as are due here to the principal according to obligations, notes and other evidences thereof; against the delinquents to proceed, all legal steps to take and execution to have issued as the case may require; for receipts acquittance to give and when required a proper accounting to render; [the principal] promising to hold good and valid whatever the attorney shall do in the matter, binding thereto his person and estate, real and personal. Done in Fort Orange, the 16th of September A°. 1658, in presence of Lowies Cobussen and Johannes Provoost.

JAN CLAESSZ BACKER

Ludouicus Cobes
Johannes Provoost, witness

Acknowledged before me,

LA MONTAGNE, *Commissary at Fort Orange*

Bond and mortgage of Jan Martensen to Daniel Verveelen (canceled)

[363] Appeared before me, Johannes La Montagne, in the service of the General Chartered West India Company commissary at Fort

Orange and the village of Beverwyck, in presence of the Honorable Jan Tomassen and Adriaen Gerritsen, magistrates of said jurisdiction, Jan Martensen, who acknowledged that he was well and truly indebted to Daniel Verveelen in the sum of seven hundred Carolus guilders in good, whole, merchantable beavers, which he, Jan Martensen, has to his content received in merchandise, and promises to pay the aforesaid sum next spring, which shall be in the year 1659; as special security for which aforesaid sum and debt he mortgages his house.[11]

Power of attorney from Jacob Hendricksen to Teunis Teunissen Metselaer

[364] Appeared before me, Johannes La Montagne, in the service of the General Chartered West India Company commissary at Fort Orange and the village of Beverwyck, in the presence of the hereinafter named witnesses, Jacob Hendericksz, who declared that he had constituted, as he hereby does constitute and appoint, Teunis Teunissen Metselaer his attorney, in the principal's name and on his behalf to collect and receive here in New Netherland all such debts and moneys as are due to the principal according to obligations, notes and other evidences thereof; against the delinquents to proceed, all necessary legal steps to take and to have execution issued as the case may require; for receipts acquittance to give, provided that the attorney shall be holden to render a proper accounting and settle with the principal, who promises to hold good and valid whatever the attorney shall do in the matter, for which he binds his person and estate, real and personal, submitting the same to all courts and judges. Done in Fort Orange, the 17th of September A°. 1658, in presence of Jan Gauw and Johannes Provoost.

This is the X mark of JACOB HENDERICKSEN, set with his own hand

This is the X mark of *Jan Gauw*, made by himself
Johannes Provoost, witness

Acknowledged before me,

LA MONTAGNE, *Commissary at Fort Orange*

---

[11] Canceled in original.

Public sale of personal property of Bastiaen de Winter

[365] Conditions on which Bastiaen de Winter proposes to sell at public sale some furniture, payments to be made in seawan, within 24 hours. This day, the 23d of September A°. 1658. Auction fees will be charged to the buyer.

Volckert Janssen, a candlestick and tongs......... *fl.*	6: —
Tryn Jochimsen, tongs and chain.................	8: —
Teeuwes Abrahamsen, a pothook and pan.........	5: —
Claes Bev[er], 18 wooden plates.................	2: 14
ditto, a kettle.................................	2: —
Jan Tomassen, an iron pot......................	9: —
Jan van Eeckelen, a salt cellar and small pewter bowl	5: 11
Jan van Aecken, a pewter cup and pitcher........	5: —
ditto, a pewter basin..........................	4: 10
Carsten Fredricksen, 4 pewter plates.............	9: 5
Volckert Janssen, 2 pewter platters..............	9: —
ditto, 2 chargers.............................	12: 2
Barent, the miller,[12] a small copper pan...........	8: —
Tomas Pouwel, one ditto and a skimmer..........	5: 10
Abram Vosborgh, a parcel of earthen dinner plates.	2: 10
The brewer of Willem Bout, for earthen ware.....	4: 5
Jurriaen Teunissen, a copper kettle...............	22: 12
Daniel V[er]veelen, a tablecloth.................	5: 13
Barent, the smith,[13] two napkins.................	6: 18
Willem Janssen Schutt, two ditto................	6: —
Tomas Pouwel, two ditto.......................	6: —
Carsten Fredricksen, two ditto...................	2: 3
Jan Harmsen Backer, a pillowcase...............	2: 8
Caspar Jacobsen, 2 handkerchiefs................	3: 7
Jurriaen Janssen, 2 ditto.......................	3: —
Poulus Dircksen, 2 unbleached bed sheets.........	10: 2
Jacob Loockermans, 2 ditto....................	11: 5
Volckert Janssen, 2 ditto......................	14: 14
Carsten Fredricksen, a piece of woolen cloth......	3: 5
Tomas Pouwel, a chimney cloth with a valance....	3: 6
	fl. 199: 0: —

---

[12] Barent Pietersen Coeymans, the miller.
[13] Barent Reyndertsen, the smith.

[366] Carried forward	*fl.*199: 0:—
Volckert Janssen, a christening robe...........	6: 5
ditto, a cloak.............................	46:—
Jan van Aecken, 3 Indian children's coats........	16:—
Jan Harmsen Backer, 3 ditto coats..............	12: 5
Volckert Janssen, 2 fur caps...................	8: 5
Jan van Aecken, 2 ditto.......................	9:—
Jacob Schermerhorn, 2 curtains and sundries......	2:—
Jan van Aecken, 2 fur caps....................	6: 5
ditto, a pair of cloth stockings................	8: 5
Jan Harmensen, a Bible.......................	8: 5
Jan Tomassen, a Bible.......................	10:—
Carsten Fredricksen, a parcel of books...........	5:—
Barent, the miller, a dark lantern...............	5:15
Volckert Janssen, an Indian coat...............	18:10
ditto, one ditto............................	18:15
Jan van Aecken, one ditto.....................	15:15
Volckert Janssen, one ditto....................	15:10
ditto, seven ditto @ *fl.*13 apiece...............	91:—
Tomas Pouwel, two small ditto.................	16:10
Volckert Janssen, a parcel of fur caps, unfinished..	8:10
Eldert Gerbertsen, some old silk stockings........	11:10
Geertie Bouts, 3 pairs of Faroe (*feerosse*) stockings	9:15
Jan van Aecken, 6 pairs of mittens.............	5: 5
Tomas Pouwel, 12 pairs of children's stockings....	13:15
Barent, the smith, a pillowcase.................	2: 7
Mattheeus Abrahamsen, 3 cravats...............	2:11
Henderick Jochimsen, a sanitary girdle and cravat.	4:—
Broer Cornelissen, a parcel of mittens...........	5:—
Mother Schaets, 12 pairs of children's stockings...	14:10
Geertie Bouts, 6 pairs ditto....................	10:14
Poulus Dircksen, an unbleached sheet...........	2: 6
Jan van Eeckelen, a parcel of laces..............	5: 1
Geertie Bouts, a child's shirt with two false sleeves	1:16
Jan van Eeckelen, a parcel of mittens...........	3: 5
La Montagne, 6 pairs of children's stockings......	7:—
Jan van Aecken, a lot of miscellany and a leather coat	6:—
Henderick Jochimsen, a parcel of galloons........	3: 8
	*fl.*635: 7:—

[367] Carried forward...................	*fl.*635: 7
Adriaen Gerritsen, a parcel of knives and box.....	6: 5
Willem Teljer, 2 pipes and an Indian shell........	7: —
Henderick Jochimsen, a lot of miscellany.........	7: —
Adriaen van Ilpendam, ditto...................	6: —
Jan Harmsen, junior, a saw and an ax............	5: —
Teunis Jacobsen, an ax, with Comans[14]..........	4: 10
Tomas Pouwel, a parcel of salt..................	3: 18
Geertie Bouts, a parcel of soap..................	14: 2
Johannes Provoost, a bed......................	57: —
Geertie Bouts, 2 scales........................	2: 5
Willem Schut, a lot of miscellany................	3: 15
Volckert Janssen, a gun.......................	21: 5
Jan van Aecken, a chest.......................	18: 4
Daniel V[er]veelen, a hammock to be paid for in beavers	53: —
	*fl.*844: 11: —

Public sale of hops on the land of Jan Jansen van Otterspoor

[368] Conditions and terms on which Teunis Teunissen *metselaer* and Jurriaen Teunissen propose to sell at public sale to the highest bidder the hops which now stand on the land of Jan Janssen van Otterspoor, deceased.

The aforesaid hops shall be delivered to the buyer as the same stand, but the buyer shall be holden to remove them at his own risk, and when the buyer shall have picked the hops, he is then to lay the poles in a heap to be returned to the seller.

Payment shall be made in good, whole, deliverable beavers, to wit, the half, and the other half in good, deliverable seawan, next year 1659, on the first of July.

The buyer shall be holden to furnish two sufficient sureties, joint and several, immediately, to the content of the seller.

If the buyer can not furnish sufficient sureties in the aforesaid time, [the hops] shall again be offered for sale at his expense and charge and whatever less they shall bring, he shall be holden to make good and whatever more they shall fetch shall not inure to his profit. The auction fees shall be a charge upon the buyer.

At the above sale, the prices being run down, Jan Helmsen

---

[14] With Barent Pietersen Comans, or Coeymans.

remained the last bidder for the hops above named, on the above-written conditions, for the sum of one hundred and two guilders, for which Jochim Wesselsen and Barent Gerritsen offered themselves as sureties and principals, binding for the payment of the aforesaid sum their persons and estates, real and personal. Done in the village of Beverwyck, the 24th of September A°. 1658.

This is the mark X of IAN HELMSEN, made by himself

JOCHEM *backer*

This is the mark X of BARENT GERRITSEN

Ludouicus Cobes
J. Provoost, witness

Conditions of public sale of the land of Jan Jansen van Otterspoor

[369] Conditions and terms on which Teunis Teunissen and Jurriaen Teunissen propose to sell at public sale to the highest bidder the land of Jan Janssen van Otterspoor, deceased, which he bought at auction of Madam De Hulter.[15]

First, the aforesaid land shall be delivered to the buyer, lying by the fourth kill; to the north Cornelis Teunissen, in breadth twelve rods and seven feet; along the river side, in length thirty rods; to the south the tile yard, in breadth twenty rods; to the west the *kreupelbosch*[16] twenty-four rods; the poles which are upon the aforesaid land remain for the benefit of the buyer.

Delivery shall be made tomorrow, being the 25th of September, but the hops standing thereon with the garden truck belong to the seller.

Payment shall be made in two payments in good, whole, deliverable beavers, the first payment on the first of July A°. 1659 and the second payment on the first of July A°. 1660.

The buyer shall be holden to furnish two sufficient sureties, jointly and severally [liable] as principals, to the content of the seller, immediately.

If the buyer can not furnish two sufficient sureties in the aforesaid time, then [the land] shall be offered for sale again at his charge and expense and whatever less it shall bring, he shall be holden to make good and whatever more it shall fetch shall not inure to his profit.

The auction fees shall be a charge upon the buyer.

---

[15] See *Early Records of Albany,* 1:57-58.
[16] Literally: cripple bush; a thicket.

Sale of the slaughter excise to Frans Barentsen Pastoor

[370] Conditions and terms on which the honorable vice director and the magistrates of Fort Orange and the village of Beverwyck propose to let the slaughter excise for the term of one year.

The farming of the aforesaid slaughter excise shall begin on the first of October of the year 1658 and end on the last of September A°. 1659.

The farmer shall receive one stiver of every guilder that the slaughtered animals, whether ox, cow, calf, bull, hog, goat or sheep, shall be worth and in case of dispute, appraisal shall be made by impartial persons.

The farmer shall be holden for the excise money to furnish two sufficient sureties to the satisfaction of the honorable lessors, a just fourth part of the excise to be paid every quarter year in good merchantable seawan; and if the former can not furnish sufficient sureties, then [the excise] shall be offered [for sale] again at his expense and charge and whatever less it shall bring, he shall be holden to make good, and whatever more it shall bring shall not inure to his benefit.

Frans Barentsen Pastoor remained the last bidder of the aforesaid excise for the sum of seven hundred [371] and ninety-seven guilders, according to the aforesaid conditions; for which aforesaid sum Cornelis Teunissen Bosch and Pieter Brouck offered themselves as sureties and principals, binding for the payment and satisfaction of the honorable lessors their persons and estates, real and personal, submitting the same to the authority of all courts and judges.

Done in the village of Beverwyck, this first of October A°. 1658, in the presence of Johannes Provoost and Lowies Cobus.

FRANS BARENTZ PASTOOR
CORNELUS THONISEN BOS
PYETER BRONCK

Johannes Provoost, witness
Ludouicus Cobes

Bond and mortgage of Jan Martensen to Daniel Verveelen

[372] Appeared before me, Johannes La Montagne, in the service of the General Chartered West India Company commissary at Fort Orange and the village of Beverwyck, in the presence of Jan

Tomassen and Adriaen Gerritsen, magistrates of said jurisdiction, Jan Martensen, who· acknowledged that he was well and truly indebted to the worthy Daniel Verveelen in the sum of six hundred Carolus guilders in good, whole, merchantable beavers, for which he, Jan Martensen, has received merchandise to his content, and promises the aforesaid sum to pay next spring which shall be in the year 1659; and to this end he mortgages his house and lot lying in the village of Beverwyck as special security for the payment of the aforesaid sum, promising the foregoing to perform, for which he binds his person and estate, real and personal, present and future, submitting the same to the authority of all courts and judges. Done in Fort Orange, the first of October A°. 1658.

      This is the mark X of JAN MARTENSEN,
        made with his own hand

Jan Thomasz
Adriaen Gerretsen

 Acknowledged before me,

  LA MONTAGNE, *Commissary at Fort Orange*

Bond and mortgage of Dirck Bensem to Willem Fredericksen Bout

[373] Appeared before me, Johannes La Montagne, in the service of the General Chartered West India Company commissary at Fort Orange, in the presence of the Honorable Fransois Boon and Ariaen Gerrits, magistrates of said jurisdiction, Dirck Bensich, inhabitant of the village of Beverwyck, who declared that he was truly indebted to Willem Fredricksen Bout in the number of ninety beavers, which he promises to pay in the year of 1659 in the month of June, binding thereto his person and estate, real and personal, present and future, especially his house wherein he dwells at present, as special security by way of mortgage, promising to warrant the same against all claims and submitting the same to all courts and judges. Done in Fort Orange, the 5th of October 1658.[17]

      This is the X mark of DIRCK BENSICH,
        made with his own hand

Françoys Boon
Adriaen Gerretsen

 Acknowledged before me,

  LA MONTAGNE, *Commissary at Fort Orange*

---

[17] This bond was the result of a judgment given against Dirck Bensem on August 26, 1658, in an action for debt brought by Willem Fredericksen Bout for money due on a yacht. See *Early Records of Albany*, 1:27-28.

Bond of Willem Brouwer to Jeronimus Ebbinck, mortgaging his house and lot as special security for the money due

[376][18] Appeared before me, Johannes La Montagne, in the service of the General Chartered West India Company commissary at Fort Orange and the village of Beverwyck, in the presence of the Honorable Françoys Boon and Adriaen Gerritsen, magistrates of said jurisdiction, Willem Brouwer, who acknowledges that he is well and truly indebted to Jeronimus Ebbinck, burgher and trader at Amsterdam in New Netherland, in the sum of nine hundred guilders and thirteen stivers for and in consideration of divers wares, goods and merchandise, as duffels, blankets, *dosyntiens*[19] and woolen cord to his content received, therefore promising the aforesaid sum of nine hundred guilders and thirteen stivers to satisfy and pay to the aforenamed Ebbinck or to the lawful bearer of this at farthest in the month of July A°. 1658 first coming punctually and without longer delay, in good, whole, merchantable beaver skins, without presenting halves or thirds in payment, and furthermore with interest thereon at ten per cent a year, commencing on the last day of June last and running until the full and effectual payment; thereto binding his person and estate, real and personal, nothing excepted, to the authority of all lords, [377] courts, tribunals and judges and especially his house and lot standing and lying in the village of Beverwyck aforenamed, adjoining and bounded on the one side by Johannes Withart and on the other side by Pieter Hartgers, for the payment of the aforesaid sum and interest and for the recovery thereof, if need be, without loss or expense; binding himself hereby in advance to confess judgment for said amount by the court of Beverwyck aforesaid, for the reason, as the debtor declares, that the said Ebbinck has done him a great favor in accommodating him with the aforesaid goods. All in good faith, this has been subscribed by the debtor. Done in the village of Beverwyck, this 12th of October A°. 1658.

WILLEM BROUWER

Françoys Boon
Adriaen Gerretsen

    Acknowledged before me,

        LA MONTAGNE, *Commissary at Fort Orange*

---

[18] Pages 374–75 contain an incomplete draft of the bond of Willem Brouwer which is canceled in the record.
[19] Probably the same as what is known in French as *draps de douzaine;* that is, light-weight cloth for summer wear and ladies' dresses.

Sale of the burghers' excise on wine and beer to Adriaen Jansen Appel

[378] Conditions on which the honorable commissary and the magistrates of Fort Orange and the village of Beverwyck propose to let to the highest bidder the burghers' wine and beer excise for the term of one year.

The farming shall begin on the first day of November A°. 1658 and end on the last day of October A°. 1659, according to the ordinances of our fatherland.

The farmer shall collect for a tun of good beer one *daelder*,[20] for a tun of small beer ten stivers, for a hogshead of French wine six guilders, for an anker of brandy, Spanish wine or liquor two guilders.

The farmer shall be holden to furnish two sufficient sureties, jointly and severally [liable] as principals, to the content of the honorable lessors, to pay the aforesaid burghers' excise, every quarter year a just fourth part of the whole sum in good strung seawan.

And in case the farmer should fail [379] in the aforesaid sureties, then the said excise shall be offered again at his expense and charge and whatever less it shall bring, he shall be holden to make good and whatever more it shall fetch shall not inure to his benefit.

At the letting of the above excise, by lowering bid (*bij afslach*), Adriaen Janssen van Leyden[21] remained the last bidder for the sum of one thousand eight hundred and seventy guilders on the aforesaid conditions and at the same time Anderies Herbertsen and Rutger Jacobsen offered themselves as sureties and principals for the payment of the aforesaid sum, binding thereto their persons and estates, real and personal, present and future, submitting the same to all courts and judges.

Done in Fort Orange, the last day of October A°. 1658, in the presence of Johannies Provoost and Lowies Cobussen.

ADRIAEN JANSZ VAN LEYDEN
ANDRIES HERBERTS
RUTGER JACOBSZ

Johannes Provoost, witness
Ludovicus Cobes

    LA MONTAGNE, *Commissary at Fort Orange*

---

[20] One *daelder*=1½ guilders.
[21] Adriaen Jansen Appel, from Leyden.

Farming of the burghers' excise continued to Adriaen Jansen Appel

[380] On this last day of October A°. 1659, the honorable commissary and magistrates have for the sake of accommodation prolonged and continued the farming of the above excise to Adriaen Janssen van Leyden[22] for the sum of one thousand and seven hundred guilders; likewise Anderis Herbertsen and Rutger Jacobsen, as sureties and principals for the satisfaction of the said sum, bind their persons and estates, real and personal, present and future, submitting the same to the authority of all courts and judges. Done in Fort Orange, as above.

A. Appel
Andries Herberts

Lease of a house from Tierck Claessen to Arent Isacksen

[381] Appeared before me, Johannes La Montagne, in the service of the General Chartered West India Company commissary at Fort Orange and the village of Beverwyck, Tierck Claesen, who declared that he had leased, as he hereby does lease, his house lying in the village of Beverwyck, for the term of one year beginning on the first of May 1659 and ending next year 1660, to Arent Isacksz, burgher and inhabitant of the city of Amsterdam in New Netherland, for the sum of two hundred guilders in good, merchantable beavers at eight guilders apiece; on condition that the lessor shall raise the ground behind the house and make a stoop in front of the house, the lessee being bound to pay each half year one-half of the aforesaid sum; for which the parties bind their persons and estates, real and personal, present and future. Thus done in Fort Orange, in presence of Jan Willemsz and Cornelis Teunissen, witnesses, the 20th of November A°. 1658.

Tierck Claesse de Witt
Arent Isackxen van den Huock[23]

This is the X mark of *Jan Willemsz*
This is the X mark of *Cornelis Teunesen*

Acknowledged before me,

La Montagne, *Commissary at Fort Orange*

---

[22] Adriaen Jansen Appel, from Leyden.
[23] Arent Isaacksen van den Houck, or van Hoeck.

Power of attorney from Pieter Jansen van Stockholm to Symon Jansen Romeyn

[382] Appeared before me, Johannes La Montagne, in the service of the General Chartered West India Company commissary at Fort Orange and the village of Beverwyck, in the presence of the hereinafter named witnesses, Pieter Janssen van Stockholm, late soldier of the aforesaid company, who declared that he had constituted, as he hereby does constitute and appoint, the worthy Symon Janssen Romeyn, trader at Amsterdam in New Netherland, his attorney, in the principal's name and on his behalf to demand and receive from the General Chartered West India Company, at the Chamber at Amsterdam, the sum of four hundred and twenty-nine guilders, nine stivers and eight pence, which the principal has earned at Amsterdam in New Netherland of the aforesaid company, as appears by the account subscribed on the debit side Carel van Brugen and on the credit side P. Stuyvesant; with power likewise one or more in his place to substitute in case the attorney shall deem this advisable; for receipts acquittance to give and in said matter to act as if the principal were present, who promises to hold good and valid whatever the attorney shall do in said matter, for which he binds his person and estate, real and personal, submitting the same to all courts and judges. Done in Fort Orange, the 23d of November A°. 1658, in presence of Johannes Provoost and Jan Cloet.

PIETER JANSSEN V. STOKHOLM

Johannes Provoost, witness
Johannsz Clute

Acknowledged before me,

LA MONTAGNE, *Commissary at Fort Orange*

Power of attorney from Rem Jansen to Teunis Gysbertsen Bogaerdt

[383] Appeared before me, Johannes La Montagne, in the service of the General Chartered West India Company commissary at Fort Orange and the village of Beverwyck, Rem Janssen, who declared that he had constituted, as he hereby does constitute and appoint, Teunis Gysbertsen Bogaerdt, his attorney, in the principal's name and on his behalf to enter upon and take possession of the principal's farm lying on Long Island, near the Manhatans, with

the oxen, cows, horses and all its appurtenances, which aforesaid farm is occupied by Henderick van Breemen, inasmuch as the tenant's term expired on the first day of November A°. 1658; promising to hold good whatever the attorney shall do in the said matter, for which he binds his person and estate, real and personal, submitting the same to all courts and judges.

Done in Fort Orange, the 24th of November A°. 1658, in the presence of Jan Barensen and Johannes Provoost, witnesses

REM YANSZEN

Jan Barentsen
Johannes Provoost, witness

Acknowledged before me,

LA MONTAGNE, *Commissary at Fort Orange*

Letting of the tavernkeepers' excise on wine, beer and distilled liquor to Adriaen Jansen Appel

[384] Terms and conditions on which the director general and council of New Netherland propose to farm out the excise on beer, wine and distilled liquor consumable by tapsters in Fort Orange and the village of Beverwyck and the appendances thereof.

First, the farming out as well as the collection[24] of the excise takes place in accordance with the praiseworthy custom of our fatherland and conformable to the printed ordinances and placards to that effect of their High Mightinesses the Lords States General of the United Netherlands (concerning Finance and Subsidies required for Public Purposes), printed copies whereof shall be placed in the hands of the honorable commissary and magistrates.

The farming shall begin on the first of November of this year 1658 and end on the last of October A°. 1659, during which time the farmer himself may collect and receive, or through his clerk or collector may cause to be collected and received, for all wines, beers and distilled liquors to be consumed or drawn by any tapster, innkeeper or retailer by the small measure in Fort Orange, the village of Beverwyck, Rencelaerswyck, in Katskil, Esopus and in

---

[24] The Dutch text repeats the word used in the first instance: "*de pachtinge soo wel als de pachtinge.*" The word intended in the first place is probably "*verpachtinge.*"

other places lying or to be established between them during that time, as follows:

For a tun of domestic beer	4 guilders
For a tun of overseas or foreign beer	6 "
For a hogshead of French or Rhenish wine	16 "
[385] For an anker of brandy or distilled liquor, malmsey, Spanish wine or Canary wines.... per anker and for larger or smaller casks in proportion	6 guilders

If, in raising or lowering the bids, two or more persons bid alike, it shall be left to the judgment of the honorable lessors to choose and to grant the excise to one of the bidders, if they please, or else to offer it again, if they should deem that advisable.

The farmer shall be holden to furnish two sufficient sureties for the excise money to the satisfaction of the honorable lessors and every year pay a just fourth part in current seawan to the receiver of the director general or their agent upon the order of the said director general and council.

To prevent all future cavil, misunderstanding, compounding and frauds, the honorable lessors stipulate and order that after the expiration of this term, when the excise shall have been farmed out anew, the new farmer shall have liberty immediately, or on the following day, or at the longest within the time of three days after the new letting, in the usual manner and in the presence of the former farmer, if he chooses to be present, to make a gaging of the wines, beers and distilled liquors which [386] remain in the hands of the innkeepers, tapsters and retailers and which were reported by them at the new letting; of which wines, beers and distilled liquors left over and found two-thirds of the receipts or excise due shall revert and be turned over by the former farmer to his successor.

The director general and council reserve the right to interpret and amplify these conditions and promise the farmer all proper help and assistance. Thus done and ratified.

At the letting of the above excise, by lowering bid (*bij afslach*), Adriaen Janssen van Leyden[25] remained the last bidder for the sum of four thousand, three hundred guilders upon the aforesaid conditions, for which said sum Anderies Herbertsen and Rutger Jacob-

---

[25] Adriaen Jansen Appel, from Leyden.

sen offered themselves as sureties, binding for the satisfaction of
said sum their persons and estates, real and personal, present and
future, submitting the same to all courts and judges. Done in the
village of Beverwyck, the 25th of November A°. 1658, in presence
of Lowies Cobussen and Johannes Provoost.

                              ADRIAEN JANSZ V: LYDEN
                              ANDRIES HERBERTS
                              RUTGER JACOBS

Ludouicus Cobes
Johannes Provoost

  Acknowledged before me,

    LA MONTAGNE, *Commissary at Fort Orange*

Conditions of sale of a horse and cart of Tjerck Claessen de Witt

[387] Conditions on which Tjerck Claessen proposes to sell at public sale to the highest bidder a horse and cart and leather harness and all other appurtenances.

Payment for the aforesaid horse and cart shall be made on the first of June of the coming year 1659, one-half in good, whole, merchantable beavers and the other half in current seawan.

Delivery shall be made tomorrow, being the 26th of this month.

The buyer shall be holden to furnish two sufficient sureties jointly and severally liable as principals, to the satisfaction of the seller, and that immediately.

If the buyer can not furnish sufficient sureties in the aforesaid time, then [the horse and cart] shall be offered for sale again at his expense and charge, and whatever less they shall bring, he shall be holden to make good and whatever more they shall fetch shall not inure to his benefit.

The auction fees shall be a charge upon the buyer.

[Canceled in the record]

Public sale of land of Jan de Groot, deceased, to Claes van Bockhoven

[388] On this 25th of November A°. 1658, Teunis Teunissen *metselaer* and Jurriaen Teunissen offered at public sale the land of Jan de Groot, deceased, whereof Claes van Bockhooven remained the last bidder for the sum of three hundred and forty guilders to be paid, one-half in good current seawan and the other half in

good, whole, merchantable beavers, in two payments, the first payment on the first of July A°. 1659 and the second payment on the first of July A°. 1660, for which aforesaid sum Cornelis Wyncoop and Willem Brouwer offer themselves as sureties and principals, binding for the satisfaction of the aforewritten sum their persons and estates, real and personal, present and future, submitting the same to all courts and judges. Done in the village of Beverwyck as above, in presence of Lowies Cobussen and J. Provoost.

This is the mark X of CLAES VAN BOCKHOOVEN,
made with his own hand

CORNELIS WYNCKOOP

WILLEM BROUWER

Acknowledged before me,

LA MONTAGNE, *Commissary at Fort Orange*

Deed from Carsten Fredericksen to Jan Harmensen, junior, of part of a lot in Beverwyck

[389] Appeared before me, Johannes La Montagne, in the service of the General Chartered West India Company commissary of Fort Orange and the village of Beverwyck, in the presence of Françoys Boon and Adriaen Gerritsen, magistrates of said jurisdiction, Carsten Fredricksen, who declared that he had conveyed, as he hereby does grant and convey, in real and actual possession, to the behoof of Jan Harmsen, junior, his heirs and assigns, a piece of a lot lying in the village of Beverwyck, which lot is a part of a patent granted by the director general and council of New Netherland to Lourens Janssen under date of the 25th of October A°. 1653, and by the said Lourens Janssen conveyed to Cornelis Steenwyck for the behoof of Gabriel Leendersen on the 30th of July A°. 1655, and again by Cornelis Steenwyck, attorney for the aforesaid Gabriel Leendersen, conveyed to Carsten and Meyndert Fredricksz on the 30th of July A°. 1655, as appears on the back of the said patent;[26] which piece of the aforesaid lot adjoins on the south side the street, on the north side Mynder[t] Fredricksen, on the east side the

---

[26] The record of this patent, like that of all other patents of the same date, is lost. It included apparently a garden lot which on July 30, 1655, was likewise conveyed to Carsten and Meyndert Fredericksen and by them on July $\frac{3}{31}$, 1668, conveyed to Jan Clute; see *Early Records of Albany*, 1:440–41.

grantor and on the west side Jan van Aecken ;[27] in length forty-three feet, in [390] breadth twenty-two wood feet, front and rear; for which aforesaid piece of a lot the grantor acknowledges that he has had satisfaction and promises to warrant the same against all claims and demands, for which he binds his person and estate, personal and real, present and future, submitting the same to all courts and judges. Done in Fort Orange, the 30th of November A°. 1658.

KARSTEN FRERICKSEN

Françoys Boon
Adriaen Gerretsen

Acknowledged before me,

LA MONTAGNE, *Commissary at Fort Orange*

Release from Carsten Fredericksen to Meyndert Fredericksen for another part of the patent mentioned in the preceding deed

[391] Appeared before me, Johannes La Montagne, in the service of the General Chartered West India Company commissary at Fort Orange and the village of Beverwyck, in the presence of the Honorable Jan Tomassen and Abraham Staets, magistrates of said jurisdiction, Carsten Fredricksz,[27] who declared that he had granted and conveyed, as he hereby does grant and convey, in real and actual possession, to the behoof of Meyndert Fredricksz, his heirs and assigns, a piece of a lot lying in the village of Beverwyck, which is a portion of the patent granted by the director general and council of New Netherland to Lourens Janssen under date of the 25th of October A°. 1653, and by Lourens Janssen conveyed to Cornelis Steenwyck for the behoof of Gabriel Leendersen on the 30th of July A°. 1655, and again by Cornelis Steenwyck, attorney for the aforesaid Gabriel Leendersen, conveyed to Carsten and Meyndert Fredricksen on the 30th of July A°. 1655, as appears on the back of said patent; which piece of the lot adjoins to the west [28] the street, breadth three rods, eleven feet, one inch; to the south Jan Dareth, length two rods, eleven feet, four inches; to the west Jan van Aecken, breadth three rods, eleven feet, eight inches; to the north Carsten Fredricksen, length four rods, one foot, three inches; for which piece [392] of a lot the said grantor acknowledges

---

[27] Jan Coster van Aecken; see deed from Carsten and Meyndert Fredericksen to the magistrates and from the magistrates to Van Aecken for adjoining lot, December 10, 1659, in *Early Records of Albany*, 1:260-61.

[28] Apparently a mistake for "east," although the word *oosten*, which occurs immediately after *westen*, is crossed out.

that he has had satisfaction and promises the same to warrant against all claims and demands, binding therefor his person and estate, real and personal, present and future, under submission to all courts and judges. Done in Fort Orange, the 30th of November A°. 1658.

KARSTEN FREDERICKSEN

Jan Thomasz
Abram Staas

Acknowledged before me,

LA MONTAGNE, *Commissary at Fort Orange*

Conditions of public sale of a house, lot and piece of land of Marten Hendricksen

[394][29] Terms and conditions on which Marten Hendericksen proposes to sell at public sale to the highest bidder his house, lot and piece of land behind the said house, adjoining to the north Tomas Janssen, to the south the colony of Rencelaerswyck, to the east a road and to the west a road.

First, the aforesaid house, lot and piece of land shall be delivered to the buyer of such length and breadth as is to be seen in the two patents thereof, but the seller reserves to himself the brewer's tools that are in said house.

Delivery of the aforenamed house, lot and piece of land shall be made on the first of May of this year 1659.

Payment shall be made in three payments, to wit: the first payment on delivery of the house, lot and land in good current seawan; the second payment on the 15th of September A°. 1659, also in good current seawan; and the third payment on the first of May A°. 1660, in good, whole, merchantable beavers.

The buyer shall be holden to furnish two sufficient sureties, jointly and severally liable as principals, to the satisfaction of the seller, within twenty-four hours.

If the buyer can not furnish sufficient sureties within the aforesaid time, the premises shall be offered for sale again at his expense and charge and whatever less they shall bring, he shall be holden to make good, and whatever more they shall bring shall not inure to his benefit.

The auction fees shall be charged to the buyer.

---

[29] Page 393 contains the first lines of another draft of the same conditions.

Conditions of public sale of the house and lot of Albert Gerritsen

[395 blank; 396] Terms and conditions on which Albert Gerritsen [30] proposes to sell at public sale to the highest bidder his house and lot lying in the village of Beverwyck.

First, the aforesaid house and lot shall be delivered to the buyer, adjoining to the north Pieter Loockermans, to the south Jan van Eeckelen, to the east the street, to the west the fence of Adriaen Gerritsen; length on the north side 85 feet, on the south side length with the house 92 feet, breadth in front on the street 24 feet and in the rear 21 feet, to wit, wood feet; furthermore, the seller shall be holden to erect a middle partition and to have a winding stairway built.

Delivery of the aforesaid house and lot shall be made on the first of May of this year 1659.

Payment shall be made in two instalments in good, whole, merchantable beavers, the first payment on the first of June of this year 1659 and the second payment on the first of June A°. 1660.

The buyer shall be holden to furnish two sufficient sureties, jointly and severally [liable] as principals, to the content of the seller, within 24 hours.

If the buyer can not furnish sufficient sureties within the aforesaid time then the premises shall be again offered for sale at his charge and expense and whatever less they shall bring, he shall be holden to make good and whatever more they shall fetch shall not inure to his benefit.

The auction fees will be charged to the buyer.

Conditions of public sale of Jan Teunissen's garden

[397 blank; 398] Conditions on which Jan Teunissen proposes to sell at public sale to the highest bidder his garden lying in the village of Beverwyck, next Mr Rencelaer's, on the river side.

First, the garden shall be delivered to the buyer as it now lies in its fence; to the west a road, length eight rods and seven feet; to the east along the river side, length eight rods and one foot; to the north on the lot of Goosen Gerritsen, breadth six rods; and on the south side, breadth three and a half rods.

Delivery shall be made at once.

---

[30] Albert Gerritsen was a carpenter by trade. He moved to the Esopus, where he was living in 1662. See *Early Records of Albany*, 1:202, 418; and *Dutch Records of Kingston*, revised translation by Samuel Oppenheim, p. 12.

Payment shall be made in two payments, in good current seawan; the first payment shall be on the first of January of this year 1659 and the second payment on the last of February A°. 1659.

The buyer shall be holden to furnish two sufficient sureties, jointly and severally [liable] as principals, to the content of the seller and that immediately.

If the buyer can not furnish sufficient sureties within the aforesaid time then [the garden] shall be offered for sale again at his expense and charge and whatever less it shall bring, he shall be holden to make good and whatever more it shall fetch shall not inure to his benefit.

The auction fees are a charge upon the buyer.

[399] On the aforesaid conditions, by decreasing bid, Willem Fredericksz Bout remained the last bidder for the sum of one hundred and fifty-eight guilders, for which he binds his person and estate, real and personal. Done in the village of Beverwyck, this 3d of January A°. 1659, in presence of Loduvicus Cobussen and Johannes Provoost.

    This is the mark X of WILLEM FREDRICKSZ
    BOUT, made with his own hand

Ludouicus Cobes
Johannes Provoost, witness

Acknowledged before me,

  LA MONTAGNE, *Commissary at Fort Orange*

Jan Teunissen acknowledges that he has received the abovementioned sum from Willem Fredricksz Bout and releases the said Willem Fredricksz from all claims and demands, for which he binds himself as above.

Done in Fort Orange, this 4th of January A°. 1659.

    This is the mark X of JAN TEUNISSEN,
    made with his own hand

Deed from Jan Teunissen to Willem Fredericksen Bout for a garden at Beverwyck (incomplete)

[400] Appeared before me, Johannes La Montagne, in the service of the General Chartered West India Company commissary at Fort Orange and the village of Beverwyck, in presence of the Honorable Jan Tomassen and Adriaen Gerritsen, magistrates of said jurisdiction, Jan Teunissen, who declared that he had granted and con-

veyed, as he hereby does grant and convey, in real and actual possession, to the behoof of Willem Fredricksz Bout, his heirs and assigns, a garden lying over against Mr Rencelaer's. [Incomplete and canceled]

Conditions of public sale of Teunis Slingerlant's house and lot

[401] Conditions and terms on which Storm Albertsen, attorney for Teunis Slingerlant, proposes to sell at public sale to the highest bidder the house and lot of the aforesaid Slingerlant, lying in the village of Beverwyck.

First, the aforesaid house and lot shall be delivered to the buyer, adjoining to the north Reynier Wisselpenningh, to the south the street, to the east Jacob de Brouwer, to the west also the street; the house is 30½ feet in length and 23½ feet in breadth; the lot is 64½ feet in length, including the width of the house, and 33 feet in breadth, in the [direction of the] length of the house, to wit, wood feet.

Delivery shall be made on the first of May A°. 1659.

Payment shall be made in two instalments in good, whole, merchantable beavers, to wit, the first payment on delivery of the house and the second payment on the first of August of this year 1659.

The buyer shall be holden to furnish two sufficient sureties jointly and severally [liable] as principals, to the content of the seller, immediately.

If the buyer can not furnish sufficient sureties within the aforesaid time then the premises shall be offered for sale again at his expense and charge and whatever less they shall bring, he shall be holden to make good, and whatever more they shall fetch shall not inure to his benefit.

The auction fees will be charged to the buyer.

Conditions of public sale of Thomas Chambers' house and lot in Beverwyck

[402] Conditions and terms on which Mr Tomas Chambert proposes to sell at public sale to the highest bidder his house and lot lying in the village of Beverwyck according to the patent thereof.

First, the aforesaid house and lot shall be delivered to the buyer, with whatever is fast by nail or earth, adjoining on the north Claes Hendericksz, to the south Abraham Vosburgh, to the east a road, to the west also a road, breadth ten rods and eight feet, length twelve rods and eleven feet.

Delivery shall be made of the aforenamed house and lot immediately.

Payment shall be made in three payments; the first payment eight days after delivery in good current seawan, the second payment on the first of July A°. 1659, in good, whole, merchantable beavers, and the third payment on the first of July A°. 1660, also in good, whole, merchantable beavers.

The buyer shall be holden to furnish two sufficient sureties, jointly and severally [liable] as principals, to the content of the seller, immediately.

If the buyer can not furnish sufficient sureties in the aforesaid time [the house and lot] shall be offered for sale again at his charge and expense and whatever less they shall bring, he shall be holden to make good and whatever more they shall fetch shall not inure to his benefit.

The auction fees will be charged to the buyer.

[Canceled in the record]

Deed from Thomas Chambers to Abraham Staets of a house and lot in Beverwyck

[405][31] Appeared before me, Johannes La Montagne, in the service of the General Chartered West India Company commissary at Fort Orange and the village of Beverwyck, in the presence of the Honorable Jan Tomassen and Françoys Boon, magistrates of said jurisdiction, Tomas Chambert, inhabitant of Esopus, who declared that he had granted and conveyed, as he hereby does grant and convey, in real and actual possession, to the behoof of the Honorable Abraham Staet[s], burgher and inhabitant of this village of Beverwyck, his heirs and assigns, a house and lot lying in the village of Beverwyck, adjoining northerly Abraham Vosburgh, southerly Claes Hendericksz, easterly the street, westerly the wagon road, length twelve rods and eleven feet, breadth ten rods and eight feet according to the patent to him, the grantor, granted by the honorable director general and council of New Netherland of date the 8th of November A°. 1658, for a certain sum, for which the grantor acknowledges that he has received satisfaction, and the aforenamed

---

[31] Page 403 contains a canceled draft of the present deed from Thomas Chambers and page 404 is blank.

grantor promises the aforesaid house and lot to warrant against all claims, demands and pretensions which may hereafter arise, for which he binds his person and estate, real and personal, present and future, submitting the same to all courts and judges. Done in Fort Orange, the 24th of January A°. 1659.

THOMAS CHAMBERS

Françoys Boon
Jan Thomasz

Acknowledged before me,

LA MONTAGNE, *Commissary at Fort Orange*

Power of attorney from Evert Pels to Capt. Jan Jacobsen

[406] Appeared before me, Johannes La Montagne, in the service of the General Chartered West India Company commissary at Fort Orange and the village of Beverwyck, Evert Pels, who declared in the presence of the hereinafter named witnesses that he had constituted and appointed, as he hereby does constitute and appoint, the Honorable Capt. Jan Jacobsen his attorney, in the principal's name and on his behalf to procure the freedom of Marritien Symons, sister of the principal's wife, dwelling in the city of New Amstel on the South river with one Pieter Pietersen Herder, in such manner as the attorney may judge best; promising to hold good and valid whatever the attorney shall do in this matter as if he, the principal, were himself present, for which he binds his person and estate, real and personal, submitting the same to all courts and judges. Done in Fort Orange, the 19th of February A°. 1659, in presence of Johannes Provoost and Jan Pietersen Muller.

EVERT PELS

Johannes Provoost, witness
Jan Pieters Mulder

Acknowledged before me,

LA MONTAGNE, *Commissary at Fort Orange*

Deed from Sander Leendersen Glen to Willem Fredericksen Bout of a lot in the village of Beverwyck

[409][32] Appeared before me, Johannes La Montagne, in the service of the General Chartered West India Company commissary at

---

[32] **Page 407** contains an unfinished draft of the present deed and page 408 is blank.

Fort Orange and the village of Beverwyck, in presence of Françoys Boon and Pieter Hartgers, magistrates of said jurisdiction, Sander Leendersen Geleyn, burgher and inhabitant of the aforesaid village, who declared that he had granted and conveyed, as he hereby does grant and convey, in real and actual possession, to the behoof of Willem Fredricksz, his heirs and assigns, a lot lying in the aforesaid village, adjoining northerly the grantee, southerly Willem Teljer, extending from the street to the path at the river, in length ten rods and in breadth seven rods, as appears by the patent to him, the grantor, given by the honorable director general and council on the 23d of April A°. 1652, for the sum of fifty good, whole beavers, wherefore the said grantor promises to warrant the said grantee against all claims and demands which may hereafter arise, binding thereto his person and estate, real and personal, present and future, under submission to all courts and judges. Done in Fort Orange, the 17th of March A°. 1659.

SANDER LENRSEN GLEN

Françoys Boon
Pieter Hartgerts

Acknowledged before me,

LA MONTAGNE, *Commissary at Fort Orange*

Deed from Willem Fredericksen Bout to Evert Pels of a house, lot and garden in Beverwyck in exchange for two sawmills in Rensselaerswyck

[410] Appeared before me, Johannes La Montagne, in the service of the General Chartered West India Company commissary at Fort Orange and the village of Beverwyck, in the presence of Jan Tomassen and Adriaen Gerritsen, magistrates of said jurisdiction, Willem Fredricksz, burgher and inhabitant of said village, who declared that he had conveyed, as he hereby does grant and convey, in real and actual possession, to the behoof of Evert Pels, inhabitant of the colony of Rencelaerswyck, his heirs and assigns, a house, lot and garden lying in the aforesaid village; the lot whereon the house stands has heretofore been used as a garden, as mentioned in the patent, and adjoins northerly Volckert Janssen, southerly Sander Leendersen, westerly the wagon road and easterly the path at the river; length eleven rods and breadth four rods and two feet; the garden is in length and breadth as stated in the conveyance made by Sander Leendersen to the grantor; and that for two sawmills,

standing and lying in the colony of Rencelaerswyck, on the east side of the river, behind the *greene bosch*;[33] the parties to this exchange mutually promising to warrant each other against all claims and demands which may arise on either side; for which they bind their persons and [411] estates, real and personal, present and future, submitting the same to all courts and judges. Done in Fort Orange, the 17th of March A°. 1659.

This is the mark X of WILLEM FREDRICKSZ
EVERT PELS

Deed from Jan Roelofsen to Pieter Hartgers of one-half of a house bought at public sale of Juriaen Teunissen

[412] Appeared before me, Johannes La Montagne, in the service of the General Chartered West India Company commissary at Fort Orange and the village of Beverwyck, Jan Roeloffsen,[34] who declared that he had conveyed, as he hereby does convey, to the Honorable Pieter Hartgers the half of his house which he bought at public sale of Jurriaen Teunissen and of which he remained the last bidder, for which the said Pieter Hartgers paid the half of the first payment; [executing this conveyance] as a token of ownership and that during his life or after his death it may appear that the aforesaid Pieter Hartgers has a full half interest in the aforesaid house, for which he binds his person and estate, real and personal, present and future. Done in Fort Orange, the 24th of March 1659.

JAN ROELOFSEN

Acknowledged before me,

LA MONTAGNE, *Commissary at Fort Orange*

Deed from Jan Dircksen van Bremen to Eldert Gerbertsen Cruyff of a farm at Catskill (incomplete)

[413] Appeared before me, Johannes La Montagne, in the service of the General Chartered West India Company commissary at Fort Orange and the village of Beverwyck, in presence of Jan Tomassen and Adriaen Gerritsen, magistrates of said jurisdiction, Jan Dircksz van Breemen, who declared that he had conveyed, as he hereby does grant and convey, in real and actual possession to the behoof of

---

[33] Literally "pine woods," afterwards corrupted to Greenbush.
[34] Jan Roelofsen was the son of Anneke Jans by her first husband Roelof Jansen from Masterland, and a brother-in-law of Rieter Hartgers.

Eldert Gerbertsen Kruyff, his heirs and assigns, his farm.[35] [Incomplete and canceled]

Conditions of sale of the late Johan de Hulter's land at the Esopus, being lot no. 1

[415][36] Terms and conditions on which Mr Jeronimus Ebbinck, husband and guardian of Madam Johanna de Laet, late widow of Mr Johan de Hulter, proposes to sell at public sale to the highest bidder a piece of land lying in the Great Esopus.

First, there shall be delivered to the buyer a piece of land comprising forty-seven morgens and two hundred and fifteen rods, lying on the hill, which is marked on the map thereof no. 1.

Delivery shall be made of the aforesaid piece of land at once.

Payment shall be made in two instalments in good, whole, merchantable beavers, or the half in good current seawan at eleven guilders in seawan for a beaver, the first payment on the first of July of this year 1659 and the second or last payment on the first of July A°. 1660.

The buyer shall be holden to furnish two sufficient sureties, jointly and severally [liable] as principals, to the content of the seller, and that immediately.

If the buyer can not furnish sufficient sureties in said time, then [the land] shall be offered again at his expense and charge and whatever less it shall bring, he shall be holden to make good, and whatever more it shall bring shall not inure to his benefit.

[416] The auction fees will be charged to the buyer.

Conditions of sale of the late Johan de Hulter's land at the Esopus, being lot no. 2

[417] Terms and conditions on which Mr Ebbinck, husband and guardian of Madam Johanna de Laet, late widow of Johan de Hulter, proposes to sell at public sale to the highest bidder a piece of land lying in the Great Esopus.

First, the aforesaid piece of land shall be delivered to the buyer,

---

[35] This farm was at Catskill. According to G. Beernink, *De Geschiedschrijver en Rechtsgeleerde Dr. Arend van Slichtenhorst en zijn vader Brant van Slichtenhorst*, p. 170, Jan Dircksen came not, as generally supposed, from the city of Bremen, in Germany, but from Amersfoort, in the province of Utrecht, van Bremen being his family name.

[36] Page 414 contains an unfinished draft of the present conditions of sale.

comprising forty-eight morgens and seventy-two rods, lying on the hill, on the survey map marked no. 2.

Delivery of the aforesaid piece of land shall be made immediately.

Payment shall be made in two instalments, the first payment on the first of July of this year 1659, and the second payment on the first of July of the coming year 1660, in good, whole, merchantable beavers or the half in good strung seawan, the seawan reckoned at eleven guilders for a beaver.

The buyer shall be holden at once to furnish two sufficient sureties, jointly and severally [liable] as principals, to the content of the seller.

If the buyer shall not furnish in said time sufficient sureties, the aforenamed land shall be offered for sale again at his expense and charge and whatever less it shall bring, he shall be holden to make good and whatever more it shall fetch shall not inure to his benefit.

The auction fees will be charged to the buyer.

Conditions of sale of the late Johan de Hulter's land at the Esopus, being lot no. 3

[418 blank; 419] Terms and conditions on which Mr Jeronimus Ebbinck, husband and guardian of Madam Johanna de Laet, late widow of Johan de Hulter, proposes to sell at public sale to the highest bidder a piece of land lying in the Great Esopus.

First, the aforesaid land shall be delivered to the buyer, comprising thirty-five morgens and one hundred and ten rods, marked on the survey map no. 3.

Delivery shall be made at once.

Payment shall be made in two instalments, the first payment on the first of July A°. 1659, the second payment on the first of July A°. 1660, in good, whole, merchantable beavers or the half in good current seawan to be paid at eleven guilders the beaver.

The buyer shall be holden to furnish two sufficient sureties to the content of the seller and that at once.

If the buyer can not furnish sufficient sureties in said time, the aforesaid land shall be offered for sale again at his expense and charge and whatever less it shall bring, he shall be holden to make good and whatever more it shall fetch shall not inure to his benefit.

The auction fees will be charged to the buyer.

Conditions of sale of the late Johan de Hulter's land at the Esopus, being lot no. 4

[420 blank; 421] Terms and conditions on which Mr Jeronimus Ebbinck, husband and guardian of Madam Johanna de Laet, late widow of Mr Johan de Hulter, proposes to sell at public sale to the highest bidder a piece of land lying at the Great Esopus.

First, the aforesaid piece of land shall be delivered to the buyer, comprising thirty-five morgens and one hundred and fifty rods, lying on the kill, marked on the survey map no. 4.

Delivery shall be made at once. Payment shall be made in two instalments, the first payment on the first of July of this year 1659, and the second payment on the first of July A°. 1660, in good, whole, merchantable beavers, or the half in good current seawan at eleven guilders a beaver.

The buyer shall be holden to furnish two sufficient sureties, jointly and severally [liable] as principals, to the content of the seller, at once.

If the buyer can not furnish sufficient sureties in the aforesaid time, then [the land] shall be offered for sale again at his expense and charge and whatever less it shall bring, he shall be holden to make good and whatever more it shall fetch shall not inure to his benefit.

The auction fees will be charged to the buyer.

Deed from Jan Andriessen from Dublin to Jan Dircksen van Bremen of a piece of land at Catskill

[422] Appeared before me, Johannes La Montagne, in the service of the General Chartered West India Company commissary at Fort Orange and the village of Beverwyck, in the presence of Abraham Staets and Pieter Hartgers, magistrates of said jurisdiction, Jan Anderiessen van Dubelingh,[37] who declared that he had conveyed, as he hereby does grant and convey, in real and actual possession, to the behoof of Jan Dircksz van Breemen, his heirs and assigns, a piece of land lying in Katskil, on the north side of the aforesaid kill, comprising six morgens, which piece of land was given to him, the grantor, by the honorable director general and council of New Netherland under date of the 16th of November A°. 1653, [by patent] signed by Johannes Dyckman and P. Stuyvesant, for which

---

[37] Jan Andriessen (John Andrews, or Anderson?) from Dublin, Ireland.

the grantor acknowledges that he has been satisfied, promising to warrant the said land against claims and demands which may hereafter arise, for which he binds his person and estate, real and personal, present and future, submitting the same to all courts and judges. Done in Fort Orange, the 10th of April A°. 1659.

This is the X mark of JAN ANDERIESSEN
VAN DUBELINGH

Pieter Hartgers

Power of attorney from Rem Jansen to Jacobus Visch, trader at New Amsterdam

[423] Appeared before me, Johannes La Montagne, in the service of the General Chartered West India Company commissary at Fort Orange and the village of Beverwyck, Rem Janssen, who declared that he had constituted and appointed, as he hereby does constitute and appoint, Mr Jacobus Visch, trader at Amsterdam in New Netherland, his attorney, in the principal's name and on his behalf to demand restitution of his farm lying on Long Island from Henderick Janssen van Breemen, at present still occupying the same, and the implements, to wit, wagons, plows and harrows, and furthermore the house roof tight and the land well fenced, according to the contract made between both parties; promising to hold good and valid whatever the attorney shall do in said matter, for which he binds his person and estate, real and personal, present and future, submitting the same to all courts and judges. Done in Fort Orange, this 15th of April A°. 1659, in presence of Arent vanden Bergh and Johannes Provoost.

REM YANSEN

Johannes Provoost
This is the AB mark of *Arent vanden Bergh*

Acknowledged before me,

LA MONTAGNE, *Commissary at Fort Orange*

Deed from Hendrick Gerritsen Vermeulen to Jan Dareth of a garden in Beverwyck

[424] Appeared before me, Johannes La Montagne, in the service of the General Chartered West India Company commissary at Fort Orange and the village of Beverwyck, in the presence of the Honorable Françoys Boon and Pieter Hartgers, magistrates of said juris-

diction, Henderick Gerritsen,[38] who declared that he had conveyed as he hereby does grant and convey, in real and actual possession, to the behoof of Jan Dareth, his heirs and assigns, a garden lying in the village of Beverwyck, behind Fort Orange, to the north Rutger Jacobsen, to the south Frans Barentsen, to the east Jan van Aecken, according to the patent granted to Rem Janssen, from whom the grantor received the said garden by conveyance; therefore, the said grantor warrants the grantee against all claims and demands which may hereafter arise, for which he binds his person and estate, real and personal, present and future, submitting the same to all courts and judges. Done in Fort Orange, the 7th of May A°. 1659.

HYNDRICK GEIRES

Françoys Boon
Pieter Hartgerts

Acknowledged before me,

LA MONTAGNE, *Commissary at Fort Orange*

Deed from Jan Dareth to Rutger Jacobsen of the garden conveyed to him by preceding deed

[425] Appeared before me, Johannes La Montagne, in the service of the General Chartered West India Company commissary at Fort Orange and the village of Beverwyck, in the presence of the Honorable Françoys Boon and Pieter Hartgers, magistrates of the said jurisdiction, Jan Dareth, who declared that he had conveyed, as he hereby does grant and convey, in real and actual possession, to the behoof of Rutger Jacobsen, his heirs and assigns, a garden lying in the village of Beverwyck behind Fort Orange, to the north the grantee, to the south Frans Barentsen, to the east Jan van Aecken, which garden the grantor received by conveyance from Henderick Gerritsen, in length and breadth according to the patent which was granted to Rem Janssen, from which the [title to] said garden arises; therefore, the grantor warrants the grantee against all claims and demands which may hereafter arise, for which he binds his

---

[38] His signature is the same as that of Hendrick Gerritsen Vermeulen in *Deeds*, 2:664–65 (tr. in *Early Records of Albany*, 1:420), and that of Hendrick Gerritsen in *Deeds*, 1:19 (tr. in *Early Records of Albany*, 1:8–9), whom Professor Pearson, erroneously, it seems, has identified with Hendrick Gerritsen van Wie. See note on page 6 of same volume.

person and estate, real and personal, present and future, submitting the same to all courts and judges. Done in Fort Orange, this 7th of May A°. 1659.

JAN DARETH

Françoys Boon
Pieter Hartgerts

Acknowledged before me,

LA MONTAGNE, *Commissary at Fort Orange*

Contract of sale between Jan van Aecken and Stoffel Jansen Abeel, attorneys for Pieter de Maecker, and Cornelis Cornelissen de Boer and Daniel Verveelen of a house and lot in Beverwyck

[426] Appeared before me, Johannes La Montagne, in the service of the General Chartered West India Company commissary at Fort Orange and the village of Beverwyck, Jan van Aecken and Stoffel Janssen, burghers and inhabitants here, being attorneys for Pieter Maecker, now at Amsterdam in the fatherland, who declared in the presence of the hereinafter named witnesses that they had sold, as they hereby do sell, to Cornelis Cornelissen de Boer and Daniel Verveelen a house and lot lying in the village of Beverwyck, with such rights and interest therein as the aforesaid Pieter de Maecker has had, to wit, the house as broad as it stands under its roof and in length twenty-five feet, with the lot in the rear, extending from the house to the kill, at the house or north end of the same breadth as the front of the aforesaid house, in length from the rear wall to the aforesaid kill sixty-five feet; behind, on the kill, from the division fence of Dirck Janssen Croon and the seller to the end of a straight line on the east side drawn from the first post to the rear line of the yard or lot, which lot is eighteen feet in breadth; with the stipulation that the buyers are to have all that is expressed in the conveyance from Cornelis Vos to the seller, and that for the sum of one thousand two hundred Carolus guilders in good, whole, merchantable beavers, in two payments, the first [427] payment on the first of July of this year 1659 and the second payment in the month of August A°. 1659, and upon the last payment the seller shall be holden to give a conveyance to the buyers, [parties] promising furthermore, each as far as he is concerned, to perform

all that hereinbefore in love and friendship is agreed upon. Done in Fort Orange, the 16th of May A°. 1659.

This is the X mark of JAN VAN AECKEN
STOFFEL JANSZ
CORNELIS CORNELISSEN DE BOER
DANIEL VERVEELEN

Johannes Provoost, witness
Acknowledged before me,

LA MONTAGNE, Commissary at Fort Orange

Conditions of sale of a house and lot of Juriaen Teunissen

[428] Terms and conditions on which Jurriaen Teunissen proposes to sell at public sale to the highest bidder his house and lot lying in the village of Beverwyck.

First, the house and lot shall be delivered to the buyer according to patent thereof.

Delivery shall be made on the first of October of this year 1659, the house and lot, earth and nail fast.

Payment shall be made in two terms in good, whole, merchantable beavers, to wit: the first payment on the last of July of this year 1659, the second payment on the last of July of the year 1660.

The buyer shall be holden to furnish two sufficient sureties jointly and severally [liable] as principals, within 24 hours, and if the buyer can not furnish sufficient sureties, [the house and lot] shall be offered for sale again at his expense and charge.

The auction fees shall be charged to the buyer.

Bond of Goosen Gerritsen, Adriaen Jansen Appel and Philip Hendricksen as sureties for Steven Jansen (incomplete)

[429] Appeared before me, Johannes La Montagne, commissary at Fort Orange and the village of Beverwyck, on the date underwritten, Goossen Gerittsz, Adriaen Jansz Appel and Philip Hendrixsz, who jointly bind themselves as sureties and principals for the payment of the fine of Steven Jansz, amounting to the sum of three hundred guilders. [Incomplete and canceled]

Conditions of sale of the house and lot and bake shop of Jochem Wesselsen

[430] Terms and conditions on which Jochum Wessels proposes to sell at public sale to the highest bidder his house and [lot] with the [bake] shop[30] as the same at present are infenced, lying in the village of Beverwyck.

First, the house and lot shall be delivered to the buyer as it now stands four square in its fence, earth and nail fast, save a copper cover belonging to the bake oven, which the seller retains for himself.

Payment shall be made in whole, merchantable beavers, in three terms or payments, whereof the first payment shall be made in the last of the month of September of this current year 1659 on the delivery of the said house.

The second payment shall be made one year thereafter in the year 1660 and on the same date.

The third payment shall be made in the year 1661, in the last of September.

The buyer shall be holden to furnish two sufficient sureties, severally [liable] as principals, within 24 hours, and if the buyer can not furnish sufficient sureties within said time, then the premises shall be offered for sale again at his expense and charge [431] and whatever less they shall bring, he shall be holden to make good and whatever more they shall fetch shall not inure to his benefit.

The auction fees shall be charged to the buyer.

Conditions of sale of a house, blacksmith's shop and horse stable of Rem Jansen

[432] Terms and conditions on which Rem Jansz proposes to sell at public sale to the highest bidder his house with a small smith's shop and a horse stable as the same are now infenced, lying in the village of Beverwyck.

First, the house and lot shall be delivered to the buyer, as the same now stand in fence, earth and nail fast, saving the smith's tools which the seller reserves for himself.

Payment shall be made in two instalments in whole, merchantable beavers, whereof the first shall be made on the first of September of this year 1659, being the just half, on the delivery of the house,

---

[30] *Sijn huys ende met de loots.*

and the second and last payment a year from that date, in the year 1660.

The buyer shall be holden to furnish two sufficient sureties, jointly and severally [liable] as principals, to the content of the seller, within 24 hours, and if the buyer can not furnish sufficient sureties within the aforesaid time, then the premises shall be offered for sale again at his expense and charge [433] and whatever less they shall bring, the buyer must make good, and whatever more they shall fetch shall not inure to his profit.

The auction fees become a charge upon the buyer.

After many offers, Jan Thomassen was the last bidder and became the buyer for the sum of ten hundred and thirteen guilders and according to the foregoing conditions he offered Volckert Jansz and Gerart Bancker as sureties, who bound themselves likewise for the performance of the conditions hereinbefore specified. In witness of the truth they have signed these with their own hands, this 16th of June 1659, at Beverwyck, in presence of Jan Hendrixsz and Herman Vedder, called as witnesses hereto.[40]

JAN THOMASZ
VOLCKART JANSZ
GERRET BANCKEN

Jan Hendericksen van Bael, witness
Harman Vedderen, witness

    LA MONTAGNE, *Commissary at Fort Orange*

Conditions of public sale of the house of Philip Pietersen Schuyler

[434] Terms and conditions on which Philip Pitersz proposes to sell at public sale to the highest bidder his house lying in the village of Beverwyck, on the hill, next the house of Piter Bronck.

First, the house shall be delivered to the buyer, earth and nail fast, with the lot according to the patent, in breadth 5 rods and in length 20 rods, being rectangular in shape.

Delivery shall be made tomorrow, being the 17th of June of this year 1659, provided that the lessee shall occupy the house until the first of May anno 1660 and the buyer receive the rent of the said house.

Payment shall be made in good, whole, merchantable beavers,

---

[40] Cf. deed from Rem Jansen to Jan Thomassen, August 3, 1660, in *Early Records of Albany*, 1:283-84.

in three payments, the first on the first of September of this year 1659, the second on the same day a year later, and the third and last payment likewise a year after the date of the second payment, being in the year 1661.

Conditions of public sale of the house and lot of Jan Lambertsen

[435] Terms and conditions on which Jan Lambertsen[41] proposes to sell at public sale to the highest bidder his house and lot lying on the plain in this village of Beverwyck.

First, the house and lot shall be delivered to the buyer, earth and nail fast, according to the patent thereof, which the buyer shall receive with the last payment. The house is 20 feet long and 20 feet broad, built up all around with a half-brick wall ceiling and floor tight; the lot is 6 rods long and 3 rods broad.

Delivery shall be made on the first of August of this year 1659.

Payment shall be made in good, whole, merchantable beavers in two terms, the first term or payment on the first of August 1659 on the delivery of the said house, being the just half; the second and last payment a year thereafter on the same date, to wit, on the first of August 1660.

The buyer shall be holden to furnish two sufficient sureties, jointly and severally [liable] as principals, to the content of the seller, within 24 hours, and if the buyer can not furnish sufficient sureties [the house and lot] shall be offered for sale again at his expense and charge and whatever less [436] they shall bring, the buyer must make up and pay and whatever more they shall fetch shall not inure to his benefit.

The auction fees become a charge upon the buyer.

Power of attorney from Dirck Jansen Croon to Tielman van Vleck

[437] Appeared before me, Johannes La Montagne, in the service of the General Chartered West India Company commissary at Fort Orange and the village of Beverwyck, on the date underwritten and in presence of the hereinafter named witnesses, the worthy Dirrick Janssen Croon, trader here at Fort Orange, who declared that he had constituted and appointed, as he hereby does constitute and appoint, Tielman van Vleck, notary public residing at Amsterdam in New Netherland, his special attorney, in the principal's

---

[41] Jan Lambertsen van Bremen; see *Early Records of Albany*, 1:299, 326-27, 376-77.

name to demand, collect and receive from Jan Gerardi, or Maria Polet,[42] his mother, as surety and principal, or the notary Mattheus de Vos, as husband and guardian of the aforesaid Maria Polet, the sum of four hundred and seventy guilders according to the bond thereof, to be paid in good, merchantable Virginia tobacco, with the interest and expenses; for the receipt acquittance to give and in case of refusal payment to secure by judicial proceedings and rigor of law; to this end all necessary legal steps to take unto judgment and extreme execution thereof; also, if need be, to proceed by attachment against the person and property and furthermore all things to do and perform that to the attorney may seem proper, promising at all times to hold good and valid whatever by the attorney shall [438] be done in the matter aforesaid, provided the attorney be holden a proper return and accounting of his transactions and receipts to make when requested. Thus done and executed in presence of Macchiel Janssen and Saccharias Sickels, as witnesses hereto called, on this 5th of July A°. 1659, who with the principal have subscribed the original minute hereof remaining in the custody of me, the commissary.

DIRCK JANSEN CROON

Machghyel Janss[43]
Sachariasz Sickelsz

Acknowledged before me,

LA MONTAGNE, *Commissary at Fort Orange*

Conditions of public sale of the house and lot of Jacob Jansen Loockermans

[439] Terms and conditions on which Jacob Janssen Loockermans proposes to sell at public sale to the highest bidder his house and lot lying in the village of Beverwyck, to the east Willem Janssen Schut, to the south and west the street.

First, the house and lot shall be delivered to the buyer with all that is fast by earth and nail, said house being fifteen feet in length and twenty-four feet in breadth, with a lean-to, the lot being as

---

[42] Marie Pollet, the widow of Philip Gérard, or Geraerdy, an early tavern-keeper of New Amsterdam. See J. H. Innes, *New Amsterdam and its People*, p. 8, 12.
[43] Michiel Jansen van Schrabbekercke; see *Van Rensselaer Bowier Mss*, p. 499, 818. Schrabbekercke, or 's-Heer-Abtskerke, is a village in the polder of Vreeland, on the island of Zuid-Beveland, in the province of Zealand, Netherlands. The children of Michiel Jansen adopted the name Vreeland as a family name.

long and as broad as it lies in its fence. The rent of the cellar till the first of May 1660 is reserved by the seller.

Delivery of the aforesaid house and lot shall be made on the first of August next coming.

The payment in two instalments, the first payment on delivery of the house and lot in good, whole, merchantable beavers and the second on the first of July 1660, also in good, whole, merchantable beavers.

The buyer shall be holden to furnish two sufficient sureties, jointly and severally [liable] as principals, immediately, to the content of the seller.

[440] If the buyer can not furnish sufficient sureties in the aforesaid time, then [the house and lot] shall be offered for sale again at his expense and charge and whatever less they shall come to, he shall be holden to make good and whatever more they shall bring shall not inure to his benefit.

The auction fees shall become a charge upon the buyer.

Public sale of hats and furniture of Jan Claessen Backer

[441] Conditions on which Jan Claessen Backer proposes to sell some hats and furniture, to be paid for within 8 days in beavers and what amounts to less than one beaver in seawan. The auction shall be charged to the buyer. In Fort Orange, the 10th of July 1659.

Philip Hendericksz, a hat	fl. 7 : 18
Luycas Dircksz, a ditto, black	11 : 10
Barent Meyndersen, ditto	11 : 10
Tomas Poulus, ditto	11 : 16
Cobus Teunissen, ditto	10 : 6
Reyer Albertsz	9 : 10
Claes Jacobsen, ditto	11 : 5
	fl. 73 : 15

Public sale of three negroes and a negress of Cornelis Martensen Potter

[442] Conditions on which Cornelis Martensen Potter proposes to sell at public sale to the highest bidder three negroes and one negress, who shall be sold separately, excepting the negress, who shall be sold with a negro.

Delivery of the same shall be made at once.

Payment shall be made in good, whole, merchantable beavers on

Monday morning next, being the 14th of this month, or today, if it can be done.

The buyer shall be holden to furnish at once two sufficient sureties, jointly and severally liable as principals, to the satisfaction of the seller.

If the buyer can not furnish sufficient sureties in said time, then the aforesaid negroes shall be offered for sale again at his expense and charge and whatever less they shall bring, he shall be holden to make good, and whatever more they bring shall not inure to his benefit.

[443] The auction fees shall be charged to the buyer.

On the aforesaid conditions, by lowering bid (*bij afslach*), Abraham Staets was the last bidder for one of the three negroes, named Augustynus, for the sum of three hundred and fifty guilders.

Bond and mortgage of Hendrick Gerritsen Vermeulen to Cornelis Steenwyck

[444] Appeared before me, Johannes La Montagne, in the service of the General Chartered West India Company commissary at Fort Orange and the village of Beverwyck, in the presence of the Honorable Anderies Herbertsen and Jan Verbeeck, magistrates of said jurisdiction, Hendrick Gerritsen, who acknowledged that he was well and truly indebted to Mr Cornelis Steenwyck, trader at Amsterdam in New Netherland, in the sum of four hundred and fifty guilders and ten stivers in good, whole, merchantable beavers at eight guilders apiece, with interest at ten per cent, beginning from the month of August A°. 1658, for every month after the expiration of the aforesaid time until the full payment of the said sum. As special security for which aforesaid sum and said interest the said Henderick Gerritsz mortgages both his houses lying in the village of Beverwyck, to the south the kill, to the north Reynier Wisselpennigh, and at present occupied by him, all for the payment of the aforesaid sum, promising furthermore to pay the said Mr Steenwyck as soon as possible, for which he binds his person and estate, real and personal, having and to have, submitting the same to all courts and judges. Done in Fort Orange, the 15th of July 1659.

HINDRICK GEIRES

Andries Herberts
Jan Verbeeck
   Acknowledged before me,
     LA MONTAGNE, *Commissary at Fort Orange*

Farming of the tapsters' excise continued to Adriaen Jansen Appel

[445] On this last day of October A°. 1659, the honorable *commis* and magistrates have for the sake of accommodation prolonged and continued the farming of the tapsters' excise according to the former conditions made on the 25th of November A°. 1659,[44] to Adriaen Janssen van Leyden, for the sum of four thousand guilders; likewise Anderies Herbertsen and Rutger Jacobsen, as sureties and principals for the satisfaction of said sum, bind their persons and estates, real and personal, having and to have, submitting the same to all courts and judges. Done in Fort Orange, as above.

A: APPEL
ANDRIES HERBERTS[45]

Bond and mortgage of Jan Labatie to Allart Anthony

[446] Appeared before me, Johannes La Montagne, in the service of the General Chartered West India Company commissary at Fort Orange and the village of Beverwyck, and in presence of Sander Leendersen Glen and Jan Verbeeck, magistrates of said jurisdiction, the Honorable Jan Labatie, inhabitant of the colony of Renselaerswyck, who acknowledged that he was truly indebted to Mr Aldert Anthony, burgher of the city of Amsterdam in New Netherland, in the sum of four hundred and fifty guilders, which sum he promises to pay, to wit, one-half in the month of July of this year A°. 1660, in good, whole, merchantable beavers, and the other remaining half in the year anno 1661, in like currency in the month of July; for which he binds his person and estate, real and personal, having and to have, especially mortgaging and binding his new house, lying in the village of Beverwyck, to the north of Sander Leendersen's house, waiving hereby all exceptions to this mortgage which might be claimed. Done in Fort Orange, the 10th of April A°. 1660.

JAN LABATIE

Jan Verbeeck
Sander Lenrsen

    Acknowledged before me,

        LA MONTAGNE, *Commissary at Fort Oranje*

---

[44] This should be 1658; see p. 90.
[45] Not signed by Rutger Jacobsen.

Farming of the burghers' excise continued to Adriaen Jansen Appel van Leyden

[447] On this 4th of November A°. 1660, the honorable commissary and magistrates have prolonged and continued the farming of the burghers' excise according to the former conditions made on the last of October A°. 1658 and considerately granted the same to Adriaen Janssen van Leyden for the sum of one thousand, eight hundred and fifty guilders, for the payment of which aforesaid sum, in case the farmer fails, Philip Pietersen Schuyler and Pieter Ryverdinck, as sureties and principals, bind their persons and estates, real and personal, having and to have, submitting the same to all courts and judges. Done as above, in Fort Orange.

                        A: APPEL VAN LEYDEN
                        PHILIP PIETERSEN SCHUYLER
                        PIETER RYVERDINGH

Acknowledged before me,
    LA MONTAGNE, *Commissary at Fort Oranje*

[END OF MORTGAGE NO. 1]

Part 2

WILLS, INVENTORIES AND SETTLEMENTS OF ESTATES JANUARY 5, 168$\frac{0}{1}$ — OCTOBER 30, 1765

RECORDED IN DUTCH IN

WILLS, PARTS 1 AND 2, 1691-1835

Record of Letters of Administration &^{a}. Begunn y^e. 6th. of Octob^r, 1691

Will of Teunis Teunissen Metselaer and Egbertie Egberts, his wife

[6] In the name of the Lord, Amen. Teunis Teunise d'Metselaer,[46] farmer, dwelling in the colony of Renselaerswyck in the county of Albany, at present sick in body but of sound mind and memory, and Egbertie Egberts, sound in body and mind, married people, who, considering the shortness and frailty of human life, the certainty of death and the uncertainty of the hour thereof, deliberately and advisedly, without inducement, persuasion or misleading of anyone, declare that they have made, ordained and determined this their respective and reciprocal last will and testament in form and manner following:

First and foremost committing their immortal souls, whenever they shall be separated from their bodies, to the gracious and merciful hands of God, their Creator and Savior, and their bodies to a Christian burial, likewise revoking, canceling and annulling all and every testamentary disposition heretofore made either jointly or severally, and herewith arriving at the principal disposition of their temporal effects to be left behind, these testators have nominated and constituted, as hereby they do reciprocally nominate and constitute the survivor of the two as his and her sole and universal heir of all their estate, real and personal, claims, credits, money, gold and silver coined and uncoined, jewels, linen and woolen clothing,

---

[46] Literally: Teunis Teunise, the mason.

household furniture, etc., nothing whatsoever excepted or reserved, thereof to dispose, so [7] long as the survivor lives, without interference or contradiction of any person, and whenever the survivor shall decease, it is the will and desire of both the testators that the estate and effects left behind which shall then be found shall be equally divided among their seven children or their heirs, to wit: Maritje, wife of Harme Lievese; Egbert Teunise; Gerrittje, wife of Andries Hanse; Dirkje, wife of Bastian Harmense; Willemtie Teunise, aged 23 years; Anna Teunise, aged twenty-one years; and Martyn Teunis, aged nineteen years; that is, each to inherit and receive a just seventh part, one no more than another; provided nevertheless that the survivor be holden properly to support and provide for their three unmarried daughters, and whenever they shall enter into the marriage estate, to give to each of them a proper outfit such as the other married sisters have had, without being holden to do more. But in case the survivor of the testators marries again, the same shall be holden to divide and apportion the whole, namely the just half of the whole estate, to the behoof of their aforesaid seven children, to be divided equally among them, no one receiving more than the others, and the other half shall be for the behoof of the survivor. Finally, the testators hereby exclude and debar (saving all honor and respect) the honorable orphan masters of this place and of any other place where the testators may die from the supervision and administration of their aforesaid children and property, not wishing that the same shall [8] meddle therewith,[47] but instead appointing as guardians of the same the survivor of the two, with power one or more persons to choose and take as fellow guardians. All that is hereinbefore written they, the testators, declare to be their last will and testament, desiring that the same after the death of either of them shall have full force and effect, whether as will, codicil, donation, gift in anticipation of death, or otherwise, as may be most consistent with the contents, notwithstanding that certain formalities of law or custom may herein be omitted, neglected, or not included or observed, requesting of all lords, courts and judges, wherever the testators may die, the enjoy-

---

[47] It was a common practice for testators to exclude the orphan masters from the administration of their estates, not because they were in any sense distrustful of these officials or wished to avoid the fees of such adminstration, but because the investments of funds by the orphan masters, which possessed a high degree of security, were as a rule less profitable to the orphans than those that were open to relatives and friends whom the testators appointed as guardians. See on that point Nicolaas de Roever Az., *De Amsterdamsche Weeskamer*, Amst. 1878, p. 35-36.

ment of the utmost benefit herefrom; one or more copies hereof to be made and delivered by me, the secretary, as the case may require. Done in Albany, at the house of Eghbert Teunise, son of the testators, on this, the seventh day of August, in the first year of his majesty's reign, Anno Domini 1685.

TEUNIS TEUNISĖ METSELAER
EGBERTIEN EGBERTS

Signed and sealed in presence of,
Cornelis van Dyck
Myndert Harmense

In my presence,

Robt. LIVINGSTON, *Cl.*

Will of Jacques Cornelissen van Slyck

[11] In the name of God, Amen. Know all men whom it may concern, that on this eighteenth of May anno sixteen hundred and ninety, at Albany, being in the second year of the reign of William and Mary, king and queen of Great Britain, Jaques Cornelisse van Slyck, residing at Schennechtady, lying here in the city aforesaid sick abed, but having to all outward appearances the perfect use and command of his understanding, faculties, memory and speech, who, considering the frailty of human life and the uncertainty of the hour of death, has of his own motion, without inducement, persuasion or misleading of anyone, but moved thereto voluntarily after mature consideration, thought it advisable not to leave this world without first having disposed of his temporal effects granted to him by the Almighty. Commending first and foremost his immortal soul into the hands of God and his body to a Christian burial, he nominates, constitutes and appoints his wife Gerritje Ryckman his sole and universal heir of all his estate and effects, in manner following:

[12] So soon as their son Herman enters the marriage state, she shall first of all let him have by way of gift fourteen morgens of land lying above Schanechtady, on the first flat, above Sassiasn, the testator's wife to have the usufruct of all the other land, grounds, houses and buildings belonging to him, but the whole of the personal estate and effects she shall be at liberty to use, spend, sell, alienate and dispose of as she pleases, in like manner as the testator in his lifetime could do, without rendering an accounting or inventory,

much less furnishing bond or security, to any relatives, to the guardians of his children or children's children, to the honorable orphan masters or constables, to the inferior and supreme courts of this government, or to any person whomsoever, all and singular of whom he excludes and shuts out, notwithstanding that some law or laws may direct otherwise, which he wills shall in this case be inoperative and of no effect, appointing her as executrix and administratrix during the time of her widowhood; but if she again enters into the marriage estate, she shall to the children begotten by them, to wit: Susanna, Grietje, Herman, Cornelis, Geertruyt, Marte, Helena, Fytie, Lidia and those who may still be procreated by them, apportion and relinquish the just half of all the estate and effects to said children then living, wherein each child shall equally participate without any difference by reason of sex, without prejudice to the donation of fourteen morgens of land to Herman as hereinbefore written. [13] And although the daughters have likewise their interest in the lands, the testator wills that said lands shall remain in the possession of the sons subject to a proper appraisal, and the value of each daughter's portion be paid within the five following years, each year a just fifth part; which lands also may not be sold or alienated by the sons but must descend to each son's male child or children, and failing of these, to the nearest relatives in the male line, who may lawfully bear the name of Van Slyck and be of the testator's lawful seed; but the male lineage failing, the nearest female line shall inherit and succeed to the aforesaid estate even as the male line, because the testator expressly wills and desires that the aforesaid land shall not be alienated from his future blood and lineage but must always return thither again.

But if his aforesaid wife marries again, she shall immediately, before the solemnization of such marriage, cause to devolve upon those who are of age their portion and (under sufficient security) retain the minor's portion and enjoy the use and profits thereof until the time of the majority of each, with the understanding that whoever is of age may demand his portion without waiting until the majority of the younger; therefore she is holden to do by those under age in all ways as an honorable, faithful mother ought to do by her child or children, without any reserve or exception.

[14] And in order that all the aforesaid conditions may in honest simplicity and justice be carried out, the testator appoints Mr Pieter Schuyler, Mr Dirk Wessells and Johannes Glenn as guardians over his minor children, who also shall be joined with his aforesaid wife,

to act as mediators in case any difference or misunderstanding arise between her and the children and to settle the same in love and friendship, so that the maternal and filial affection be not extinguished and that the testator's aforesaid will be not broken and violated; which burden, by the testator's humble request, their honors will please take upon themselves, since Christian duty obligates us to assist the widows and orphans by word and deed. All that is hereinbefore written the testator declares to be his testamentary disposition and last will, which he desires to have effect from the weightiest to the least article thereof, whether as will, codicil, gift in anticipation of death or among the living, or any other bequest however it may be named, notwithstanding that all the formalities required by the laws of this government may not be observed herein, desiring that the utmost benefit of the law may be enjoyed herein for the maintenance of the same.

Thus done, signed and sealed on the 8th of May 1690, at Albany as aforesaid.

This is signed A C K E S by JAQUES CORNELISE VAN SLYK with his own hand (L. S.)

Signed and sealed
in our presence,
A. Appell
Jacob Staets, chirurgeon
In my presence,
JAN BECKER

Will of Andries Hendricksen

[17] In the name of God, Amen. By the contents of this present public instrument know all men that in the year after the birth of our Lord and Savior Jesus Christ 168$^9_0$, on the fifth day of the month of January, before me, Adriaen van Ilpendam, notary public residing in New Albany, admitted by the Right Honorable Edmont Andross (in behalf of His Royal Highness James, Duke of York, governor general over all his territories in America), and before the afternamed witnesses, came and appeared the worthy Andries Heyndrickse, born at Ootmars in Twent,[48] dwelling at present at the Kinderhook, to me, the notary, well known, being at present of sound body, going and standing, having full use and power of his

---

[48] Ootmarssum, a small town in the district of Twenthe, province of Overysel, Netherlands.

senses, reason, memory and understanding according to all outward appearances, which appearer, considering the shortness and frailty of human life, the certainty of death and the uncertainty of the time and hour thereof, and desiring therefore to dispose of his temporal effects to be left behind, (while he yet by God's grace may do so) and which he does of his own free will and motion, without the suggestion or misleading of anyone, has now ordained and concluded this his last will and testament in manner following:

First and foremost committing his immortal soul (whenever it may be separated from his body) to the gracious and merciful hands of God, his maker and redeemer, and his body to a Christian burial, he, the appearer and testator, declares that he has nominated and constituted, as he hereby does, Jan Gilbertz, or in case of Jan Gilbertz' death before that of this testator, Jan Gilbertsz' wife, named Cornelia Arents, or in case of the death of both of them their surviving child or children, as the sole and universal heir [or heirs] of all his estate, personal and real, nothing excepted, which the said testator at his death shall leave behind, without contradiction or gainsaying by any person, and the testator promises to hold the foregoing binding and valid and nevermore to make a will or bequest in favor of any other person, provided that if the testator be taken sick or become incapacitated, or in his old age be not able to earn his living, said Jan Gilbertz, or his wife, or his children, shall be bound properly to provide him with food, clothing and service his life long.

All which aforesaid provisions the appearers declare that they hold good, binding and valid, notwithstanding that certain formalities required by law or custom may not be observed herein, desiring that the utmost benefit herefrom may be had.

Thus done and delivered at the house of Jan Gilbertsz in New Albany, in the presence of Jacob Martense and Evert Wendel, junior, called as trustworthy witnesses hereto, who with the appearers have subscribed this instrument with their own hands in New Albany, the year, month and day above written.

After collation this was found to agree with the original in my custody. In New Albany, January 5, 168$\frac{7}{}$.

Quod attestor

ADRIAEN VAN ILPENDAM, *Not. Pub.*

Recorded in Alb. y^e 18 January 169$\frac{3}{4}$

Inventory of the estate of Neeltie Claes, widow of Hendrick Gardenier

[31][49] Inventory of the estate of Neeltie Claese, widow of the late Hend: Gardnier, the 7th of April 1695.

First, the half of the two mills at Shotak, on the east bank of Hudson's river, the other half of which said mills Cornelis Claese has bought, being valued by said Cornelis Claese and And[s]. Gardinier, guardians of the children, at fifty-five beavers seawan	*fl.* 1320: —
The four lots of land lying on Shotak's island and in the jurisdiction of said Shotak, being valued at eight beavers seawan	1920: —
The lot at Shinnechtady, lying between the lot of the late Domine of Shinnechtady and the lot of Pottmann, being valued at fifteen beavers seawan....	360: —
By a horse which was sold to Phillip D'More, but not yet paid	120: —
By a colt	84: —
By his hardware, viz, a crowbar, 2 augers, 1 try square, 1 broadax and 1 chisel	48: —
	fl. 3852: —

A statement of the debts to be paid out of the aforesaid estate. Albany, April 7, 1695.

To Evert Banker	20	beavers	*fl.*	480: —
Claes Rosevelt	10	"		240: —
Arent Shuyler	17½	"		420: —
Jan Spoor	1¾			42: —
Abraham Kip	7			168: —
Andries Arentse Bratt	3			72: —
Jan Janse Mulenaer[50]	8	" 3 gl.		195: —
Adam Vrooman			*fl.*	12: —
And[rs]. Gardenier for 110 boards @ 1 gl. 10st				165: —
Gerrit Gysbertse				16: 10
Hend: Coenraedtse	5	beavers		120: —

---

[49] Page 30 contains letters of administration in English to Andries Gardenier and Cornelis Claese upon the estate of the late Hendrick Gardenier, dated April 7, 1695.
[50] Doubtless intended for *Meulenaer*, or *Molenacr*, meaning "the miller."

The estate of Jacob Janse Gardenier, dec'd, for a bowl, kettle and spoon..........	*fl.*	19:—
for 26 skipples of peas @ 5 sk. per beaver and carting @ 9 beavers, total........		320:—
for the house on the land at Shotak 7½ beavers, and purchase of the house and barn, *fl.* 60:—, total.....		240:—
also 1½ months of the *waterloot* [51]		28:10
	fl.	607:10
	fl.	2538:—

Will of Captain Sander Glenn

[40] In the name of God, Amen. Know all men whom it may concern, that on the 19th of July sixteen hundred and ninety, at New Albany, being the second year of the reign of William and Mary, king and queen of Great Britain, Capt. Sander Glenn, residing at Schenectady, sound and hearty of body, able to walk and stand, having to all outward appearances the full use and command of his understanding, senses, memory and speech, who, considering the shortness of human life and the unforeseen hour of death and wishing not to depart hence without having first disposed of the temporal estate granted to him by Almighty God, and that without the inducement, persuasion or misleading of anyone, but of his own motion, commending in the first place his soul into the hands of God and his body to a Christian burial, nominates, constitutes and appoints hereby his wife, Antje Glenn, his sole and universal heir of his whole estate and effects, real and personal, money, claims and credit, nothing in the world reserved and excluded, the same to be used, granted, alienated and sold in such manner as the testator if living might do, saving that the land now occupied by the testator and half of the land which he bought of Jan Luykasse, and two negroes named Pieter and Wouter shall not be alienated or sold, but the usufruct thereof be enjoyed during her lifetime. *Item.* So soon as it is known that the testator is dead, his wife shall permit all the

---

[51] Perhaps intended for *water loop*, meaning rent for water privilege.

linen and woolen that have belonged to his body and also all the arms to be equally divided among the sons of his two brothers, but the son of his brother Johannes, named Sander, shall first receive his shotgun that Mr Teller brought from Holland. Furthermore [41] it is his will that she shall not be troubled by the blood relations, or the guardians of the minors, constable or constables, the honorable orphan masters, the court of this county or city of New Albany or any high or low court, or judge of this province, of what name soever, to deliver an inventory of the estate, much less to furnish security or sureties, notwithstanding any law or laws, custom or customs of this province may otherwise direct, desiring that the same shall herein be suspended and without effect, making her to this end administratrix and executrix of the whole of the aforesaid estate and effects in manner and on conditions as aforesaid during the time of her widowhood; but entering the marriage state again, she shall give up the just half of the effects and personal estate as the same may be found to the behoof of his deceased brother Jacob's children and of his brother Johannes or, if deceased, of his child or children, said just half to be divided between both sides into two like parts. But the aforesaid lands and two negroes she shall have use of during the time of her life, without having the power of encumbering, much less of alienating or selling the same; but after her death they shall go to the lawful sons of his brother Jacob and to his brother Johannes, or in case of their deaths before partition to their son or sons, to wit, the one equal just half to the sons of his deceased brother Jacob Glen and the other half to his brother Johannes, or in case of his decease to his son or sons, with this understanding, that the half of the aforesaid land that falls to the son or sons of his brother Jacob shall be lawfully valued and appraised by impartial persons in order that their just portion be paid over in wheat or money to the sister or sisters, as the testator wills and desires that each of the said children shall participate to the same extent in the appraised land but that the son or sons shall possess the same (provided that they make a proper compensation to their sister or sisters), in order that it be not alienated by the next of kin lawfully bearing the name of Glen, which the testator likewise wills to apply to the son or sons of his brother Johannes, if he happen to die before the aforesaid land is divided. The two aforesaid negroes, namely Piet and Wouter, shall also be divided, whereof the one [42] shall go to the children of his deceased brother Jacob and the other to his brother Johannes or, in case of his death before the partition, to his children. *Item.* The share in the grist mill standing at Shennectady and all the real estate acquired by him through inheritance on his aforesaid wife's side, his aforesaid wife shall have and retain for herself, with power in all respects to do therewith and to dispose thereof, alienate, use and sell the same even and in like manner as the testator might do. Likewise the testator grants to his said wife administration of his affairs during his absence to Canada. All that is hereinbefore written the testator declares to be his testamentary disposition and last will which he desires to have full effect from the least to the weightiest article, whether as will, codicil, gift in anticipation of death or among the living, or any other bequest however it may be named, notwithstanding that all the formalities required by the laws of this government may not be observed herein, desiring that the utmost benefit may be received for the maintenance of what is hereinbefore written.

In witness of the truth of which, without craft or guile, he has subscribed and sealed this with his own hand on the 19th of July at New Albany aforesaid.

Was signed,
SANDER GLENN (L.S.)

Signed and sealed in presence of us,

Willem Ketelheyn
Joh: Becker Junr. } 1690, the 28th July
J. Becker

The land which I bought with my brother Johannes Glenn from Jan Luykase, it is my will that my brother Johannes' son named Sander shall receive by privilege [and], in case of his death, his brother Johannes.

Signd
SANDER GLENN

As witnesses

This is the mark IoS of *Isaak Switts*

Dirk Bratt[52]

---

[52] Page 43 contains letters of administration in English to Annetje Sanders on the estate of her late husband Sander Glenn, dated February 20, 1696.

Will of Pieter Winne

[44] In the name of God, Amen. By the contents of this present public instrument know all men that in the year after the birth of our Lord and Savior Jesus Christ, one thousand six hundred and eighty-four, on the 6th of July, about midday, and in the thirty-sixth year of his majesty's reign Charles the second, before me, Robt. Livingston, secretary of Albany, colony of Renselaerswyk and Shinnechtady, etc., and before the hereinafter named witnesses, came and appeared the Honorable Mr Pieter Winne, magistrate, born in the city of Gent in *d Landeren*,[53] at present sick in body but of sound memory and understanding as is clearly apparent, who, considering the shortness and frailty of human life, the certainty of death and the uncertainty of the time and hour thereof, therefore wishing to dispose of his temporal effects to be left behind while he yet by God's grace is able, and doing so of his own free will and motion, without the inducement or misleading of anyone, he now ordains and determines this his last will and testament in form and manner following:

First and foremost commending his immortal soul (whenever it shall be separated from his body) to the gracious and merciful hands of his Creator and Savior and his body to a Christian burial, likewise [45] canceling, revoking and annulling thereby all and every such testamentary disposition and bequest as he before the date hereof may have made and executed, especially that will by himself and wife made under date of the 1st of June 1677, written by Mr Adriaen van Ilpendam, notary public, holding the same null and of no effect and now making a new disposition, this testator declares that he has nominated and instituted, as he does nominate and institute hereby, his worthy and beloved wife Tannetje Adams as his sole and universal heir of all his lands, property real and personal, claims, credits, money, gold, silver coined and uncoined, jewels, clothing, linen, woolens, household furniture, etc., nothing excepted, so long as she remains in her widowed state, without her being called upon or annoyed by any one of the children, or anyone for them, for an inventory or anything appertaining to the estate and after her death shall his estate be equally divided among the children whom they have begotten together, share and share alike. But if his wife enters the marriage state again, then she shall be

---

[53] Intended for Gent in Vlaenderen, Ghent in Flanders.

holden to divide and apportion the whole estate; that is to say, a just half thereof as it then may be found to the behoof of the children whom he has begotten by his present wife aforenamed, namely, Adam Winne, Livinus, Frans, Allette, wife of Casper Leendertse Tenyn,[54] Killiaen, Tomas, Lyntje, Marte, Jacobus, Eva, Daniel and Rachell Winne; and the other half [46] to the behoof of his wife, with this reservation that she remain holden the minor children to bring up in the fear of the Lord, and cause them to learn reading and writing and a trade or handicraft wherewith in due time they may, by God's favor, with honor obtain their subsistence, the legitimate portion of said minor children remaining so long in the hands of their mother aforesaid and the rents and profits thereof being by her received until they arrive at maturity and enter into matrimony, she giving good security that the portions of the minor children be not lessened; and to the other children who may be already married and have arrived at their majority to pay over their portions pro rata, as their shares in the estate may be, share and share alike, no more to the eldest than to the youngest; she being holden to deliver an inventory of the whole estate and confirm the same, if necessary, by oath. The testator wills and ordains hereby that after his death his oldest son Pieter Pieterse Winne, dwelling in the Sopus, shall out of the common estate receive once for all the sum of ten beavers in place of his legitimate portion and entire inheritance, wherewith he shall be content, without any more, not willing that he or anyone for him shall make the least claim any more upon the testator's estate, directly or indirectly.

The testator further desires that if it please God the Lord both him and his wife to remove, both now being sick, the whole estate shall be kept together, without any division or partition, until the youngest child shall attain her majority or enter the marriage state, and then be divided among the aforesaid twelve children, share and share alike, the portion of that child or children who die in their nonage to go to the survivors.

[47] The testator excludes herein the honored orphan masters (saving all honor and respect) and in their place requests and constitutes, as he hereby does Mr Marte Gerritse and Mr Cornelis van Dyck (who have accepted the same) to see the contents of this his last will and testament promptly and uprightly carried out in all its parts and provisions. All which he, the testator, declares to be

---

[54] This should be Conyn.

his last will and testament, desiring the same after his death to have full force and effect whether as will, codicil, donation, gift in anticipation of death, or otherwise, as the same may be last maintained, notwithstanding that some formalities demanded by law or custom may not have been fully observed herein; desiring the utmost benefit hereof to be received, and one or more copies hereof to be made and executed as occasion may require. Thus done and executed at Bethlehem, lying in the county of Albany on Hudson's river, two miles to the south of the city of Albany, at the house of the testator, which [will] he has signed and sealed in the presence of Mr Marte Gerritse and Mr Cornelis van Dyck, magistrates called as witnesses hereto, the year, month and day aforenamed.

Was signed:

P^R. WINNE (L.S.)

In my presence,

ROB^T. LIVINGSTON, Sec^y.

Marten Gerritse
Cornelis van Dyck

Release by Pieter Winne, junior, of his share of his mother's estate

[48] I, the undersigned, Pieter Winne, junior, eldest son of my father Pieter Winne, senior, acknowledge and declare that in love and friendship, without persuasion or deceit, I have well and truly agreed with my aforesaid father respecting the inheritance from my mother deceased; also that after my said father's death neither I, nor any of my heirs or assigns shall make any further claim thereto, either directly or indirectly, with or without legal proceedings, inasmuch as I acknowledge that I have received from my aforesaid father all that was heretofore agreed upon. I therefore thank him for good payment and release him and his heirs from all claims, the provision heretofore made in my father's will regarding that portion of the inheritance that was to come to me being hereby canceled and annulled. In witness of the truth of which, I have subscribed and sealed this without fraud or deceit, on the fourteenth day of September at New Albany, 1689, being in the first year of

the reign of our sovereign majesties of Great Britain, William and Mary.

Was signed:

P^r. WINNE JUN^r. (L.S.)

Signed, sealed and delivered
  in our presence,

Dirk Wessels ⎫
Alb^t. Ryckman ⎬ Justices of ye Peace[55]

Will of Marten Gerritsen van Bergen

[50] In the name of God, Amen. I, Marten Gerritsen van Bergen, dwelling in the county of Albany, being at present in good bodily health and of sound mind and memory, considering the shortess and frailty of human life, the certainty of death and the uncertainty of the hour thereof, and wishing to anticipate the same, therefore make and ordain this my last will and testament in manner and form following.

First and foremost I commend my soul, whenever it shall be separated from my body, to the hands of God Almighty, hoping through the suffering and death of my Savior, Jesus Christ, to obtain a full forgiveness of all my sins and the inheritance of eternal life, and my body I commend to a Christian burial in the earth. And as regards the disposition of all such temporal estate as it has pleased Almighty God (far above my deserts) to grant me, I give and dispose thereof as follows:

First, I will and desire that all my debts and burial expenses shall be paid out of my personal estate.

Item, I give to my sister's son, Claes Ziverse, fifty acres or twenty-five morgens of land lying at Koxhaghje, fit to be plowed, the limits and bounds thereof can not at present be indicated since I still own and possess the aforesaid land in company with Jan Bronk and do not know where my portion will be; I also give to the aforesaid Claes Ziverse four horses and four cows or cattle, on the express understanding that if [51] my estate shall become notably diminished, whether by war, fire or otherwise, he shall receive no more than the twenty-five morgens or fifty acres of land.

---

[55] Page 49 contains letters of administration in English to Livinus van Schaik and Casper Leendertse on the estate of their late father Pieter Winne, senior, dated February 26, 169$\frac{5}{6}$.

Item, I give to my eldest son, Gerrit van Bergen, all my horseman's accoutrement, namely, saddle, bridle, holsters, pistols, sash and side arms. The remainder of my personal estate, comprising all my property, movable and immovable, claims and credits, gold and silver coined and uncoined, jewels, linen and woolen clothing, household furniture, etc., nothing excepted or reserved, I give to my beloved wife Neeltje Mynders, my sole and absolute executrix of this my last will and testament, to do therewith and dispose thereof as is hereinafter further expressed.

First, she shall be holden honorably to bring up and rear in the fear of God, my children (whom we together have procreated and begotten in wedlock), to have them learn writing, reading and a proper trade or handicraft whereby they with honor may earn their living, to wit, my eldest son, Gerrit van Bergen, aged now about three years, my other or second son, Myndert van Bergen, aged about one and a half years, and if God should please to grant us in our married state still other children, then my wife shall be holden to do by them as by my two aforesaid children.

My wife shall not have power to sell, grant or alienate any of my real estate or the appurtenances thereof (as lands, houses, barns, ricks, negroes, horses, cattle and other animals, farm implements and whatever else belongs to the same), but she shall enjoy all the profits and income thereof in the form of rents, increase, fruits etc.

Whenever my youngest son Myndert van Bergen shall have attained his majority or entered the married state, my wife shall be holden to restore and turn over to my aforesaid children whom we have now and to those whom we may yet have by each other (to be divided equally among them) all my lands and farm implements at Katskill, with their appurtenances, such as houses, barns, ricks, horses, cattle and other animals and whatever else belongs thereto, a great part of which is now rented by Gerrit Teunise and Jonas Volkertse; *item,* my lands and rights at Corlaers kill, my lands and rights which I now possess in company with Jan Bronk, the land on the Bevers kill and my house and lot standing and lying in the city of Albany, according to the patents thereof.

As regards my farm (now occupied by me), lying on the west side of Hudson's river, to the south of Casteels island, with all its appurtenances, such as houses, barns, ricks, farm implements, negroes, horses, cattle and other animals, my wife shall hold and enjoy the same as long as she lives, and after her death my eldest son Gerrit van Bergen shall have and enjoy the same with all its belongings as above mentioned, in acknowledgment of his right of primogeniture, provided that on the receipt of the same he shall be holden to make over and pay to his brother Myndert van Bergen a sum of two hundred pieces of eight, current money of this province.

After my death, my wife shall be holden to give to the guardians of my children above named a true inventory of all my real estate and appurtenances, such as lands, houses, barns, ricks, negroes, horses, cattle and other animals, farm utensils and other belongings. As to the negroes on the farm now occupied by me, my wife shall receive the increase thereof after my death, without however being holden to make good the number if any happen to die. Of the two little negro boys, sons of the negress Mary, the eldest named Jan shall be for my son Gerrit van Bergen and the other named Willem for my son Myndert, each [son] to have and receive his negro boy when he becomes of age or enters the marriage state.

[53] The number of horses, cattle and other animals and farm utensils belonging to all my aforesaid lands, my wife shall be holden to keep entire, that my children at the appointed time may receive the same as found at my death, except the same be destroyed by war, fire, or otherwise (which may God avert). My further personal estate and effects shall wholly remain and be at the disposal of my wife, without her being obliged to give an inventory or accounting of the same to anyone, save that she shall be holden to pay all my debts out of the same as aforesaid. If any of my children happen to die, their right of inheritance shall pass to the other child or children, and if they all happen to die before they become of age or enter the marriage state, their right of inheritance shall be equally divided between my relatives and my wife or her relatives. Furthermore, I nominate and appoint as guardians over my children Gerrit Teunise and Claes Siverse, and in case one of them during the minority of my children happens to die, the survivor of the two shall have power to nominate and appoint another. If my children can not agree with each other regarding the division of the estate left by me, it is my will and desire that the guardians be umpires and apportion to each his part of the inheritance, without the interposition of any judge or judges (saving their respect).

All that is hereinbefore written I, the testator, declare to be my last will and testament, revoking, annulling and canceling hereby all former testamentary dispositions heretofore ever made or executed by me, whether oral or written, desiring that after my death the same may have full force and effect, whether as will, codicil, donation, gift in anticipation of death, or otherwise, as may be most suitable, [54] notwithstanding that certain formalities demanded by law or custom be herein omitted, neglected, or not inserted and observed, asking of all judges and courts before whom these presents may come, that the utmost benefit from this my will may be enjoyed. In witness whereof I have signed and sealed this my last will and testament, written upon seven sides of paper and numbered from one to seven, in Albany in America, this 6th day of January, in the second year of their majesties' reign and in the year of our Lord 169$^0_1$.

Was signed:
MARTE GERTSE VAN BERGEN (L.S.)

Signed and sealed in presence of,
Pieter Schuyler
L. V. Schaik

I, Marte Gerritse van Bergen, residing in the county of Albany, being at the present time in good bodily health and of sound mind and memory, considering the shortness and frailty of human life, the certainty of death and the uncertainty of the hour thereof, have therefore made and herein inclosed my last will and testament, written upon seven pages of paper, desiring that the same shall be opened after my death and have full force and effect, whether as will, codicil, donation, gift in anticipation of death, or otherwise, as may be most suitable, although certain formalities required by law or custom may herein be omitted or not observed, requesting all courts and judges before whom these may come that the utmost benefit thereof may be enjoyed. In witness of the truth of which, I have signed and sealed the same in Albany, this 6th day of January in the second year of their majesties' reign and in the year of Lord 169$^0_1$.

Was signed:
MARTEN GERRITSE VAN BERGEN (L.S.)

Signed and sealed in presence of,
P^r. Shuyler
Livinus V. Shaik[56]

---

[56] Page 55 contains letters of administration in English to Neele van Bergen on the estate of her late husband Marten Gerritsen van Bergen, dated December 3, 1696.

Inventory of the estate of Marten Gerritsen van Bergen

[56] Inventory of the estate left by Marte Gerritse van Bergen, deceased in the county of Albany this 6th day of May 1696, according to the provision of his last will and testament that after his death an inventory should be taken of his real estate, to wit, of lands, houses, barns, ricks, cattle and all other animals and farming utensils. This 3d of June 1696, in Albany.

First, the land lying at Catskill, a part of which is in the possession of Gerrit Teunissen and Jonas Volkertse,[57] according to the patent;[58] eight horses, to wit, six mares, one gelding and one stallion; eight cows; a half-worn wagon and a plow, eight traces, four lines, four whiffletrees, four stirrups, two bits, an iron neckyoke, a fan, an iron chain, all of which are on the aforesaid farm occupied by G^t. Teunis and Jonas Volkertse.

Second, the lands lying at Corlaers kill, in partnership with the heirs of the late Mr Corn. van Dyck, comprehended in Coxhachy patent.[59]

Third, all the land at Coxhachy in partnership with Jan Bronk,[60] comprehended in the same patent of Coxhachy. An old, dilapidated house and a barn in the possession of Helmer Janse, with a cow.

Fourth, a sawmill lying on a kill called Marte Gerritse's kill, included in the aforesaid patent of Coxhachy.

The land on the Bevers kill, according to the patent thereof.[61]

The house and lot lying in this city of Albany, according to the patent or groundbrief thereof.

[57] The farm lying at the south end of Castells island,[62] at present in the possession of Neelle van Bergen,[63] the widow of the late Marte Gerritse van Bergen, on which were found six cows, also four cows bequeathed to Claes Siverse, as appears by the last will and testament of the deceased; six hogs ½ year old, six geese,

---

[57] Gerrit Teunissen van Vechten and Jonas Volkertsen Douw, who had leased the land, according to Marten Gerritsen's will.

[58] Patent of March 26, 1680, to Capt. Sylvester Salisbury and Marten Gerritsen for five flats on both sides of the Catskill creek, purchased of the Indians on July 8, 1678.

[59] No such patent seems to be recorded.

[60] See deeds from Jan Bronck and Johannes Clute and others, *Early Records of Albany*, 1:455, 479–80.

[61] Patent dated November 12, 1677.

[62] Castle island, now called Westerlo island. In the Dongan charter of Albany it is called "Martin Garetsons Island."

[63] Neeltje Mynders, the second wife of Marten Gerritsen.

twelve hens, a brew kettle, a half-worn plow with appurtenances and traces, a cart and a harrow with iron teeth, six horses, viz, three mares and three geldings; six sheep, three Flemish scythes with snaths and grain hooks; a house, a barn and two ricks, a journal box and iron support, a half-worn fan, a wooden sled, two axes, four forks, a dung fork and sled, an auger, a hammer, a brace, two iron wedges, a negro named Samson, a negress named Marya with four children, to wit, three boys named Jan Tap, Will and Harma and a girl named Sara.

The above inventory was made by the guardians Capt. Gerrit Teunise and Claes Siverse in the presence of us, the undersigned, in Albany, the 3d of June 1696.

P^r. Schuyler
Dirk Wessells
Kill: van Renselaer

Will of Jan Juriaensen Becker

[58] In the name of God, Amen. In the year of our Lord 1694, the 31st of August, at Albany, being in the sixth year of the reign of William and Mary, king and queen of England, Scotland, France and Ireland, defenders of the faith, I, the undersigned, Jan Becker, senior, residing in the aforesaid city, considering the frailty of life and the unknown hour of death, have thought fit not to depart hence without first disposing of my temporal estate granted me by the Almighty. Therefore, being hale and sound in body, going and standing, having the full possession and use of my mind, memory, understanding, senses and speech, as outwardly appears, and acting without the persuasion, inducement or misleading of anyone, but of my own free will and motion, I commend first and foremost my soul to the gracious protection of the Most High and my body to a Christian burial and hereby canceling, annulling and rendering void all testamentary dispositions and bequests heretofore made, now make a new disposition as follows:

My son Johannes after my death shall receive first the sum of one hundred guilders seawan value, that is 50 shillings;[64] he shall also have all my linen and woolen [59] [clothing] that has belonged to my body, not comprehending therein anything else. My daughter

---

[64] Thus in the original.

Martina shall have all my other movable estate, including my bed, sheets, blankets and other appurtenances; also all my credits and outstanding claims, nothing whatever reserved or excepted.

My garden lying behind the old fort and now by me occupied shall be equally divided between my son and daughter, that is, each to have one-half; the debts which I shall leave behind and my burial expenses and whatever is connected therewith shall be a lien upon my house and ground which I now possess, but it is my express will that my daughter shall not let the cost of the funeral and incidental expenses exceed thirty pieces of eight at the most. My daughter shall have full ownership of the aforesaid house and ground belonging thereto, to do therewith as she pleases, in all respects as I in my lifetime might do, without her husband or anyone else having anything to say in the matter or making her do ought but what she intends to do, the same as about all other things which she by virtue of this will of mine shall inherit, but she shall be holden to turn over to her brother one hundred pieces of eight within three years after my death, a third part to be paid every year, all my debts and funeral expenses to be [60] also at her charge.

It is also my express will and desire that the aforesaid one hundred pieces of eight which I give to my son, shall not be taken, attached, claimed or received by any of his creditors under any pretext whatever, but that he shall receive and dispose of the same for his own benefit and use as he pleases.

Also, if either of my aforesaid children be not satisfied with the aforesaid provisions, he or she shall be deprived of what they otherwise would have had, the same to inure to the benefit of the one who is satisfied.

All that is hereinbefore written, I declare to be my testamentary disposition and last will, which I desire to have full effect from the least to the most important article thereof, whether as will, codicil, gift in anticipation of death or among the living, or any other bequest of whatsoever nature it may be, notwithstanding that all the formalities required by law or laws of this province may not be fully observed herein, desiring that said laws may be held not to apply and be not enforced in this case, desiring that the most favorable construction may be allowed for the maintenance of what is hereinbefore written. In witness of the truth of which I have deliberately signed, sealed and executed this on the said 31st of August 1694.

J. BECKER [L. S.]

Signed and sealed in our presence,

Laurens van Ale
Evert Banker, Ald^n.
Warner Castense

The reason why I apparently give more to my aforesaid daughter than to my son, is not that I bear less affection to him than to her, but because of the great service which from her youth onward she has faithfully rendered in the household and to her mother in health and sickness, yes, to the hour of her death, whereby she has saved much money, for which the mother (my wife) in her last hours promised a reward and recommended the same to me, and because since her mother's death she has, [61] as occasion demanded, rendered me great service to this day and undoubtedly will continue to do so; yes, I am in truth bound to say that without her diligence I could not have put my estate (small as the same may be) in so good a posture, all of which it is not necessary for me to particularise, but is best known to me and after my death it is very apparent her brother will not or very little take into consideration. Nevertheless, in consideration hereof, knowing that it is the truth and that through untoward circumstances I could not reward her according to her merit, I have given to her what is comprised in my aforesaid will. Done in Albany, the 31st of August 1694.

Was signed,
J. BECKER [65]

Inventory of the estate of Jan Cock

[63] Inventory of the estate left by Jan Cock, a young man, who by the bursting of a cannon in their majesties' fort at Albany was killed on the 9th of February 16$\frac{89}{90}$, when the French destroyed Schenectady, made by Albert Ryckman and Jan Lansing, aldermen of the city of Albany.

1 hammock
4 shirts

---

[65] The remaining part of page 61 and page 62 contain letters of administration in English to Martina, wife of William Hogen, on the estate of her father John Becker, deceased, dated December 16, 1697.

1 linen breeches
1 plush breeches
1 broadcloth breeches
1 coat of cloth with handsome buttons
1 old cloth coat ⎱ sold by Katelyntie for 15 skipples of wheat
1 old broadcloth coat ⎰
1 bombazine waistcoat
1 cloth waistcoat without sleeves
6 pairs of white thread stockings
3 pairs of silk stockings, 1 white and 2 colored
1 pair of sayette stockings
1 pair of sleeves without lace
2 pairs ditto with lace
4 cravats with lace
6 ditto without lace
1 silver spoon
1 hat, sold by Katelyntie for 2 pieces of eight
2 transverse flutes
1 razor
1 barrel and 1 lock for a gun
1 iron-bound chest
1 small trunk
3 pairs of gold buttons for shirts
1 small compass
5 dozens and 10 silver buttons for a waistcoat
1 gold ring
2 silver *scruffies* (small screws?)

[64] 30 pieces of eight and 6 quarter-guilders
8 pieces of eight that are due from Harp^t. Jacobse
1 old *Oeffeninge der Godtsaligheyt* (Exercise of Godliness)
1 horse pasturing in the woods
The half of a yacht appraised by Jacob Lokermans and Hendrick
  Martense at thirteen hundred and twenty guilders seawan
By cash received for him by Catelyntie Jacobse, 131 gl. seawan
6 *loot* (4 ounces) baroque pearls
By cash due to him by Samson Bensing, 228 gl. seawan
By 30 gl. due to him from Killiaen van Renselaer

Will of Hendrick van Wie

[80] God be praised in the highest. Hendrik van Wie, being quite infirm, but in full possession of his mind, walking and standing, has declared to us his last will and desire as follows:

First, Hendrik van Wie wills that his wife shall remain in full possession of his estate so long as she lives, on condition that she bring up the children to the best of her poor ability,[66] and after her death the lawful heirs begotten of them shall share alike, except that the eldest son shall first of all have a horse. But whenever his wife shall marry again, an inventory shall be made of all there is, in order that the estate be not diminished. In witness hereof he has signed this with his own hand.

This is the X mark of HENDRIK VAN WIE
This is the X mark of *Gerrit Gysbertse*
H I by me, *Pieter Winne*

Albany ye 3^d. of June 1701

Then appeared before mee Johannis Cuyler & Peter van Brugh Esq^{rs}. Justices of ye Peace Gerrit Gysbertse & helmer Janse of ye County of Albany aforesaid wittnesses as abovewritten who declare upon ye holy Evangelist that some time about ye year of our Lord 1690 they saw ye signing of ye abovementioned Instrument by hendrik van wie of ye said County as his last will or Testament who Dyed in ye year 1690 as aforesaid.

JOHANNIS CUYLER Justice
PETER VAN BRUGH Justice

Recorded ye 8th of octob^r. 1701

Will of Dirck Teunissen van Vechten

[89] In the name of the Lord, Amen. Know all men whom it may concern, that in the year sixteen hundred and eighty-seven, the fourth day of April, being in the second year of the reign of James, king of England, France and Ireland, defender of the faith, sovereign and proprietor of the colony and province of New York, appeared before me, Jan Becker, notary public residing at y, admitted by His Excellency the Right Honorable Thom⸺ ⸺n, captain general under his majesty aforesaid in the provi⸺ New

---

[66] *nae haer krank vermogen;* translated by Professor Pearson according to her ability in her infirmity," which may be the correct ⸺pretation.

York and the dependencies thereof in America, residing at New
York aforesaid, the worthy Dirk Teunise van Vechten, residing in
the county of Albany in Katskill, on a farm to him belonging, who
being now at Albany, sound in body, walking and standing, having
full possession and use of his understanding, faculties, memory and
speech, as outwardly appears, who, considering the frailty of life
and the unforeseen hour of death and not wishing to depart hence
without first having disposed of his temporal effects granted him
by the Almighty and that without the persuasion or misleading of
any person whomsoever, but of his own motion, deliberately causes
the following to be drawn up in manner following: In the first
place, commending his soul into the hands of God and his body to
a Christian burial and declaring that heretofore he has made no
testamentary disposition, he appoints, as he hereby does appoint,
his respected wife, named Jannetie Michiels, his sole and universal
heir of all his estate and goods which at his death he shall leave
behind, as well fast, lying, standing as movable and immovable
property, the furniture and household stuff, claims and credits,
nothing whatsoever excepted of whatever nature or kind it may
be, with power to do therewith in every manner as the testator in
his lifetime might have done, and [90] to this end makes her administratrix and executrix of the aforesaid whole estate and desires
that she shall not deliver any appraisal or inventory thereof, much
less be obliged to give any surety or bond to the children, to wit,
Jannetie aged about twenty-seven years, Weyntie about twenty-five
years, Michiel about twenty-three years, Neeltie about twenty-two
years, Johannes about twenty, Theunis about eighteen, Annetie
about sixteen, Fytie about fifteen, Samuel about fourteen, Sara
about twelve and Abraham about eight years, nor that during their
minority or in case of death their children, blood relations,
guardians, the honorable orphan masters, constable or constables,
the court of this city or any other authority or authorities, or any
supreme or inferior court or judge (saving their respect) shall
interfere therein, one and all of which the testator expressly debars
and excludes, notwithstanding that some law or laws may direct
otherwise, which laws he desires shall not be applied and enforced
in this case as long as she remains unmarried. And whereas among
the testator's children hereinbefore mentioned there are some who
are married and who have received outfits, his wife, having become
his widow, shall likewise give the other child or children entering
the married state an outfit according to her station and condition

from the whole estate, but with the understanding that farms, lands, houses and all their appurtenances may not be sold or alienated by her, but must be occupied or rented by his wife, who is to have the use of the rent or income therefrom. And in case his widow happens to die, then the aforesaid lands shall remain unsold and undivided until the youngest child becomes of age, the same to be meanwhile supported out of the income thereof; and when the children shall all have attained their majority, the aforesaid lands with their appurtenances and all that is fastened by nail and earth shall be appraised by impartial persons, excepting the best horse, [91] which the eldest son shall first of all receive out of the common estate. The aforesaid farm and lands with their appurtenances being so appraised, the children shall equally participate therein, the eldest [son receiving] no more than any of the other children; so also with the movable estate, which shall likewise be divided into equal shares immediately after the mother's death and each son who then shall be unmarried shall first receive for an outfit as much as the married sons have received and each daughter for an outfit as much as the married daughters at their marriage received out of the common estate, always understanding that in the possession of the lands the son or sons shall have the preference over the daughter or daughters and to prevent disputes, the sons shall draw lots among themselves as to who shall possess the aforesaid lands and their appurtenances, with the understanding that those to whom they shall fall, shall give sufficient security for the amount at which they have been appraised (excepting his own part), but before the lots are drawn the children shall in love and friendship agree upon decent and reasonable terms for the payment; but if one or more of the aforesaid children happen to die without leaving lawful issue before the lots are drawn, then the portion of the deceased shall go to the other children and if all the testator's sons die before the lots are drawn without leaving lawful issue, then the daughters shall draw lots therefor in the same way as has hereinbefore been stated with respect to the aforesaid sons.

If the testator's wife desires to marry again, then all the movable goods and effects shall be equally divided into two parts between her and the children (except the best horse out of the common estate as hereinbefore stated), the one half for the testator's wife and the other half for the children, to be divided equally among them, but first of all a portion of the common estate shall be reserved for the outfits of the unmarried children as aforesaid and the portions of those under age shall remain in the care of his wife until their [92] majority, provided that she give sufficient security therefor.

As regards the lands, farms and their appurtenances and all that is fastened by earth and nail, his wife shall occupy or rent the same and during her lifetime receive and enjoy the income thereof, without making any accounting thereof or turning over any part thereof to the testator's child, children, heirs, or any other person whomsoever, but she be holden to keep the building in good repair and honorably to rear and bring up the minor child or children until they become of age without lessening the capital, and after her death the real estate shall be disposed of as aforesaid.

The testator appoints as guardians of his minor children Mr Marte Gerritse van Bergen, Gerrit Teunise,[67] Elias and Enoch Michielsz,[68] either all four together, or two in particular, and if so be that two are far away and one of those nearby should fail by reason of death or otherwise, then the one who is nearest may, if he sees fit, associate another person with him, in order that the minor children may be properly maintained in their rights according to the testator's will. All that is hereinbefore written the testator declares to be his testamentary disposition and last will, desiring that the same shall have effect from the least to the weightiest article thereof, whether as testament, codicil, gift in anticipation of death or among the living, as may be most suitable, notwithstanding that all the formalities required by law may not have been observed herein, desiring the utmost benefit [of the law] for the maintenance of what is herein written.

Thus done at N. Albany, on the date above written and by the testator signed and sealed in the evening about six o'clock, at the house of his son-in-law Gabriel Thomas.

Dirk Teunise van Vechten   (L.S.)

Signed, sealed and delivered
    in our presence,

Gerrit Visbeek
Wouter Albertse
    In my presence,

        J. Becker, *Not. Pub.*

---

[67] Gerrit Teunissen van Vechten.
[68] Elias and Enoch Caljer, or Collier.

Certificate of Probate

[93] Dirk Wessels Esqr. one Judge of the Inferior Court of Common Pleas held for ye Citty and County of Albany To all to whom these Presents shall Come or may Concerne Greeting Know Yee that on ye one and Thirtieth day of March In ye year of our Lord one thousand seaven hundred and three Before mee and other Justices of ye said Court Thee will of Dirk Teunise van Vechten Late of the said County to these Presents Annexed was Prooved approoved and Insinuated haveing while he Lived and at ye time of his death Goods Rights and Creditts in Diverse parts of the said County for the obtaining whereof ye administration of all and singular the goods Rights and Creditts of the said Deceased and his Last will in any manner of ways Concerning was Committed unto his wife Jannetie Michiels Executrix In ye said will named well and faithfully to administer ye same and to Render a plean and true Account thereof In testimony whereof I have hereunto sett my hand & Caused ye seale of this City to Bee hereunto affixed dated In Albany ye one and Thirtieth day of March In ye second Year of ye Reign of our Souveraign Lady Anne by ye grace of God of England Scotland france and Ireland Queen Defender of ye faith &^{a}. A^o. ·1703

was Signd

DIRK WESSELSE JUDGE

Will of Evert Wendel, junior

[95] In the name of the Lord, Amen. Know all men whom it may concern that on the twenty-fourth of November, at New Albany, in the year sixteen hundred and ninety, being in the second year of the reign of William and Mary, king and queen of Great Britain, the worthy Mr Evert Wendel, trader residing here, hale and sound of body, walking and standing, having the full use and possession of his mind, memory and speech as outwardly appears, considering the frailty of life and the unforeseen hour of death, not wishing to depart hence without first having disposed of his temporal effects granted him by Almighty God, and that without the persuasion, inducement or misleading of anyone, but of his own free will and motion, commending first and foremost his soul to the gracious keeping of the Most High, and his body to a Christian burial, hereby nominates, constitutes and appoints his respected wife

Elisabeth [60] his sole and universal heir of all his estate and goods,
lying here in New York, in England, Holland, or elsewhere, as well
real as personal, movable as unmovable, nothing whatsoever
reserved and excepted, however it may be named; not willing that
she shall be called upon to deliver an inventory or statement to either
child or children by them procreated, to wit, Susanna, Robert,
Ephraim, the first aged about nine years, the second about seven
and the third about two years, or by those likewise whom they may
hereafter procreate together, or during their minority by blood
relations, guardians, the honorable orphan masters, constables, the
court of this city and county or any high or low court or judge, or
any other authority of whatsoever nature or quality it may be, much
less to give se-[96]curity or bond, inasmuch as he altogether excludes
and debars the same, notwithstanding certain laws or law, customs
or custom may otherwise direct, which laws and usages he desires
shall herein be inapplicable and of no effect, as he appoints his
aforesaid wife executrix and administratrix of the whole of his
aforesaid estate and goods during the time of her widowhood. But
if she again marries, he wills that the just half of his estate (as it
then be found) shall be set aside for the behoof of the child or
children then surviving; and in order that all things may be arranged
orderly the testator appoints as guardians of his child or children
his brother M[r] Johannes Wendel and M[r] Jan Herberdingh, residing
at New York, and whatever she may agree upon with them shall
be valid under proper security and bond that neither her nor the
child's or children's just half shall be diminished, fully commending
the care thereof to the aforesaid guardians, whom he trusts in all
things. Likewise, the testator deliberately binds himself, in case he
should marry again after his aforesaid wife's death, to set aside a
like and similar portion for the behoof of his child or children, over
which the aforesaid guardians shall have the same supervision and
as much to say as if the testator had died first and his wife had
entered again into the married state, with the express understanding
that the eldest son shall first of all receive four pounds money of
this province, and then all the children shall share a-[97]like; and
if a minor shall die, his portion shall be shared equally by the other
child or children: All that is hereinbefore written the testator
declares to be his testamentary disposition and last will, which he
desires to have effect from the least to the weightiest article, whether
as testament, codicil, gift in anticipation of death or among the

---

[60] Elisabeth Sanders.

living, or any other bequest of whatsoever name and nature; notwithstanding that all the formalities of the laws of this government may not be herein observed, desiring that the utmost benefit may be received herefrom; and in witness of the truth hereof he has signed and sealed this with his own hand on the 24th of November 1690, at New Albany as aforesaid.

Signed: EVERT WENDEL [L. S.]

Signed and sealed in our presence,

Evert Wendel, senior
Robert Sanderse

In my presence,

J. BECKER

Registered the 4th Feb. 170$\frac{3}{4}$.[70]

Release of the heirs of Pieter Winne for their respective portions of their father's estate

[99] Whereas Pieter Winne of the city and county of Albany, deceased, by his last will and testament dated the 31st of December 1688 did bequeath and devise his estate, real and personal, remaining after his and his wife's death and the payment of all his debts, to his youngest son Daniel Winne, on condition that he pay to his brothers and sisters within six following years, each year a just sixth part, [their portion of the estate] according to appraisal made by impartial persons, [said estate] to be divided among said brothers and sisters share and share alike; and whereas the court of Albany has appointed as administrators of the estate Livinus Winne and Casper Leendertz, and as appraisers Jacob Lokermans, Luykas Gerritz, Gerrit van Ness and Anthony Bratt, who have appraised the same at the sum of two hundred and forty-one pounds, sixteen shillings current money; and whereas there are eleven heirs, to each of whom there is coming for his portion £ 21-19-7½, and after the appraisal some debts against the estate have come in amounting to £ 6-12, so that there remains due to each £ 21-7-7½; and whereas Eva Winne died after having received five yearly portions and

---

[70] Page 98 contains the certificate of probate of the will of Evert Wendel, junior, which is in English and identical in form with that of the will of Dirck Teunissen van Vechten, printed on a preceding page. The present certificate is dated December 27, 1703, and names Elisabeth Sanderse as executrix.

Frans Winne, as guardian of her children, has received the sixth or last part, being £ 3-2, and Marte Winne has deceased and left a child to whom there is due as his inheritance £ 11-14, which Frans Winne, guardian of the aforesaid child, has received; and whereas Adam Winne, eldest son of the testator, died before the appraisal or partition of the estate was made, so that Livinus Winne, guardian of the children of his brother Adam Winne, deceased, has received the full portion of the inheritance left, to wit, £ 21-7-7½; therefore we, the undersigned, heirs of the estate of Pieter Winne, deceased, acknowledge and [100] declare that we have been fully satisfied for our inheritance, real and personal, that we have no further claims, whether large or small, against the estate, and that this shall serve as a general acquittance for the same. Given under our hands in Albany this 29th day of January 170¾.

Was signed:

his
LIVINUS L W WINNE
mark
his
CASPER K L LEENDERSE
mark
FRANS WINNE
JELLES VONDA
HENDRIK JANSE
his
JACOB I W WINNE
mark
her
TEUNTIE T WINNE
mark
his
DANIEL X WINNE
mark

Will of Gerrit Teunissen van Vechten

[112] In the name of God, Amen. Know all men by these presents that I the undersigned, Gerrit Teunisen van Vechten,

inhabitant of the colony of Renselaerswyk, in the county of Albany, healthful in body and of sound mind, memory and speech, considering the frailty of life, the certainty of death and the uncertainty of the hour thereof, desiring therefore to dispose of his temporal effects to be left behind, first and foremost commending his soul to the gracious hands of God, his Creator and Redeemer, and his body to a Christian burial, annulling and canceling all former testamentary dispositions, therefore disposes as follows: 1 That after the death of the testator, his respective wife Grietie Volkertsen Dow shall remain in full possession of his whole estate, whether lands, houses, barns, ricks, money, gold, coined or uncoined, cattle, etc., without inventory to be given to anyone, for the time of one year and six weeks after his decease and then shall all the lands of the testator lying in the colony aforesaid, or elsewhere, having or to have, go to his two sons Johannes and Volkert van Vechten, children of lawful age (the first procreated by the testator's first wife Antie Janz, deceased, the second by his present wife) in two like parts, to wit, the land in the colony shall the aforesaid sons divide and if they can not agree, then it shall be done as nearly evenly as possible by four impartial men, with the understanding that Johannes shall have the first choice, to dwell on the south or north side where his part shall be, and then each shall possess his part in fee with his portion of all the structures, cattle, plow and wagon, and all that appertains to the land, except the free residence, etc., which the testator's wife must have as hereinafter written; the remainder of the lands to be divided among his sons [113] without first choice, provided that the same must pay all the debts, the mother being free therefrom, with the express will of the testator that none of his lands shall ever be sold to strangers, but that the same shall always go to and remain in the possession of the lawful heirs. Regarding the land and inheritance which comes to Johannes on the side of his mother deceased, it is his alone; likewise whatever may come to Volkert from his mother's side shall be for him; against this the testator's wife shall have a free dwelling and homestead in the colony on the farm where the testator now dwells, the household furniture and other effects (except the clothing, etc. belonging to the testator's body, which shall go to the sons six weeks after his death); also his wife shall select a negro and negress to serve her and each of his sons shall be holden to deliver to the mother, the aforesaid Grietie, the fourth sheaf of all the grain grown on the lands, free, under proper covering and such that it can be threshed; likewise shall she have four horses, four cows, six sheep, six hogs and six geese with the necessary stabling therefor, all this during her widowhood, but at her death all her effects shall go to the aforesaid sons.

2 In case of marriage of his aforesaid wife, she shall, before her marriage day, convey and make over to the sons said dwelling, together with the negro, if either of the sons happen to have no negro and instead of the fourth sheaf she shall receive the just part of the rent for which the land shall be appraised, during her life, and no longer, and the negro woman, horses and other stock specified shall be at her disposition, as well as the negro if she keeps him.

3 Johannes, before any partition, shall have in lieu of his right of primogeniture the sum of five pounds current money of this province.

4 Pieter, the son of Jonas Dow, shall have the negro, Fransisco, when he, the said Pieter, marries. [114] All that is hereinbefore written the testator declares to be his last will and testament, requesting of all lords, courts, tribunals and judges that after his death the same may be observed and maintained in every particular. In witness whereof the testator has subscribed and sealed this with his hand in Albany at the house of Johannes Cuyler, this eighth day of March and in the twelfth year of the reign of our King William, over England, Scotland, France and Ireland, Defender of the Faith, annoque domini 170 0/1.

                        his
       GERRIT   X   TEUNISEN VAN VECHTEN [L. S.]
               mark and seal

Signed and sealed in presence of

Wessel ten Brook, justus
Joh: Cuyler, justus

Memorandum that the thirteen words in the last part of the first article on the other side to wit: " but at her death all her effects shall go to the aforesaid sons," were inserted and written, likewise the word " appraised " in the second article was erased, before signing, sealing and delivery, whereupon the testator acknowledges his aforesaid signature and again seals and delivers this as his last will and testament as aforesaid; thus done at the house of the aforesaid testator in the colony of Renselaerswyk aforesaid, this twelfth day of March 17c¾.

Thus signed, sealed and delivered in presence of,

J. Abeel, Justis.
David Schuyler, Justus,
Johannes Cuyler, Justis
Wessel ten Brook [71]

Will of Gysbert Gerritsen van Brakel

[130] In the name of God, Amen. In the year of our Lord and Savior, Jesus Christ, the 10th of December, and in the eighth year of their majesties' reign annoq: domini 1709, Gysbert Gerritse van Brakel, of the village of Schonhechtade, in the county of Albany, in the province of New York, husbandman, considering the frailty of life, the certainty of death and the uncertainty of the time thereof, is inclined to dispose of his temporal effects, which God far above his deserts has granted him, before he departs out of this world, in form and manner following:

First and foremost I offer up my soul to God my Creator and to Jesus Christ my Savior after I shall have left this world and my body to a Christian burial, hereby annulling all former testament or testaments, gift or gifts of whatsoever nature, and make this my last will and testament. First, it is my will that after my death my son Gerrit Gysbertse van Brakell shall have that lot on which my said son Gerrit Gysbertse's house now stands, lying next to Jan Vroman's and Arent Danielse's lots, also one pound in money of this province or twenty shillings, without returning anything therefor, [*Nota bene* — I give my son Gerrit Gysbertse the aforenamed lot on which his house stands and one pound in money for his birthright, he being my eldest son]; further it is my will that my son Gerrit shall have my parcel of land called *Jufferows Landt* and the half of the pasture to me belonging in the village, provided that said land and pasture land shall be appraised by two impartial persons and the money be divided among all my children, except my youngest son Gysbert, who shall have no part or portion thereof, but my said son Gysbert shall for his whole portion have my present house and lot and half of said pasture without returning anything to any of the other brothers and sisters or heirs; furthermore it is

---

[71] A translation of the will follows on pages 114–16.

my will and desire that my beloved wife Elisabeth Gerritse, and it is so expressly stipulated, shall have all my personal estate to be [131] used for her maintenance during her life or until she shall marry again, when she shall have the sum of fifteen pounds current money of this province and no more, which shall be paid to her within six weeks after her marriage; further it is my will that all my household stuff and movable property of whatsoever nature and kind it may be shall be given to my youngest son Gysbert, provided that my said son Gysbert shall pay all my debts and in case my son Gerrit Gysbertse after receiving said estate as above mentioned can not pay the said appraised value thereof to his brothers and sisters as above within the time four years, he shall be holden to pay its proper interest until the money shall be fully paid; it is also my desire that my son Gerrit Gysbertse and Volkert Symonse be the administrators of my estate for my children, that each may have his rights as above written.

Given under my hand and seal at Schonh[echtade], the 10th of December 1709.

    Was signed

      The mark G V B of GYSBERT [L. S.]
      GERRITSE VAN BRAKEL

Signed and sealed in presence of

Philip Schuyler
Johannis Mynderts
Arent Danielse

      Albany the 7th. June 1710

This day appeared before me Dirk wessels Esqr. Judge of the Inferior Court & Albert Ryckman & John Schuyler Esq^{rs}. Justices of the Said Court, Elisabeth van Brakell wife of gysbert gerritse van Brakel Dec^d. & Produced the within Last will & Testament of ye s^d. Dec^d., the witnesses thereunto Sworn on the holy Evangelist, & Desired to have ye s^d. will approved, and we have therefore hereby Proved approved & Insinuated ye s^d. will & Testament and orderd the Same to be Enterd into the Publick Records held for such Instruments

      was Signd

      DIRK WESSELS. Judge

Recorded ye 10 June 1710

Will of Marten Cornelissen van Buren

[132] In the name of God, Amen. Know all men by these presents that I, the undersigned, Mart Cornelise van Beuren,[72] husbandman and inhabitant of the colony of Renselaerswyck, in the county of Albany, hale and sound of body, having full possession of my mind, memory and speech, considering the frailty of life, the certainty of death and the uncertain hour thereof and therefore desiring to dispose of my temporal effects, commend first of all my soul to the gracious hands of God, my Creator and Savior, and my mortal body to a Christian burial, annul and cancel all former testamentary dispositions and now make and determine this my last will in the form hereinafter written:

First, I appoint as my sole and universal heirs all my six surviving children and my child's child, to wit, Cornelia Martense van Beuren, wife of Robert van Deusen; Peter Martense van Beuren; Marte Mertense van Beuren; Maria Martense van Beuren, wife of Cornelis Gerritse;[73] Catelina Martense van Beuren, wife of Jonathan Janse;[74] Magdalena Martense van Beuren and Tobyas Cornelise van Beuren, of all my estate, real and personal, lands, houses, lots, cows, horses, farm implements, beds, bolsters, household furniture, gold, silver coined and uncoined, nothing whatsoever excepted. It is furthermore my will and desire that after my death my son Peter aforenamed, before any partition is made, shall first have six morgens of the Great Parcel's flat (*grotstucks fley*), together with that lot of woodland that was apportioned in company with the participants Peter Vosburgh, Jan Teysen and Van Alle, lying to the north without the fence of the land called the Great Parcel (*het grote Stuck*), in consideration of any prior right he may have by reason of his being now my eldest son.

It is further my will and desire that [133] my son's son, Tobias Cornelise aforenamed, in consideration of any claim he might make on account of the fact that his father was my eldest son, shall have a horse with saddle and bridle.

It is further my will and desire that my daughter Magdalena shall first have for her outfit what her sisters have had, together

---

[72] In Pearson's *Genealogies of the First Settlers of Albany*, he is erroneously identified with "Black Marten," a nickname applied to Marten Cornelissen van Ysselsteyn.
[73] Cornelis Gerritsen van den Bergh, according to the account of Marten Cornelissen van Buren in the above-mentioned *Genealogies*, though under the name Van den Bergh he is entered as Cornelis Gysbertse.
[74] Jonathan Jansen Witbeck.

with the sum of nine pounds current money of this province; and that furthermore my whole estate as it then may be found, after the debts shall be paid, shall then be divided into seven equal parts among them, it being well understood that my son Peter aforenamed and my daughter Cornelia, wife of Robert van Deusen, shall have the preference of my lands lying at the Kinderhoeck with house, barn, ricks and all that appertains thereto, acquired by me from Dirk Wessellse, only excepting what I have heretofore given to my son Peter as aforementioned, and that the same shall be appraised by four impartial persons therefor first chosen, and Peter and Cornelia shall then pay the appraised value placed upon it by said impartial persons within the six after-following years, every time a just sixth part to be divided equally among the seven of them.

It is the testator's will and desire that his son Marten aforenamed shall have for himself and his heirs forever the half island with all the rights thereunto belonging, house, barn and rick, now occupied by the testator, provided that he shall pay therefor within the six after-following years after the death of the testator one hundred and sixty-five pounds current money of this province, say £165, every time a just sixth part to be apportioned equally among the seven of them.

And I appoint as guardians and administrators my sons Peter and Marte aforenamed, together with Mr Albert Ryckman and Mr Dirck Wessells, that this my last will and testament may be observed in all its parts. All that is hereinbefore written, the testator declares to be his last and ultimate will, desiring [134] that after his death it may be observed and maintained in all its parts by all lords, courts, tribunals and judges. In witness whereof the testator has subscribed and sealed this in the manor of Renselaerswyck, at the house of Capt. Gerrit Teunise, this tenth day of April in the second year of the reign of our queen Anne, over England, Scotland, France and Ireland, defender of the faith, A°. D°. 1703.

his
MARTE X CORNELISEN
mark

Signed and sealed in presence of,
his
Gerrit X Teunise
mark

Wessel Ten Broek
Dirk Wesselz, Justice

Albany the 7th. June 1710

Then appeared before me Dirk wessels Esqr. Judge of ye Inferior Court of Common Pleas & Albert Ryckman & John Schuyler Esq^{rs}. Justices of ye said Court Peter & marte van Beuren Sons of marte Cornelise van Beuren Dec^d. and Produced the Last will & Testam^t. of the Said Deceased, the witnesses thereunto Sworn on the holy Evangelist and Did Desire to have y^{e}s^d. will & Testament prov'd, and we do therefore hereby Prove approve & Insinuate the S^d. will & Testament and orderd to be Enterd in the Publick Records held for Such Instruments,

was Signd

DIRK WESSELS Judge

Recorded ye 10th. of June 1710

Will of Lucas Gerritsen Wyngaert and Anna, his wife

[139] In the name of Almighty God, Amen. We, the undersigned, married people, now aged and infirm, but of sound mind and memory, as is evident, considering the certainty of death and the uncertainty of the hour thereof, desire not to depart this world without first commending our souls to the hands of the Creator and after our deaths our bodies to a Christian burial and furthermore betimes to dispose of our temporal effects as follows:

First, we announce and declare hereby that we appoint and nominate the survivor of us as our sole and universal heir to all our property, movable and immovable, having and to have, rights and credits, nothing excepted, consisting chiefly of real estate, namely, a house and lot standing and lying in the city of Albany and a house at the Kinderhoek, which houses and lot the survivor of us may and shall possess, occupy, use or rent at his [or her] pleasure; furthermore we, the testator and testatrix, will that the said house and lot at Albany after the death of both of us shall go to our youngest son named Luycas, for the sum of one hundred and nine pounds current money of this province, to be paid in five equal instalments, the first instalment or fifth part on his taking possession of said house and lot and the second instalment within a year thereafter, and so on. And the residue of the money after the creditors are paid shall be equally divided among our nine children or their heirs, that is, their lawful and direct descendants and heirs, with this reservation-that our eldest son Gerrit, for his primogeniture, shall before any partition is made receive twenty shillings current money and no more, and in case of his death this money [140] or prior right shall devolve upon his eldest son named Luycas Gerrits; we will further that when the first instalment is received by the heirs for the house and lot, each shall reserve from his share six shillings for our youngest daughter Marya for reasons moving us thereto; likewise the heirs shall be holden on receipt of the last instalment a sufficient and binding conveyance to deliver to their brother Luycas for the aforesaid house and lot; furthermore the survivor may make partition of the furniture and movable goods among our children according to his pleasure. All the foregoing we declare to be our last and ultimate will without the misleading or persuasion of anyone and we will and desire that all things shall be exactly performed to the greatest tranquility after our death, and also that all this shall be held valid by all courts and judges and by all Christian people. In witness of the truth of which we have lawfully subscribed and sealed these with our own hands in presence of the hereinafter named witnesses called thereto, Pieter Vosburgh, justice, Jacobus Turck and Johannis van Alen, at Kinderhoeck, in the county of Albany, this 30th of October 1709, being in the eighth year of the reign of her majesty, Anne, queen of Great Britain.

LUYCAS GERRITS (L.S.)
This is the X mark of ANNA LUYCAS,
made by herself (L.S.)

Pieter Vosburgh, Justice
Jacobus Turck
Johannes van Alen

Will of Johannes de Wandelaer, senior

[143] In the name of God, Amen. On the 20th day of June, in the fourth year of her majesty's reign and in the year of our Lord one thousand seven hundred and five, I, Johannes de Wandelaer, senior, trader in Albany, now indisposed and sick in body, but of sound mind, senses, memory and speech, God be praised for His grace; considering the certainty of death but not of the time thereof, therefore not wishing to depart hence without having disposed of my [144] temporal estate and effects, real and personal, that the Great God has granted me far above my deserts, hereby revoking, annulling and canceling all former wills, gifts or bequests heretofore made, [declare] this to be my last and ultimate will and testament drawn up in form and manner following:

1 I commend my immortal soul to the gracious hands of Almighty God my Creator, hoping and only trusting for grace and pardon

for my manifold sins and transgressions in the bitter suffering and death of the blessed Savior and Redeemer, Jesus Christ, my Deliverer and Savior, and my body to the earth in a Christian burial in hope of a glorious resurrection at the last day.

2 I give my son Anderis the sum of twelve shillings current money for his birthright, because he is my eldest son, to be paid to him by my overseers or administrators when the estate shall be divided among my heirs at the time hereinafter specified.

3 My will is that all my minor children shall be maintained out of the whole estate until the youngest then living shall become of age or marry; provided they be taught a good trade or handicraft and go to school and that no partition shall be made before the youngest child then living shall become of lawful age and that my minor children shall dwell in my house with my son Johannis until my youngest child becomes of age or marries. But if it happen that one or more marry before [145] the youngest child becomes of age or marries, then they shall no longer receive lodging; and upon the majority or marriage of my youngest child, my son Johannis shall have the refusal of said house at the valuation set upon it by two impartial persons, to wit, the house and lot standing and lying here in Albany on Browers street.[75]

4 My will is that my minor children, before any partition is made, shall each have a proper outfit in reasonable burgher style, and each one who marries before the youngest child becomes of age shall receive [his or] her outfit at once.

5 My will is that the four daughters hereinafter named shall have all my household furniture, finished woolen and linen goods, and other household stuff, save that to my body belonging, to be equally divided among them share and share alike, excepting these in particular, to wit: my daughter Sara shall have my large closet (*Kass*) that is in York; my daughter Catharina shall have my large table that is likewise in York; my daughter Anna shall have my chest of drawers and my youngest daughter Alida shall have my little glass closet, and what one article is considered worth less than another shall be made up out of the other furniture; and if one or more of these my above-named daughters happen to die before their marriage then their portions shall be equally divided among the survivors of my daughters.

6 My will is that my house in New York standing and lying in Queen's street shall be let until an opportunity shall present itself

---

[75] Brouwers, or Brewer's street, now Broadway.

to sell the same to the best advantage of my heirs, as my administrators shall think best and advisable; so also my garden lot lying in Albany on the plain is to be sold when they find it for the advantage of my heirs, together with all my merchandise, as well [146] dry as wet, and an inventory thereof to be made and sold as they, my administrators, shall deem advisable; also all my coined money, gold and silver, book debts and obligations which shall be found after my death with the above proceeds from the aforesaid house and garden lot and merchandise shall be put out on interest as my administrators shall judge proper until my youngest child shall become of age and whatever money remains over as aforesaid shall be equally divided among my eight children, save the aforesaid birthright, to wit, to each one an eighth part, to Anderis an eighth, to Johannis an eighth, to Adrejaen an eighth, to Pieter an eighth, to Sara an eighth, to Catharina an eighth, to Anna an eighth, to Alida an eighth, to one no more nor less than to another or to his heirs.

7 Lastly, my will is that every article in this my last will shall be observed without one article's annulling another, but according to the just intent and meaning of everything herein specified, and my desire is that my son Johannis and Thomas Williams shall be administrators of my estate and guardians of my minor children, with express power to administer and execute every article herein mentioned without contradiction or giving account to any of my said children or any other person, only at the end of their administration to give a statement to the majority of my aforenamed children or to the majority of those who may then be living in the province of New York, hereby giving to my administrators Johannis De Wandlaer and Thomas Williams of this city of Albany full power to sell and dispose as aforesaid and then the same to convey or make over, which [conveyance] shall be holden by them [147] or any of my aforenamed children or their heirs as valid and inviolable. In witness of the truth of which I, Johannes De Wandlaer, senior, have subscribed and sealed this in Albany, the day and date first above written.

    Was signed:

      JOHANNES DE WANDELAER (L.S.)

Signed and sealed in presence of.
Hend: Hansen, Justice
Johannis Mingael, Justice
Evert Jansen

Will of Andries Gardenier

[151] In the name of God, Amen. Know all men by these presents that I, the undersigned, Andries Gardinier, of the village of Kinderhoeck, in the county of Albany, in the province of New York, hale and sound of body, having perfect understanding, memory and speech, considering the frailty of this life, the certainty of death and the uncertainty of the hour thereof, desiring therefore to dispose of my temporal goods granted me by the Almighty, commending first and foremost my soul to the gracious hands of God my Creator and Jesus Christ my Savior and my body to a Christian burial, [152] thus, without the persuasion or misleading of anyone, but of my own motion, dispose as follows:

After my death, my beloved wife Eytje Gardinier shall remain in full possession and continue to dwell upon my farmland where I now dwell at Kinderhoek aforesaid and draw the income thereof for the maintenance of our children until my eldest son reaches his majority, when my aforesaid wife must yield up the aforesaid land and surrender the same with all my right in the adjoining woodland, together with the house, barn and other buildings thereon, to my eldest son Andries Gardinier, aged about eleven years, my wife aforesaid to have then a small piece of land out of my certain parcel of woodland on the east shore of Hudson's river, beginning on the north side of Jan Hendrickse Bruyn, northward along said river, three morgens broad,[76] and so eastward into the woods, also three morgens, containing nine morgens, with free range for her cattle and wood for herself during her life and no longer; likewise she must erect a proper dwelling upon said parcel of land for her and her family, together with a stable for her cattle, which shall be in lieu of what the law allows her. And I furthermore will that this said small parcel of land after her death shall go to my second son Jacob Gardinier and that my aforesaid wife shall have no power to incumber, much less to sell any of my land.

2 My son Jacob Gardinier aforesaid, now aged about nine years, shall out of my aforesaid woodland have the full width to the shore, to wit, from said J. H. Bruyn's right to the south line of the [153] colony of Renselaerswyck and into the woods eastward to Mutsjes kill, with the understanding that the little parcel land for my wife aforesaid shall be included therein and after her death go to said Jacob as aforesaid, with the reservation that Jan van Wye, out of

---

[76] Thus in the original.

the land of Jacob, shall have a little piece of land beginning from the patroon's south line southward, in breadth two hundred and fifty paces from the west side of the Mutsies kill aforesaid, westward to the *spruyt* which empties into the round swamp (*Creupel boss*) keeping there the same breadth, with free range for said Jan's cattle and wood for himself and his heirs.

3 My youngest son Arye, aged about seven years, shall have the remainder of my aforesaid parcel of woodland as by my deed it shall be found described and the lands herein severally bequeathed to my three sons Andries, Jacob and Arye Gardinier shall, when my youngest son becomes of age, be severally appraised by three or five impartial persons and they shall compensate each other in money for the difference in value. It is also to be understood that the land given to my three sons aforesaid, or whatever other land I may yet obtain, shall be for them and their heirs, it being my express will that none of them shall ever alienate any of it, but only have liberty to sell to the next heir of the name of Gardinier; and if Jan van Wye should desire to give up his said land, he or his heirs must also sell it to the next heir of my three aforesaid sons.

4 Six weeks after my death, my aforesaid wife shall be holden to deliver to the guardians hereinafter named a true inventory of all movable goods and effects, whatever they may be, with the understanding that whatever she shall declare she brought into the estate, she shall have the right to draw out, the rest to be for my three children, each of whom is to receive a just [154] third part when he reaches his majority or marries, but before any partition is made, my eldest son, for his birthright, is to have a cow or a horse at his choice, and whenever my children during the lifetime of my wife come to marry, the mother shall give them an outfit according to her means.

5 All that is hereinbefore written I, the testator, declare to be my last will and testament, desiring earnestly that after my death it may be observed and carried out in all particulars, to which end I appoint my aforesaid wife administratrix and executrix and as guardians my brother Samuel Gardinier and Mr Andries Coeymans, and in case of death of either of the said guardians, Pieter Coeymans shall be the second guardian of my aforesaid children, begging each of them as far as he is concerned to perform his duties conscientiously. Thus with my hand subscribed and sealed in the city

of Albany, this last day of July and in the third year of her majesty's reign A° D° 1704.

his
ANDRIES X GARDINIER (L. S.)
mark

Signed, sealed and delivered in presence of us,

Johannes Roseboom, Justice
Johannes Cuyler, Justice
Abraham Cuyler.

N. B. the word "*undertussen*" (meanwhile) was erased between the fifth and seventh lines, before signing, etc.

Albany the 13th. August 1717

Then appeared before Robert Livingston Junr. Esqr. may^r. of ye City of Albany Johannis Roseboom Johannis Cuyler & Abraham Cuyler Esq^{rs}. witnesses to this Instrument who declare on ye holy Evangelist that they saw Andries Gardenier sett his marke and seale to this as his Last will and Testament and y^t he was in perfect sense at ye same time.

Robt. LIVINGSTON JUN^r.

Will of Dirck Wesselsen Ten Broeck

[155] In the name of God. Amen. On the fourth day of February in the first year of the reign of our sovereign King George, of Great Britain, &c., and in the year of our Lord one thousand seven hundred fourteen and fifteen, I, Dirck Wesselez Ten Broeck, late of Albany, now of the manor of Livingstoen in Dutchess county, being sound in body having perfect possession and use of my understanding, memory and faculties, but considering the shortness and frailty of human life, the certainty of death and the uncertainty of the hour thereof, have after careful consideration, of my own motion, without the inducement, persuasion or misleading of anyone, made, ordained and determined this my last will and testament, revoking, canceling and annulling hereby all and every testament heretofore made and executed by me and desiring that this alone be taken as my last will and testament, in form and manner following:

First, I commend my immortal soul when it shall depart from my body to the gracious and merciful hands of God my Creator and Savior and my body to the earth whence it came, in Christian burial, there to remain until my soul shall be reunited to the body upon the joyful day of resurrection, to be made partaker of that insatiable joy of our salvation which God of His grace through the merit of Jesus Christ has prepared and promised for all who have true penitence and faith in Him.

First. Respecting such temporal goods as the Lord, above my deserts, has pleased to grant me, I give and dispose of the same in manner following:

Second. I give to my oldest son Wessel Ten Broeck for his birthright as my first born son the sum of three pounds current money of New York, who I desire shall make no further claim to any part of my estate, save an equal portion with his sisters and brothers as is hereinafter expressed.

[156] *Third.* Furthermore it is my will and desire that after my death my just debts to any and all persons shall in due time be paid by my heirs.

Fourth. I appoint my well-beloved wife Christyna Wesselz Ten B[r]oeck after my death as executrix and administratrix of my whole estate, as well movable as immovable, lands, houses, lots, obligations, claims, rents, gold and silver coined and uncoined, jewels, clothing both linen and woolen, horses, cattle, negroes, negresses and other property, nothing whatsoever excepted or reserved from my whole estate, as well here in this country, in England, Holland or elsewhere, wherever they may be situated or be found, to administer thereon without interference or contradiction of my children or anyone else, or without being held to give any inventory or accounting during the time of her widowhood, but on the express condition that she shall not have power to sell, alienate or dispose of my real or immovable estate wherever it may lie, as lands, houses, lots, and rents, but shall only receive the usufruct and yearly income thereof during her widowhood; but if she marry again, she shall be holden before she enter into the marriage state an inventory of my whole estate to deliver to my sons, to wit: Wessell Ten Broeck, Samuel Ten Broeck, Johannes Ten Broeck and Tobias Ten Broeck, whom I appoint as executors of my whole estate, as well movable as immovable, to administer upon the same, which administrators shall be holden to pay to my said wife a third of the yearly income during her life; the other two-thirds, after all the expenses incurred shall have been deducted, it is my will shall be equally divided yearly among my eleven children or their heirs, namely: Wessel Ten Broeck; Elsje Ten Broock, wife of Johannes Cuylaer; Catatyntje Ten Brock, wife of Johannes Lissjer; Cornelia Ten Brock, wife of Johannes Wynkook;[77] Geertruy [157] Ten Brock, wife of Abraham Schuylaer; Christyna Ten Broeck, wife of Johannes van Alen; Elisabeth Ten Brock, wife of Ant[o]ny Costers; Lidia Ten Broeck, wife of Volkert van Vechten; Samuel Ten Brock; Johannes Ten Broeck; Tobias Ten Broeck; to each a just eleventh part.

Fifth. After my wife's death, I give and bequeath to my eldest son Wessell Ten Brock two-thirds of all my lands lying in Sarachtoge, in the county of Albany, and the other third part of said lands I give and bequeath to my daughter Geertruy Schuylaers, wife of Abraham Schuylaer, which lands aforenamed are a just seventh part of the whole of Sarachtoge according to patent in company with Col. Piter Schuylaer and others; which I give to my aforenamed eldest son and daughter Geertruy as aforewritten, to wit, two-thirds for the aforenamed Wessel and his heirs forever, provided that such shall serve in payment and satisfaction of the aforenamed Wessel's portion of the inheritance of my estate to the amount of one hundred and twenty-five pounds New York currency, likewise to my daughter Geertruy aforenamed the just third part of the land aforesaid in payment of the sum of seventy-five pounds like currency of New York, to be deducted from her inheritance, which aforesaid third part I give to her and her heirs for the aforenamed sum forever after my wife's death.

Sixth. Furthermore I give to my sons Samuel Ten Brock and Tobias Ten Broeck all my lands in the aforesaid manor of Livingstoen according to conveyance to me given by Mr Robbert Livingstoen, to be divided in two equal parts, whereof my son Tobias shall have the choice of one half and the other half for my said son Samuel, for them and their respective heirs forever, besides which I give to my two sons Samuel and Tobias aforewritten four horses, four cows, four sheep, four hogs, [158] one of my negroes at their choice, all farm implements which then shall be found on my farm, for which I will that my sons pay to the aforenamed executors each the sum of one hundred and ninety pounds New York money, being together three hundred and eighty pounds, provided that each of the two shall have liberty to deduct from the aforenamed sum in his full portion of the inheritance of my whole

---

[77] Thus in the record.

estate, that is to say if their inheritance does not amount to so much as this aforenamed sum, then they must pay up and turn over the deficiency to my administrators, but if their inheritance comes to more then they shall be paid out of the estate, but they shall not lay claim to this bequeathed land before my aforesaid wife's death, when they shall receive the lands with house, barn, ricks, farm and all rights therein forever.

Seventh. After my wife's death I give to my son Johannis Ten Broeck my two houses and lot lying in the city of Albany, on the north side of the *Jounkeer straet*,[78] on the west side of the *Gangh straet*,[79] on the east side of the house and lot of Antony Coster and to the south of said Coster, according to conveyance thereof for him and his heirs forever; also I give the said Johannis all my right in lands lying on the east of Hudson's river, on a kill called Kinderhoeck kill, that now remain unsold, according to patent of Sir Edmond Andros and Col. Thomas Dongan, for him and for his heirs and assigns forever, for which houses and lot and rights of lands upon the Kinderhoek kill, valued by me at two hundred pounds current money of New York, it is my will that he shall reimburse the estate to the same amount, on condition that he may deduct therefrom as much as the eleventh part of the whole estate [159] shall come to and pay the rest to my executors for the benefit of my other heirs, but if his part amounts to more, the balance is to be turned over to him by the administrators.

Eighth. It is my will and desire that all my other lands, houses and lots, save what I have hereinbefore bequeathed at the prices stipulated to my aforementioned sons and daughter Geertruy, wherever they may be situated and to which I have lawful title, with all my negroes, negresses, cattle and other goods of whatsoever nature, found after my and my aforenamed wife's death, I give to my aforenamed eleven children to be sold to each other, and the entire sum together with the aforesaid sums which my sons and daughter Geertruy are to pay for the appraised lands and houses shall be added together and divided equally among my aforenamed eleven children, with the understanding that my said sons and daughter Geertruy of the appraised valuation of their lands shall pay no more than the amount in excess of the eleventh part of my whole estate.

Ninth. It is further my will and desire that none of my real

---

[78] Jonker or Jonkheer street, now State street.
[79] Literally: alley street, now James street.

estate shall be sold to a stranger, but shall always remain in my family.

Tenth. It is my will and desire that Christina Legget whenever she shall come to marry, shall have a proper outfit. All the foregoing conditions I declare to be my last will and testament, desiring that the same shall have full force and effect in all respects. Thus done and concluded on my farm in Dutchess county in the manor of Livingstoen and subscribed and sealed with my own hand in the year $17\frac{14}{15}$, the fourth day of February.

Was signed,

DIRCK WESSELS TEN BROECK (L.S.)

Signed and sealed in presence of the undersigned witnesses,

Jan Vosburgh
William Scott
Pietr Vosburgh

[160] Pursuant to an order from his Excellency Robert Hunter Esqr. Capt. Generall & Govr. in Chiefe of y^e provinces of New York New Jersey &^{a}. dated the sixth day of Novemb. last appeared before me Johannis Cuyler Esqr. Recorder of the City of Albany Jan vosburgh William Scott & Peter vosburgh the wittnesses to the above will & Testament of Dirk Wessells Ten Broeck Late of the County of Albany Esqr. Deceased who declared on the holy Evangelists that they saw the said Dirck Wessells Ten Broeck sign seale & publish the same as his Last will & Testament and that to ye best of their knowledge he had at the signing & sealing of ye said will his perfect sences and understanding, as also appeared before me the said Johan^s. Cuyler Christyna Wessels Ten Broeck Executrix of the said Last will & Testament Chiefly therein named who took the oath of Executrix for the due Execution & performance of the said will & Testament Given under my hand in Albany this sixth day of february in the fourth year of his maj^{es}. Reign A^o. D^o. 1717/8.

was Signd
JOH^s. CUYLER

Will of Arent Slingerlandt

[161] In the name of the Lord, Amen. Know all men by these presents that I, Aarent Slingerlandt, in the colony of Renselaerwyck, at present weak and sick in body but yet having the perfect use of

my senses and memory, God be praised therefor, considering the shortness and frailty of human life, the certainty of death and the uncertain hour thereof and being desirous to set all things in order, do make this my last will and testament, hereby annulling, canceling and revoking all such will or wills, testament or testaments heretofore by me made or declared, whether by word of mouth or writing, and [intending] this only to be held as my last will and testament, and no other.

Imprimis. I commend my soul to God my Creator, to Jesus Christ my Redeemer and to the Holy Ghost my Sanctifier, and my body to the earth from whence it came to be buried in a Christian manner, there to rest until the same shall be reunited with the soul at the last day and receive the everlasting joy of immortality which God has prepared for all those who unfeignedly believe and with a true heart and trust in Christ; and as regards such temporal estate as of lands, houses, slaves, cattle, money and other goods, which the Lord far above my deserts has been pleased to grant me, I give and dispose of the same in form and maner hereinafter written.

2 It is my will and desire that all my just debts shall in due time be paid out of my aforesaid estate.

3 I give to my eldest son Teunis Slingerlant the net sum of three pounds current money [162] of this province in consideration of his right of primogeniture.

4 It is my will and desire that my beloved wife Geertruy Slingerland shall remain in full possession and retain the use and income of my whole estate for the maintenance of her and my children during her widowhood, but if my aforesaid wife come to marry again she shall give up my whole estate only keep for herself all my household furniture, bedding, linen and woolen, save that the clothing belonging to my body shall be for my two sons Teunis and Gerrit Slingerland.

5 It is my will and desire and I ordain that six months after the death of my aforesaid wife or after her remarriage my whole immovable or real estate, with negro slaves, horses and cattle, plow, wagon and other implements for tilling the land or belonging to the mill shall be appraised by three impartial persons therefor appointed by my executors and my children, which estate I desire that my eldest son shall receive for him, his heirs and assigns forever provided and with this understanding that he or his heirs pay to my other children, Gerrit Slingerland, Engeltie Slingerlandt

and Sarah Slingerland, to each of them, their heirs or assigns, a just fourth part of the value of said estate according to the before ordered appraisal, within the time of five years after the remarriage or death of my aforesaid wife; and in case any of my aforesaid children happen to die in their minority, then shall their portion devolve upon and go to my surviving children, share and share alike, and my eldest son Teunis Slingerlant dying during his minority, the afore- [163] said estate shall go to my aforesaid son Gerrid Slingerland, his heirs, or assigns, provided he pay the parts and portions to my aforesaid daughters, their heirs, or assigns, according to appraisal and direction hereinbefore written.

6 I constitute and make my dear and worthy friends and brother Albert Slingerlant, Johannis Mingaal and Casper van Hoesen my executors of this my last will and testament, and desire that all that is herein comprehended according to its true meaning may be performed. Thus subscribed and sealed and declared the twenty-eighth day of January in the year of our Lord one thousand seven hundred and twelve and thirteen.

mark
AARENT X SLINGERLANT
of

Signed, sealed and declared his last will and testament in presence of us,

Johannis Mingal
Casper van Hoesen
Albert Slingerlant
Rutger Bleecker

Will of Adam Dingeman

[170] In the name of the Lord, Amen. By the contents of this present public instrument, know all men that in the year seventeen hundred and twenty and twenty-one, the twenty-first of January, in the seventh year of the reign of our sovereign lord, King George, I, Adam Dingeman, born at Haerlem in Holland, sick and weak of body, but having the perfect use of my senses, memory and understanding, make this my last will and testament, without the inducement, persuasion or misleading of anyone, in manner following: Commending first and foremost my immortal soul whenever it shall depart from my body to the gracious hands of my Creator and Savior and my body to a Christian burial; and as regards such

estate [171] as I on my decease shall leave behind, I give and bequeath it to my children, as well daughters as sons, to be equally divided among them, share and share alike, to the one not more than to the other, whether it be my real estate or my personal property, money, furniture, household goods, rights and credits, all goods, movable and immovable, nothing excepted, annulling hereby all former testaments by me made, and [intending] this alone to be accepted as my last and final will; hereby making my son-in-law Peter Cool sole executor of this my last will and testament, with power to sell and convey the real estate of lands, etc. and the proceeds thereof to divide equally among my children, and further to do all that executors by the laws of this province are permitted to do. Thus done and executed at the house of Peter Cool aforesaid in the manor of Livingston, the year, month and day aforenamed and with my hand and seal subscribed and sealed.

Was signed,

ADAM DINGMANS (L.S.)

Signed, sealed and declared in presence of us

Willem Halenbeck
Gysbert Osterhout
Dirk Halenbeek

Appeared before Robt. Livingston Junr. Peter van Brugh Esqr. Judges, Evert Bancker and Myndert Schuyler Esq^s. Justices of the Inferior Court of Comon pleas for the City and County of Albany William hawlingbeek, Gysbert oosterhout and Dirk hawlingbeek wittnesses to the within Instrument who declare on the holy Evangelists that they saw adam Dingman sign & seal it and Declare the said Instrument to be [172] his Last will and Testament and that at the same time as it seemd to them he had his perfect sences In Testimony whereof the Judges of the said Court have hereunto sett their hands in Albany this fourteenth day of March in y^e seventh year of his maj^{es}. Reign annoq^e D^o. 172$\frac{0}{1}$.

was Signd

ROB^t. LIVINGSTON JUN^r.
PIETER VAN BRUGH

Will of Harmen Jansen Knickerbacker

[176] In the name of the Lord, Amen. Know all men by these presents that on this seventeenth day of January in the year of our

Lord and Savior Jesus Christ one thousand seven hundred and seven and eight I, Harmen Janse Knickerbacker of Dutchess county in the province of New York, being in reasonable health and having full power of mind and understanding (the Lord be praised), considering the shortness and frailty of human life, the certainty of death and the uncertainty of the hour thereof, and being desirous to set all things in order, make this my last will and testament in form and manner hereinafter written, revoking, canceling and annulling by these presents all such testament or testaments, will or wills heretofore made or executed whether by word of mouth or in writing and [intending] this alone to be acknowledged as my last will and testament, and no other.

First. I commend my soul to God Almighty my Creator and to Jesus Christ my Redeemer and to the Holy [177] Ghost my Sanctifier, and my body to the earth from whence it came, to be buried in a Christian manner and there to rest until my soul and body shall be united at the last day and receive the everlasting joy of immortality which God through His grace and the sole merit of our Savior has promised and prepared for all those who unfeignedly believe in Him and from the heart repent.

2 And as regards such temporal estate of houses, lands, goods, debts, horses, cattle, money, gold and silver coined and uncoined, and whatever else appertans to my estate (which the Lord far above my deserts has been pleased to grant), I order, give and dispose thereof as follows:

3 I order that all my just debts in a due time shall be paid.

4 It is my will and desire that my worthy wife Elizabeth Knickerbacker shall have and enjoy the income and profit of my whole estate, real and personal, during my aforesaid wife's life and that at her death my aforesaid estate shall belong to my heirs hereinafter written in manner following:

5 I give to my seven children lawfully procreated with my aforesaid wife, to wit, Johannes, Lowrens, Cornelis, Evert and Pieter Knickerbacker, Jannetie Lansing, widow of Hendrick Lansing, junior, and Cornelia [178] Knickerbacker, my whole aforesaid real and personal estate, to be divided equally among them and their heirs after the death of my aforesaid wife, on this condition, however, that none of my heirs shall have the right to sell his portion of the real estate to anyone but the aforesaid Knickerbackers, only it is my will that my eldest son Johannis shall first draw three shillings current money for his right of primogeniture, without making any further claim on that account.

6 It is my will that if I before my death happen to set off any portion of my land for one or more of my children, then, after the death of my aforesaid wife, such portion or portions shall belong to that child or children to whom I shall have set it off, provided it shall appear under my hand, [written] in the presence of two or more witnesses, what and how I have set it off.

7 I appoint as executors of this my last will and testament my aforesaid wife and my two sons Johannis and Lowrens Knickerbacker, desiring that what is hereinbefore written shall in all respects be followed and observed. Thus done at my house in the aforesaid county, the day and year as above.

Was signed,

HEERMEN JANSEN KYNCKBACKER (L.S.)

Signed, sealed and declared by Harmen Janse Knickerbacker this to be his last will and testament in presence of us.

Jan I P *Ploeg,* his mark
Pieter P P *Pile,* his mark
D' Meyer Clarke

Will of Marcelis Jansen

[180] In the name of God, Amen. Know all men whom it may concern that on the eleventh day of June at New Albany, sixteen hundred and ninety, being the second year of the reign of William and Mary, king and queen of Great Britain, Marcelis Janse, dwelling in the aforesaid city, hale and sound in body, walking and standing, having perfect possession and use of his senses, memory, understanding, reason and speech as outwardly appears, who considering the frailty of life and the unforeseen hour of death, unwilling to depart hence without first having disposed of his temporal effects by the Almighty granted him and that without the persuasion, inducement or misleading of any persons but of his will and motion, commending first his soul to the hands of God and his body to a Christian burial, hereby nominates [181] appoints and chooses his lawful wife Annetie as his sole and universal heir of his whole estate and property, whether orchard or orchards, ground or grounds, lot or lots, house or houses, his movable goods, rights and credits and all that he may leave behind at his death, nothing whatsoever reserved and excepted, but with the understanding that (after the testator's death) she shall have the usufruct of the real estate during the time of her life, without being at liberty to alienate, encumber or sell the same, but after her death it shall go to their

children lawfully procreated by them, to wit, Gysbercht, Huybertje, Sytje, Judith and Aasuerus, to be divided among them equally, without regard to male or female sex or, in case of their death, to the grandchildren, taking the place of their deceased parent or parents; except that the eldest son before any partition shall receive the value of six guilders in beavers, but with the understanding that the aforesaid real estate and houses shall go to the aforesaid youngest two children, the value of which, at a lawful and proper appraisal, the aforesaid youngest two children shall pay (their just portion being deducted) in the time of the six following years, every year a just sixth part, to begin from the time of the appraisal; but as regards the movable estate, the testator's wife may sell, alienate, consume and dispose of the same in every way, just as the testator could do while alive, without delivering any statement or inventory to any child or children, or in case of infancy or death of the same, to the children's children, blood relations, guardians, the honorable orphan masters, constable or constables, the court of this city or govern[182]ment, whether high or low, judge or judges, or to any other person whomsoever much less giving surety or bond,. inasmuch as the testator excludes and debars them all, jointly and severally, and wills and desires that his aforesaid wife shall have full administration and to this end makes her administratrix and executrix in the fullest manner possible, notwithstanding that some law or laws, custom or customs of this government may otherwise direct, which laws and customs, he wills shall herein be inoperative and of no effect. All that is hereinbefore written the testator declares to be his testamentary disposition and last will, which he desires to have effect from the weightiest to the least article thereof; whether as testament, codicil, gift in anticipation of death or among the living, or any other bequest, however it may be named, notwithstanding all formalities required by law may not be observed herein, desiring the utmost benefit of the law for the maintenance of what is above written. Thus done and signed and sealed by the testator's own hand, on the aforesaid 11th of June, at New Albany, A°. 1690.

    Was signed:

            MARCELUS JANSEN (L.S.)

Signed and sealed in presence of

Cornelis Swart
Johannes Becker, Junr.

    In my presence, JOHANNES BECKER, SENIOR
    Kingston in the County of ulster may the 22^d. A°. 1722

Then appeared before me Jacob Rutsen Esqr. Judge of the Comon pleas for the said County in the presence of Eghbert Schoonmaker & John Rutsen Esq^{rs}. Justices, Cornelis Swart of Kingston aged seaventy years being Sworn on the holy Evangelist declareth that his name being hereunto Sett as an Evidence to this will & Testament is his own hand writeing.

was Signd

JACOB RUTSEN
EGHBERT SCHOONMAKER
J^{No}. RUTSEN

Will of Jeronimus Barheyt

[183] 1713, the 22d of August

This is the last will and desire of Jeroon Barheyt. First, that his wife Rabecke during her widowhood shall remain in possession [of the estate?] and the negro Aslerrsu.[80]

Second, that his son Wouter shall have the whole estate and effects, on condition that he shall give to his sister the sum of one hundred pounds and the negro Harry [the same] to be paid within 10 years. All this without craft or guile signed in presence of the hereinafter named witnesses.

his
JEROON   X   BARHEYT
mark

Jacob Schermerhorn
Myndert Marseles
    his
Hendrick   H W   *van Wie*
    mark

Albany the 23th. February 1722/3

Appeared before Peter van Brugh Esqr. one of the Judges of the Inferior Court of Comon pleas for the City & County of Albany, Jacob Schermerhoorn Mynder Marcelis and Hendrick van wie the wittnesses to the within Instrument who Declare on the holy Evangelists that they saw Jeronimus Barheyt sign & seale it and Declare the said Instrument to be his Last will & Testament and that at the same time as it seemd to them he had his perfect sences and understanding.

was Signd

PIETER VAN BRUGH

---

[80] Ahasuerus?

Will of Abraham Schuyler

[187] In the name of God, Amen. Know all men by these presents that I, the undersigned, Abraham Schuyler, burgher and inhabitant of the City of Albany in the province of New York, hale and sound in body and having full possession of my understanding, memory and speech, considering the frailty of this life, the certainty of death and the uncertain hour thereof, wishing therefore to dispose of the temporal effects which God Almighty has granted me, commending first and foremost my soul to the gracious hands of God my Creator and Savior and my body to a Christian burial, dispose as follows:

1 That after my death my respected wife Geertruy Schuyler shall remain in full possession of my whole estate and effects, that is real and personal estate, nothing therefrom excepted, during her widowhood.

2 That on the remarriage of my aforesaid wife, before her wedding day, she shall relinquish all my real estate, as well houses and lots as lands, to my five children, to wit, David aged about seventeen years, Christyna aged about fifteen years, Dirck aged about ten years, Abraham aged about five years and Jacobus aged about three years, together with the child or children which in this present wedlock we may yet have, to the end that the same may be equally divided among my children, share and share alike, except that my eldest son David shall for his birthright [188] have the sum of five pounds current money of this province, with the understanding and my will is that my house and lot lying here in Albany in the *Brouwers straet*,[81] at present by me occupied, shall go to my two sons David and Jacobus aforesaid, share and share alike, which house and lot they shall receive by appraisal of three impartial persons, in order that the just portion may be turned over to the other child or children when each child attains his [or her] majority or marries; with the further understanding that if my aforesaid wife marry again, she may nevertheless remain in occupancy of the little house on the street and have the use of a lot in the rear of the breadth of said house, for the term of seven years beginning from such marriage day and no longer.

3 My wife remains holden on the marriage of each of my children to give a proper outfit according to the value of the estate.

4 I nominate and appoint as guardians and executors of my

---

[81] Literally: Brewer's street, now Broadway.

children and whole estate aforesaid my two brothers David and Myndert Schuyler with my two brothers-in-law Wessell and Samuel Ten Bro[e]ck, to the end that my foregoing will in all its parts may be observed and maintained. All that is hereinbefore written the testator declares to be his last will and testament. Thus with my own hand subscribed and sealed in Albany this fifteenth day of December annoq. domini one thousand seven hundred and [189] nine.

ABRAHAM SCHUYLER (L.S.)

Signed, sealed and published
in presence of

Andries Coeyemans
Joh'. Cuyler
Pieter van Brugh

Will of Dirck Goes

[192] In the name of God, Amen.

On the first day of June in the fifth year of the reign of our sovereign king George the second, over Great Britain, France and Ireland, defender of the faith, &c, in the year of our Lord and Savior Jesus Christ one thousand seven hundred and thirty-two, I, Dirck Goes, of Kinderhook in the county of Albany and in the province of New York, being weak and sick of body, but having sound and perfect memory and understanding (God be thanked for the same), considering the uncertain condition of this life, and that all flesh must die whenever the Lord shall please to call, and being desirous to set my affairs in order, make this my last will and testa-[193]ment in form and manner following: In the first place I commend my soul to Almighty God my Creator, to Jesus Christ my Savior, to the Holy Ghost my Sanctifier, and my body to the earth from whence it came therein in a becoming and Christian manner to be buried, to rest until my soul and body shall again be reunited, on the day of the general resurrection to become partaker of the insatiable joy of immortality, which God of His grace through the merits of Jesus Christ alone has prepared and promised for all such as have true penitence and faith in Him. As regards such temporal goods as the Lord far above my deserts has been pleased to bestow upon me I give and dispose of the same in manner and form following:

First. It is my will and desire that my wife Elizabeth Goes shall be altogether master of my whole estate as it is now in use, during her widowhood.

2 I bequeath to my son Johannis Goes after my death one of my cattle according to his choice in order that he may make no further claim upon my estate by reason of his primogeniture than shall hereinafter be bequeathed to him.

3 I bequeath to my son Luyckas Goes my house, barn, homestead and orchard as I now have them in possession, for him and his heirs and assigns forever.

4 I bequeath to my two aforenamed sons Johannis Goes and Luyckas Goes to them and their heirs and assigns forever the remainder of all my real estate, arable land, mills, meadow and swamp, to each an equal half and no more, (saving a piece of land called the *Maiezhoek*, that I give to my daughter Anna, wife of Tobias van Bure [n], to her and her heirs and assigns forever).

5 I bequeath my vote in the Common patent of Kinderhook to my three children to wit, Johannis and Luyckas Goes and Anna, wife of Tobias van Beuren, to each a third part, to them and their heirs and assigns forever.

6 I bequeath all my title and claim which I have at Claverack to my son Johannis Goes and my daughter Anna van [194] Beuren, for them and their heirs and assigns forever, to be divided among them and their heirs, to the one no more than to the other.

7 I will that my sons Johannis and Luyckas Goes shall each pay twenty-five pounds current money of New York to my daughter Anna van Beuren, wife of Tobias van Beuren, to her or her heirs, four years after my wife's death.

8 If my son Luyckas should die without heirs, it is my will that what I have herein bequeathed to him shall go to my son Johannis and my daughter Anna, wife of Tobias van Beuren, to them and their heirs and assigns forever, to one no more than to the other.

9 I give to my son Luyckas Goes my negro Toby, and my negress Bettie, for him and his heirs and assigns, after my wife's death.

10 I will that after my wife's death my three children, to wit, Johannis and Luyckas Goes and Anna, wife of Tobyas van Beuren, shall have equal parts, each a third part of all my movable goods to wit, furniture, beds, bolsters, horses, cows, sheep and everything else (save what has already been herein bequeathed).

11 I bequeath to my sons Johannis and Luyckas Goes, to them and their heirs and assigns forever, all my waterpower on the Kinderhook kill with shoot, dam and all other property and rights and privileges belonging to the mill aforenamed standing on the great fall, now belonging to me and Coenraed Borghard, with ground and orchard thereto belonging.

In acknowledgment of the truth of which I have hereunto set my hand and seal the day and year above written, in presence of these

his
DIRCK △ GOES (L.S.)
mark

Witnesses

A. V. Dyck
Cornelis van Schaack
       his
Jan Tysen I G *Goes*
      mark

Albany the 5th Augt. 1732

Appeared before Philip Livingston one of his Majesties Councill for the Province of New York Arent van Dyck one of the Subscribeing wittnesses to the within written Will of Dirk Goes and made oath on the holy Evangelists of Almighty God that he saw the said Dirk Goes seale Publish & Declare the within to be his Last will & Testament, and that at the same time he was of sound Disposeing mind & memory to the best of his knowledge and that he saw the other wittnesses sign thereto, to the best of his Remembrance

PH: LIVINGSTON

Will of Francis Hardick

[207] Know all men by these presents that upon this nineteenth day of December one thousand seven hundred and thirty-seven, in the eleventh year of his majesty's reign, King George the second, of England, Scotland, France and Ireland, defender of the faith, I, Francis Hardik, in good health and having full power and use of my understanding, senses and memory as outwardly appears, considering the shortness and frailty of human life, the certainty of death and the uncertain hour thereof, and being desirous to set all things in order, make this my last will and testament in form and manner hereinafter written:

First of all commending my soul to God Almighty my Creator, to Jesus Christ my Redeemer and to the Holy Ghost my Sanctifier, and my body to the earth from whence it came to be buried in a Christian manner, there to rest until my body and soul shall be reunited at the last day and enjoy the eternal bliss of immortality which God of His grace has prepared through the merit of our Savior for all those who unfeignedly repent and believe in Him; and as regards such temporal estate of lands, goods, horses, cattle, credits, etc., as the Lord has been pleased far above my deserts to grant me, I order, give and dispose of the same in manner hereinafter written:

[208] *First*. It is my will and desire that all my just debts in proper time shall be paid.

2 I give to my eldest son Jan Hardick for his birthright as my eldest son thirty shillings current money of New York.

3 I give to my son Jan Hardick a certain piece of land lying on the east side of Hudson's river, now partly in his possession, beginning at a certain place called the *Noorder Boght* (north bend) at an elm tree at the corner of the fence, stretching thence into a *vley* (flat) by the first kill which is called the *Diepe Leeghtese Kill* (Deep Valley creek), then up along the south side of said kill to the fall on said kill, thence up to the corner of the fence or the land now already in his possession, thence to a bridge called the *Pople* (Poplar) bridge, thence to a bridge called the *Swarte* (Black) bridge, which bridge lies over a *Spruyt* (brook), thence along the north side of said *spruyt* to the land which my son Willem Hardick has bought of him, thence along the fence to the aforesaid elm tree, which I give him for him and his heirs and assigns forever.

4 I give and bequeath to my son Willem Hardick all my right, title and interest in and to my land lying at Claverack, excepting what I have already granted or bequeathed, for him, his heirs and assigns forever, on condition that he shall pay to my daughter Sarah Hardick, wife of Jonatan Rees, or her heirs the sum of thirty pounds current money of New York, and to the three children of my deceased daughter Gerrite, wife of Domine Iustus Valkenaer, deceased, fifteen pounds current money of New York, or else he can satisfy them by [giving] each twenty-five morgens of woodland, more or less, it being left to his choice to give either money or land, for them, or their heirs and assigns.

5 It is my will and desire that my son Willem Hardick shall have one year and six weeks after my death in which to pay my abovesaid daughter Sarah and the three children of my abovewritten daughter Gerritje, deceased, or their heirs, the portion aforenamed.

6 I give to my son Willem Hardick, or his heirs, all my movable

estate, that is, horses and cows and furniture, excepting the older furniture which I desire shall be divided among my five children, or their heirs, [209] namely: Jan, Willem, Sarah, Gerritje and Volkje Hardick, wife of Leendert Rees.

7 I appoint as executor of this my last will and testament, my above written son Willem Hardick. In witness whereof I have signed this in presence of witnesses in Claverak in the county of Albany, the day and year as above.

his
FRANCIS X HARDIK (L.S.)
mark

Signed and declared this to be
his last will and testament.
The word *Koningh* (king)
interlined before signing.

Samuel Ten Broeck
Dirk W. Ten Broeck

    his
Evert E. B. *Bout*
   mark

Albany the 3 day of Nov. 1742

Be it Remembred that on the day and year above written personally appear'd before me Myndert Schuyler being thereunto Deligated and appointed, Samuel Ten Broeck and Evert Boudt Two of the Subscribing wittnesses to the within will of Fransis Hardick, and made oath on the Holy Evangelists of Almighty God That they Saw the said Francis Hardik Sign and Seal publish and declare the same to be his Last will and That at the Time thereof he was of Sound disposeing mind and memory to the best of their Knowledge and further declared they Saw the other wittness Derick Ten Broek sign as wittness thereunto in the presence of the Testator

MYNDERT SCHUYLER

Recorded in the Book of Records of wills held for the City and County of Albany page 206, 207 & 208, the fourth day of November 1742

P^r me PHIL LIVINGSTON JUN. D. *Clk*

Will of Volckert van Vechten

[216] In the name of God, Amen. Know all men by these presents that upon this fifteenth day of July in the year of our Lord one thousand seven hundred and forty-seven, I, Volkert van Veghte, dwelling in the colony of Renslaerswyck in the county of Albany, in the province of New York, being old in years, but having my memory and understanding perfect, and considering the shortness and frailty of human life, the certainty of death and the uncertainty of the time and hour thereof, and being desirous to set my affairs in good order, make this my last will and testament, hereby annulling, canceling and revoking all wills or testaments heretofore made and declared by me, whether by word of mouth or in writing, and [desire] this to be held as my last [217] will and testament.

Imprimis. I commend my soul to God my Creator and Savior and my body to the earth to be buried in a Christian manner, and respecting such temporal estate as belongs to me, money obligations, goods, rights and credits, nothing excepted where and whatsoever it may be, I order and dispose thereof as follows:

Item, I give and bequeath to my son Gerrit Teunise's son Volkert Van Veghte in consideration of his father's birthright and right of primogeniture fifteen pounds current money of this province.

Item, I give to my wife Liedia Van Veghte my whole estate during her widowhood or lifetime as I possess and occupy the same, nothing whatsoever excepted.

Item, I give and bequeath after my wife Liedia Van Veghten's death my whole estate as it may be found after her death to my six afternamed children and children's children, that is to say, my farm, house, barn, ricks, a fourth interest in the sawmill and all other appurtenances belonging to the farm lying in the colony of Renslarswyck on the east side of Hudson's river over against *Papsknee,* bounded north by the south end of the land of Jannetje Witbeeck and south by the north end of the land of the heirs of Johannis Van Veghten, dec^d. and west by *Papsknee's* Kill; and also my just eighth part of the land of the Hoosieck patent to me devised and bequeathed by my father's last will and testament, and furthermore my whole estate and effects, negroes, negresses, negro children, [218] horses, cows, and everything without exception, to my son Dirck Van Veghte, his heirs or assigns a just sixth part of my whole estate and of all the above-named property, nothing whatsoever excepted.

Item, I give and bequeath to my daughter Magrieta Van Den Bergh, wife of Gerrit C. Vanden Bergh, her heirs or assigns, a just sixth part of my whole estate and of all that is above mentioned, without any exception.

Item, I give and bequeath to my son Gerrit Teunisse's two children, Volkert and Angenietje Van Veghte, to them and their heirs, each a just sixth part of my whole estate above named, nothing excepted.

Item, I give and bequeath to my son Ephraim's daughter, Liedia Van Veghte, to her and her heirs, a just sixth part of my whole estate above named, nothing excepted.

Item, I give and bequeath to my son Johannis Van Veghten's heirs, to them and to their heirs, a just sixth part of my whole estate, without exception.

Item, I give and bequeath[82] that in case any of my aforenamed children or children's children happen to die before they or any of them attain their majority what is hereinbefore bequeathed to them shall pass to the above-named surviving children, or their heirs, to be divided [219] equally among them.

Item, I will and desire that my farm or whole estate six weeks after my and my wife's death shall be sold to one of my children if he shall be able to buy the same, or else to someone else whom my hereinafter named three executors shall consider fit and able to buy the same, and I authorize and empower my executors or two of them to convey the same after such sale and that their conveyance, signed and sealed by them, shall pass and stand as a perfectly lawful title to anyone as if the same was done by me personally.

Item, I will and desire that the share of the minor children's children in my whole estate shall be secured by obligation for their behoof until the time they shall come of age and then be given to them, and the income of said obligations shall yearly be given to the mothers of the children for the maintenance of their children and the principal of the obligations shall remain in the hands of the executors.

Item, I desire and order that if my aforesaid children or any of them may not be satisfied with their just sixth part of the whole and all that belongs to me, which I have above bequeathed and given to them, but seek to make further claim or pretension to any part of my estate, or any portion thereof here or elsewhere of whatsoever

---

[82] Read: I will and desire.

nature it may be, those who come to do that shall be completely deprived of their inheritance bequeathed to them above.

Item, Lastly I nominate my two sons Dirck Van Veghten and Gerrit C. Van Den Bergh [220] and my friend Petrus Douw as my executors of this my last will and testament and desire that they my just debts which I may leave behind shall pay in proper time out of my whole estate. In witness of the truth of which I have subscribed and sealed these and declared these to be my last will and testament, the day and year above written.

VOLCKERT VAN VEGTE (L.S.)

Signed, sealed and the above written declared by Volkert Van Veghte to be his last will and testament, in presence of us as witnesses.

Hend[r]. Beeckman
Johannis De Wandelaer
Pieter De Wandelaer

On the back of the above will was written as follows viz

Albany the 15 Ap 1749

Be it Remembered, that on the Day & Year above written personally appeared before me Myndert Schuyler being thereunto Deligated & Appointed Hendrick Beekman & Joh[s] De Wandelaer two of the Subscribeing Witnesses to the Within Written Will of Volckert Van Veghten Deceased, And made Oath on the holy Evangelists of Almighty God that they saw the Said Volkert Van Veghten Sign Seal publish & Declare the Same to be his Last Will & That of the time thereof he was of Sound Disposeing Mind & Memory to the best of their knowledge & also further Declare that they Saw Pieter Dewandelaer one Other of the said Witnesses to the s[d] Will Sign as Witness to the Same in the Presence of the Testator

MYNDERT SCHUYLER

Recorded Ap: 27th 1750
P[r] John Colden Clerk

Will of Dirck van Vechten

[235] In the name of the Lord, Amen. Know all men by these presents that I, Dirck van Vechten, of Schagtekoek in the county of Albany, husbandman, being sick in body, but in possession of

my understanding and senses, God be praised therefor, and being desirous to set all things in order, make this my last will and testament in manner following:

Imprimis. I commend my soul to God my Creator and Redeemer and Savior and my body to the earth to be buried in a Christian manner; and concerning the temporal property, including lands, horses and cattle and whatever else belongs to my real and personal estate which the Lord far above my deserts has been pleased to grant me, I order and dispose of the same as follows: I desire that all my just debts shall be paid out of my aforesaid estate.

Item. I give to my eldest son Harmen van Vechte my large Bible containing the Old and the New Testament, &c., for and in consideration of his right of primogeniture.

[236] *First.* My will is that my well-beloved wife Maragrieta van Vechten shall hold and possess my whole estate, my land, houses and buildings, cattle and all my movable goods, slaves and outstanding obligations during her widowhood and her natural life, nothing excepted, and if my aforenamed wife have occasion during her widowhood, she may sell or dispose of my slaves, negroes and negresses, as well as of my outstanding obligations, to whom she may think fit, but none of my real estate, land and houses, shall my aforenamed have power to sell or dispose of, but shall have the use and income thereof during her widowhood; but if my aforenamed wife marry again, then it is my will that she deliver up and hand over my whole estate to my son or the heirs whom I shall hereinafter specify, also to give up all my personal property to my children or their heirs, saving one of my negresses whom I give to her during her life and after her death, the negress shall revert to my children or their heirs.

Second. I give and bequeath to my son Theunis van Vechten my farmland, houses, barn, ricks, orchard and all outbuildings, where I now dwell at Schagtekoek, in the county of Albany, lying north of the land of Johannes Knickerbacker, and according to writings and as it came to me, and all my farming implements together with two gelding horses, two mares, three cows, three sheep and three sows, which I give to my aforenamed son Theunis van Vechten for him and his heirs and assigns forever, for which I will that he shall pay after my aforesaid wife's death, and six years after he comes to occupy, receive and peacefully till the land, to my four children or to their heirs, to wit, to Harmen van Vechten the sum of twenty-five [237] pounds, to Anna van Vechten, wife of Hendrick Fonda, the sum of twenty-five pounds, to Philip van Vechten the sum of twenty-five pounds, and to Benjamin van Vechten the sum of fifty pounds, all current money of New York.

Third. It is my will that my youngest son Benjamin van Vechten shall have, after my brother Leendert van Vechten's death without natural heirs, the fifteen morgens of land called the *Boght,* lying at Schagtekoek on the Great Kill, according to writings thereof, which I give to the aforenamed Benjamin van Vechten, for him and his heirs and assigns forever.

Fourth. I further give and bequeath after my wife's death all my movable goods, household furniture, etc., nothing excepted, to my five children or their heirs, Harmen van Vechten, Theunis van Vechten, Anna van Vechten wife of Hendrick Fonda, Philip van Vechten and Benjamin van Vechten, to be divided equally among them, except the large Bible which I now have in my house, that I give to my son Theunis van Vechten or his heirs forever.

Lastly. I appoint and make my well-beloved wife Maragarieta van Vechten executrix of this my last will and testament during her widowhood, who is to have the administration of all my movable goods, as an administratrix is required to do by the laws of the government. Furthermore, I appoint my good friends Livynes Lewisse and Dirck Ten Bro[e]ck to be guardians and overseers over my children that each may have and receive his rights, and to assist my beloved wife in the administration.

Thus signed and sealed with my own hand at my farm at Schagtekoek in the county of Albany the seventeenth day of August and in the thirteenth year of the reign of our King George the [238] Second of England, Scotland, France and England, etc. Annoque Domini 1739.

his
Dirck X Vechten (L.S.)
mark

Signed, sealed and declared by the testator to be his last will and testament in presence of

Barent Egbertsen
Harmen Kneckerbacker
Dirck Ten Broeck

Albany den 17th. of October 1752

Be it remembered that on the Day & Year above written personally Appeared before me Myndert Schuyler being thereunto

Deligated and Appointed Hermen Knickerbacker one of the Subscribing witnesses to the within written will of Dirick Van Veghten and made Oath on the holy Evangelist of Almighty God that he Saw the Said Dirick van Veghten Sign and Seale publish and declare the Same to be his last will and that att the Time thereof he was of Sound Disposing Mind and Memory to the Best of his knowledge And also further Declared that he Saw Barent Egbers & Dirck Ten Broeck Sign as witnesses thereunto in the presence of the Testator

Myndert Schuyler

Recorded this 29 Day of December 1756

P^r Ha: Gansevoort *Clerk*

Will of Pieter Hoogeboom

[242] In the name of God, Amen. On this twentieth day of June one thousand seven hundred and forty-six, I, Peter Hogeboom, of Claverack in the county of Albany in the province of New York, being of sound mind and memory, God be praised for the same, considering the frailty of my body and well knowing that it is appointed that all men must die, thus make and ordain this my last will and testament, that is to say, principally, I first give my soul into the hands of God the Lord who first gave it, and my body I commend to the earth to be buried in a Christian manner.

First. I give to my eldest son's son Peter Hogeboom for his birthright as eldest son the sum of ten pounds York money.

Second. I give to my eldest son's son Pieter Hogeboom and his heirs the neck and the strip (*streek*) at Canaan and all that lies between that and the old farm for his inheritance, on condition that he pays six years after my death to his sister Rachel Hogeboom and to his brother Cornelis Hogeboom to each per head thirty pounds York money.

Third. I give and bequeath to my son Barth. Hogeboom and to his heirs the old farm at Canaan as the deed shows on the record and also sixty acres lying upon the east side of the *Coninghs pat* (King's path), and also thirty-five acres on the south next the heirs of the widow Beldins and Sam[11]. Robens which lies undivided with Abram Halenbeek, on condition that Bartholomeus Hogeboom and his heirs shall pay six years after my death to Catrynte Hogeboom, wife of Ph: Conyn, and her heirs, the sum of fifty-five pounds York money, and to my daughter Hillatie Hogeboom, the wife of Jochem Radcliff, and her heirs, the sum of fifty-five pounds York money, and to my daughter Arriatic Hogeboom, the wife of Low^r. van Alee, deceased, and her heirs, the sum of fifty-five pounds York money, [243] and to my daughter Geertruy Hogeboom, the wife of Willem Van Ness, and her heirs, the sum of fifty-five pounds York money.

Fourth. I give and bequeath to my son Johannis Hogeboom and to his heirs the east or rear end of the farm at Claverack in the manor of Renselaer, as the division fence now stands, right through north and south so far as my right extends and as the deed shows, on condition that Johannis Hogeboom and his heirs pay six years after my death to Catryntie Hogeboom, wife of Ph: Conyn, and her heirs, the sum of thirty-two pounds, ten shillings York money, and to my daughter Hilletie Hogeboom, wife of Jochem Radcliff, and her heirs, thirty-two pounds, ten shillings York money, and to Arriantie Hoogeboom, wife of Lowerens van Alle, deceased, and her heirs, the sum of thirty-two pounds, ten shillings York money, and to Geertruy Hogeboom, wife of Willem van Ness, and her heirs, the sum of thirty-two pounds, ten shillings York money.

Fifth. I give and bequeath to my son Jeremyas Hogeboom and his heirs the foremost or westerly end of the farm with all the buildings thereon, at Claverack, straight through as the division fence now stands north and south so far as my right extends as the deed shows, on condition that Jeremyas Hogeboom pays six years after my death to Catryntie Hogeboom, wife of Ph: Conyn, and her heirs, the sum of forty-two pounds, ten shillings York money, and to my daughter Hilletie Hogeboom, wife of Jochem Radcliff, and her heirs, the sum of forty-two pounds, ten shillings York money, and to my daughter Arriantie Hogeboom, wife of Lou^w. van Alle, deceased, and her heirs, the sum of forty-two pounds, ten shillings, York money, [244] and to Geertruy Hogeboom, wife of Willm. van Ness, and her heirs, the sum of forty-two pounds, ten shillings York money.

Sixth. I give and bequeath to my daughter Marytie Hogenboom, wife of Jochem van Valckenburgh, and her heirs, the bush farm where Bart^h. Hogeboom now dwells, the old and the new for which I have conveyance and for which I have no conveyance as yet: just as it is with all my right and title, for her inheritance; and if so be that Bartholomeus Hogeboom will not deliver it up peaceably, then he shall be cut off from the farm at Canaan, and if it happen that the farm where Bart^h. now dwells shall be lost through any process of law, then shall the ten heirs be holden to make good again to Marytie and her heirs, her inheritance and if Bartholomeus keeps it for his portion, then shall all the heirs be holden if he lose it by process of law also to make good his inheritance to him, but the heirs shall be holden to make good the inheritance for no longer time than 6 years, after my death.

Seventh. I order that Geertruy Hogeboom, wife of Willem van Ness, and her heirs, shall be holden to pay six years after my death the sum of ten pounds York money to all my ten heirs, to each twenty shillings, before she receive the lot of ground.

Eighth. My daughters, Catryntie and Hilletie and Arriantie and Geertruy shall all be holden six years after my death when they shall have received their inheritance as aforenamed to pay the four of them, twenty pounds York money to Marytje Hogeboom, the wife of Jochem Valkenburgh, and her heirs.

Ninth. I give to my son Jeremyas Hogeboom a negro called Sees and a plow with all its appurtenances which I left there on the farm and three cows and three mares and three geldings from the stock which I have left on the farm.

[245] *Tenth.* I bequeath to all my children, my eldest son's son Piete, and Bartholomeus and Johannis and Jeremias, to my daughters Catryntie and Hilletie and Ariantie and Marytie and Geertruy and Annatie all my negroes and negresses, big and little, young and old, and all my horses and cattle and furthermore all my movable goods from the largest to the smallest that may be found after my death, to each his just tenth part, and furthermore all the heirs shall be held after my death to contribute equally until all my debts which may then appear shall be paid.

Lastly, I order and appoint my three sons Bartholomeus, Johannis and Jeremias all three as executors of this my last will and desire, to direct matters as I have desired them in this my last will and testament that my children may receive each what is provided for him individually and in the fear of the Lord use the same.

N. B. If there be any heirs who should [wish to] sell their estate, they shall be holden to sell to the nearest heirs if they will give as much as anyone else.

PIETER HOGENBOOM (L.S.)

To which I set my hand and seal in the presence of these witnesses:

Johannys Ten Eyck
Abram Vosburgh Jn
Pietter Soundhard

City & County } Be it Remembred that on the 23 day of February
of Albany } one Thousand and seven hundred and fifty Eight
personally Came and Appeared before me John De peyster Surrogate of the Said City and County Johannis Ten Eyck of the Manner of Livingston in the Said County of Albany and being duly Sworn on his Oath declared that he did See [246] Peter Hogeboom Sign and Seal the above written Instrument Porporting to be the will of the Said Pieter Hogenboom bearing date the 20 day of June 1746 And heard him Publish and declare the Same to be and Contain his Last will and Testament That att the Time thereof he the Said Pieter Hogenboom was of Sound disposing Mind and Memory to the best of his knowledge and Blief of him the deponant and that his name Subscribed to the Said will is of his Respective proper handwriting which he Subscribed as wittness to the Said will in the Testators presents, and that he the deponent Saw Abraham Vosburgh Junr. and Pieter Lounhard the other witnesses to the Said will Subscribe there names as witnesses thereunto in the Testators presents.

JOHN DE PEYSTER *Surrogate*

Recorded the 23 day of February 1758

p^r. HA: GANSEVOORT *Clerk*

Will of Jannetje, widow of Martin Cregier

[285] In the name of God, Amen. On this twentieth day of August in the year of our Lord one thousand seven hundred and thirty-four, I, Jannetie Cregier, widow of Martin Cregier, of Albany, in the province of New York, being weak and sickly in body, but having my senses and understanding, the Lord be praised and thanked, and considering the shortness and frailty of human life, the certainty of death and the uncertain time and hour thereof, make this my last will and testament, hereby revoking, annulling and canceling all former will or wills, testament or testaments heretofore by me made or published whether by word of mouth or in writing and [desire] these presents to be held as my last will and testament and none else.

First I commend my soul to God and my body to the earth to be buried in a Christian manner and there to rest in expectation of a blessed resurrection at the last day; and as regards such temporal estate as the Lord far above my deserts has been pleased to grant me, I dispose of the same in manner following:

First. I will and order that all my just debts shall be paid in proper time out of the rents of my real and immovable estate in manner following, that is to say, that all my real and immovable estate shall be leased for the time of six years after my death or until my debts are paid, by my executors hereinafter named.

Item. I give to my son Martynus Cregier ten shillings current money of New York for his right of primogeniture.

Item. I give and bequeath to my said son Martynus Cregier the full and complete half of my farm lying at Knistageione in the county of Albany, to wit, the easterly portion with the homestead as I have it in use with the full half of the pasture, cripple bush and woodland behind the home- [286] stead and farm, west of the *Fuyck* or Albany path, to him my aforesaid son Martynus Creiger, his heirs or assigns forever, provided that my son Martynus or his heirs or assigns pay or disburse therefor two hundred fifty pounds current money of New York, to wit, to my daughter Elizabeth, wife of Daniel van Olinda, or her heirs or assigns the sum of fifty pounds thereof within the time of one year after my death, and to my daughter Annatie, wife of Victoor Becker, or her heirs or assigns the sum of fifty pounds thereof within the time of two years after my death, and to my daughter Geertruy, wife of Ulderick van Francke, her heirs or assigns, the sum of fifty pounds thereof within the time of three years after my death, and to Enogh Vreelandt and Marya Vreelandt, children of my deceased daughter Marya Vreelandt, the sum of one hundred pounds, that is to them or their respective heirs or assigns to each fifty pounds, all current money of New York in the time of four years after my death.

Item. I give and bequeath to my son Samuel Cregier the full and just half of my said farm and land at Kanistagone, to wit, the westerly portion thereof with the homestead at present by him occupied and used with the full half of the pasture, cripple bush and woodland lying behind the homestead and farm to the west of the *Fuyck* or Albany path, to him my aforesaid son Samuel Cregier his heirs or assigns forever; also a third part of the orchard fruits for the time of six years after my death, provided that he, my said son Samuel, or his heirs or assigns pay and disburse therefor the sum of two hundred pounds current money of New York, to wit, to my aforesaid daughter Elisabeth, wife of Daniel van Olinda, or her heirs or assigns the sum of fifty pounds within the time of one year after my death, and to my daughter Annatie, wife of Victoor Becker, or her heirs or assigns the sum of fifty pounds within the time of two years after my death, and to my daughter [287] Geertruy, wife of Ulderick van Francke, or her heirs or assigns the sum of fifty pounds in the time of three years after my death, and to Enoch Vreelandt and Maria Vreelandt the sum of fifty pounds, that is, to each of them or their respective heirs or assigns twenty-five pounds, all current money of New York, within the time of four years after my death.

Item. I give and bequeath to my said daughter Elisabeth, wife of Daniel van Olinda, the half of my house and of the lot of ground lying in Albany on Jonker street, between the house and lot of Patroon Jeremiah van Renselaer and Jacob Glen, that is to say, the westerly half part of the house and lot, with the overhang over the alley up to the garret (but the alley under the floor is to be in common between her and her sister Geertruy, to each the half), to her my aforesaid daughter Elizabeth and to her heirs and her assigns forever, provided that in case it shall be sold or made over to anyone by my said daughter Elizabeth, her daughter Maritie shall have the sum of fifty pounds current money of New York after the death of her mother, my daughter Elizabeth.

Item. I give and bequeath to my said daughter Geertruy, wife of Ulderick van Francke, the easterly half of my aforesaid house and lot in Albany on Jonker street, bounded easterly by the house and lot of Patroon Jeremiah van Renselaer, that is to say the most easterly half of the whole lot, with the half alley heretofore mentioned, the overhang over which belongs to the westerly portion of the house bequeathed to my daughter Elizabeth; which aforesaid easterly half of the house and lot and alley in common under the floor I bequeath to my aforesaid daughter Geertruy, her heirs and assigns forever.

Item. I grant to my aforesaid daughter Elizabeth, wife of Danjel van Olinda, the right to dwell in the house now standing upon the back part of the aforesaid lot, on the west side thereof, during the time of six years after my death, with some ground to the south thereof, now a garden, without any rent to be paid therefor to my executors or any of them.

Item. I give and bequeath to my aforenamed daughter Annatie, wife of [288] Victor Becker, all that land lying at Knistageioene to the east of the *Fuyck* or Albany path beginning and bounded on the shore by the homestead of my son Samuel Cregier and thence down the river to Schurlynen kill with the island and thence into the woods so far as my right extends on the east of the *Fuyck* path or [the land] belongs to me, to her my aforesaid daughter Annatie during her life and after her death to her children, to wit, Martynus, Nicholas, Hendrick and Janetie respectively, to their respective heirs and assigns, to each a just fourth part thereof forever.

Item. I give and bequeath to my aforesaid two sons Martynus and Samuel Cregier to each the half of my portion and right, being the just half of a certain parcel of land at Knistigone, abutting westerly on my farm between the little kill and the *Steene* (Stone) kill, to them my aforenamed sons, their respective heirs and assigns forever.

Item. I desire that my daughter Elizabeth together with my daughter Geertruy shall have a third of the apples out of the orchard at Knistigone (bequeathed to my two sons) for the time of six years after my death.

Item. And in case my two sons Martynus and Samuel or either of them should decline to take the aforesaid land at Kniestigeioene hereinbefore mentioned and bequeathed to them and to pay or turn over the money therefor hereinbefore mentioned to my daughters Elizabeth, Geertruy, Anna and to the two children of my deceased daughter Marya, to wit, Enoch Vreelandt and Maria Vreelandt according to the true intent and meaning of this my last will and testament, then I will that my aforenamed daughters with the two aforenamed children of my deceased daughter Marya shall be entitled to enter upon and share an equal portion of the real and immovable estate with him who refuses to pay according to my desire.

[289] *Lastly,* I appoint and make my sons Martynus Cregier and Samuel Cregier and moreover my daughters, namely, Elizabeth, Annatie and Geertruy, executors of this my last will and testament. Thus signed, sealed and declared to be my last will and testament in presence of the witnesses named below, the day and year first above written.

JANNETJE CREGIER (L. S.)

Signed, sealed and declared by the
  testatrix to be her last will and testament in presence of us, as witnesses, signing hereto in the presence of the testatrix

Stephanus van Rensselaer
Gerardus Bancker
Jn°. de Peyster

Albany ye 10 day of June 1741 Be it Remembred that on the day and Year above written personally appeared before me Myndert Schuyler being thereunto deligated and appointed Stefanus van Renselaer and John de Peyster two of the witnesses to the within written will of Jannetie Cregier and made Oath on the holy Evangelist of Almighty God that they Saw the said Jannetie Cregier Sign seal publish and declare the same to be her last will and that at the time thereof she was of sound disposing mind and memory to the best of their knowledge and Also further declare they saw Gerr^d. Bancker one of the other of the witnesses to ye abovesaid will Sign as witness thereunto in the presence of the Testatorix.

MYNDERT SCHUYLER

Recorded and Examined the 12th October 1763

p^r. HA: GANSEVOORT *Clerk*

Will of Arent Vedder

[294] In the name of God, Amen. I, Arent Vedder, now of the village of Schoneetendy in the county of Albany, husbandman, having at this time my senses, knowledge, memory and understanding perfect, thanks be to God for the same, but considering my highly advanced age, the mortality of the body, the certainty of death and the uncertain time and hour thereof, do therefore this tenth day of August in the twentieth year of the reign of our King George the second and in the year of our Lord one thousand seven hundred and forty-six make, ordain and publish this my last will and testament, to wit, of all my immovable and movable worldly estate wherewith the Lord has been pleased to bless me in this life, after my lawful debts and burial expenses are paid or satisfied, I give, bequeath and dispose of in the following manner and form:

First. I give to my eldest son Harmen Vedder, his executors, or administrators, the sum of three pounds current money of this province to be paid to him out of my estate for his right of primogeniture, wherewith he must be content and make no further claim to my movable or immovable estate as heir at law.

Second. I give to my wife Sarah all my movable and immovable estate during her widowhood, or so long as she lives and remains my widow, she not to incumber or alienate the same, but only to have, receive and take the rents, income and profits thereof during the time above mentioned for her sustenance and maintenance and immediately after my wife's death, she being my widow, or immediately after her remarriage, whichever occurs first, I give, bequeath and dispose of my movable and immovable estate as follows, to wit: To my son Seymon Vedder and to his heirs and assigns forever I give and bequeath the easterly part of my land lying and being on the south side of the Maakwasse river,[83] in the Woestyne,[84] where I now live, with the house, barn and homestead, beginning at [295] the division between me and Jan Wemp and running up the river to the Kromme kill,[85] and a morgen on the height over or on the west side of the Kromme kill, between the ditch and the river, and thence with a straight line where the uppermost or most westerly line of that morgen of land comes over the Kromme kill from the river to the king's highway, with the woodland that lies toward my house from the aforesaid Kromme kill, between the hill and the lowland, to be held by him, the aforesaid Seymon Vedder, his heirs and assigns, forever.

To my son Harmen Vedder, or to his heirs or assigns I give and bequeath the westerly portion of my arable land, lying and being on the south side of the Maakwasse river in the Woestyne in the county of Albany, whereon he has now built, with his house and barn thereon standing; beginning on the west side of the Kromme kill where my son Seymon's [land] ends and running up the river so far as my right extends along said river, with all the woodland that lies between the lowland and up the hill to the south of the land that I now hereby give to him, to be held by him, the aforesaid Harmen Vedder, his heirs and assigns forever; and it is my express will, order and desire that my son Harmen Vedder therefor shall pay yearly and every year forever the quantity of four and a half skipples of wheat to the trustees of the village of Schnectendy, or to their order:

To my youngest son Albert Vedder, jun[r]., I give and bequeath, to him, his heirs and assigns, my house and lot lying in the village of Schonectendy wherein he now dwells, with all that thereto belongs, bounded southerly by the lot of Myndert Veeder, northerly by the house and lot of Hendrick Brouwer, and easterly by the [Washington] Street and westerly by my son Harmen Vedder, also my two morgens, more or less, of lowland lying on the arable land in the village of Schonectendy, as I now have it in possession, bounded

---

[83] Mohawk river.
[84] Literally: "the desert," opposite Hoffman's ferry. See *History of the Schenectady Patent*, p. 201, where part of this will is quoted.
[85] Literally: "Crooked creek," or "Winding creek."

northerly by the king's [296] highway, easterly by the land of Harmanus Vedder, southerly by land of Corset Vedder and westerly by land of Abraham Maby; also my little hay meadow, being about a fourth part of a morgen, lying in the low ground on the south side of the village of Schonectendy, bounded southerly, westerly and northerly by meadow of the heirs of Law^r. van der Volgen and easterly by the road, to hold for him the aforesaid Albert Vedder, jun^r., his heirs and assigns forever.

To my seven daughters, to wit, Antje, Rebecca, Angenietje, Maria, Susanna, Sarah and Elizabeth, or to their executors and assigns, I give and bequeath the sum of one hundred and five pounds current money of this province, that is to say, to each one of my above-named daughters or to their heirs the sum of fifteen pounds current money as above said and it is my express will, order and desire that my three above-named sons, Harmen, Seymon and Albert Vedder, jun^r., or their heirs, the above-named sum pay equally to my above-named daughters, or to their heirs, seven years after my and my wife's death, that is, each of my above-named three sons the sum of thirty-five pounds current money as aforesaid; furthermore, it is my will and desire that my three above-named sons, to wit, Harmen, Seymon and Albert Vedder, jun^r., together pay my and my wife's burial expenses, the one no more than the other, but each the full lawful third part thereof.

To my son Seymon Vedder or to his heirs I give and bequeath my negro Thom; to my sons Harmon Vedder and Seymon Vedder and to their heirs and assigns I give and bequeath all my woodland or wood ground that lies to the south of my son Harmen Vedder's land which I hereinbefore have bequeathed to him, that is, from where my son Harmen Vedder's land ends up on the hill to the southerly end of my right of my woodland, to hold for them, my aforesaid sons Harmen Vedder and Seymon Vedder, their heirs and assigns forever: it is my express will and desire and I bind my three sons Harmen, Seymon and Albert Vedder, jun^r., hereby that if one or two of my aforesaid sons may hereafter be put to any [297] expense in relation to any portion of the land hereby to them bequeathed, my three aforesaid sons shall together bear the expense among them, the one no more than the other, and if any one of them by some trouble comes to lose any part of his land here above to him bequeathed or given, the other two of my sons whoever they may be, shall pay a full third part of the value of the land so lost on appraisal by three honest persons, to him who loses it, without any sort of trouble or opposition; and if it happen that my daughter Maria remain unmarried during her life and she be unable to support herself, then she shall choose with which of my sons she wants to dwell and my three sons, to wit, Harmen, Seymon and Albert Vedder, jun^r. shall together maintain her so long as she lives, one contributing no more nor less than the others. It is further my express wish and desire that when the survivor of me and my wife shall come to die, my son Seymon Vedder shall freely and peaceably mow the crop or grain that shall have been sowed upon any part of my land by him without any trouble or hindrance from my two other sons above mentioned, and draw the same away and dispose thereof for his own use.

To my son Seymon Vedder and to his heirs I give all my farming tools, sleighs, carts, plow, harrow with all their belongings, axes, adzes, forks, etc., nothing excepted.

To all my children, sons and daughters, to wit, Harmen, Seymon, Albert Vedder jun^r. and my daughters hereinbefore named, to wit, Antje, Rebecca, Angenietje, Maria, Susanna, Sarah and Elizabeth, I give and bequeath all the residue and remainder of my movable estate of whatever nature it may be, hereinbefore not disposed of, such as my furniture or household goods, linen and woolen, my horses and cows, oxen, calves, foals, mares, sheep, lambs, hogs, pigs, hens, etc., of whatsoever nature they [298] may be, to be divided among all my children or their heirs, as well sons as daughters, no one to have anything more or better than another.

Lastly, I make and appoint my son-in-law William Brower and Major Jacob Glen executors or trustees of this my last will and testament to have the same carried out according to my true intent and meaning and I revoke and annul all other testaments heretofore made by me, so that this, and no other heretofore made by me, I declare to be my last will and testament. In witness of the truth of which I, Arent Vedder, have hereunto set my hand and seal, the day and year first above written.

ARENT VEDDER (L.S.)

Signed, sealed and published by the said Arent Vedder as and for his last will and testament in the presence of us,

Albert Vedder
Vredrhek van Petten
John Sanders

City & County } Be it Remembred that on the 1st Day of March of Albany } 1755 personally Appeared before me Myndert Schuyler Surrogate of the said County frederick van petten & John Sanders two of the Subscribing witnesses to the within written will of Arent Vedder and being Duely Sworn on their oaths Declare that they and Each of them Did See the said Arent Vedder Sign and Seal publish and Declare the same to be his Last will and that at the Time thereof he was of sound Disposing mind & memory and further Declared that they Saw the other witness Albert Vedder Sign as witness thereunto in the presence of the Testator

MYNDERT SCHUYLER

Recorded and Examined The 1st Day of February 1764

P^r. HA: GANSEVOORT *Clerk*

Will of Thomas van Alstyne

[302] In the name of God, Amen. Know all men by these presents that on this fifteenth day of November in the year of our Lord one thousand seven hundred and sixty-four, I, Thomas van Alstyn, of the township of Kinderhook, in the county of Albany, in the province of New York, being advanced in years, but having my memory and understanding perfect, considering the shortness of human life, the certainty of death and the uncertain hour thereof, have determined this to be my last will and testament in manner following.

First, I commend my immortal soul whenever it shall depart from my body to the gracious and merciful hands of God my Creator and Savior and my body to a Christian burial in the earth from whence it came, there to rest until my soul and body be reunited at that joyful day of the resurrection to be made partaker of that insatiable joy of our salvation which God by His grace through the merits of Jesus Christ has prepared and promised for all those who have true repentance and faith in Him. And as regards such temporal estate, as money, obligations, goods, rights and credits, nothing in the world excepted, where and whatsoever they may be, I order and dispose thereof as follows. I desire that all my just debts shall first be paid out of my above-mentioned estate.

[303] *Item*, I give and bequeath to my son Wiliam Van Alystyn in consideration of his right of primogeniture of being my eldest son, my large shot gun.

Item. I give and bequeath to my son William Van Alstyn and his heirs forever the farm which he now has in his possession and dwells upon, with all the rights thereto appertaining, lying in Claverack in the manor of Rensselaerswick and in the county of Albany upon this condition that my son William or his heirs therefor pay the sum of one hundred pounds current money of this province, which is still owing on that land, and furthermore, after my wife's death, that my son William pay or disburse to my daughter Cathariena Hofman, widow of Petrus Hoffman, or her heirs, the sum of forty pounds current money of this province, if it goes well with the woodland which I have conveyed to my five children; if not, my son William must pay to the aforenamed Cathariena the sum of sixty pounds current money aforenamed.

Item. I give and bequeath to my son Lambarth Van Alstyn and his heirs forever the farm which he now possesses and occupies, lying in the township of Kinderhook in the county of Albany.

Item. I give and bequeath to my son Peter Van Alstyn and his heirs forever my whole farm as I now possess the same, with all the farm implements thereto belonging, after the death of my wife, on this condition that my son [304] Peter or his heirs pay therefor to my son Lambarth or his heirs the sum of four hundred pounds current money of this province, the first payment of one hundred pounds two years after my death, the second payment also of one hundred pounds four years after my death, the third payment again of one hundred pounds six years after my death, the fourth payment again of one hundred pounds eight years after my death; from this time forth my son Peter is to have the half of the whole income of my farm and is also to be at half of the expense of the whole and after my death my son Peter is to have the whole income of my farm, provided that he is to give to my wife during her life the fourth of the income, and also a free dwelling, also pay all my debts. Furthermore my son Peter or his heirs must pay or disburse to my daughter Maria or her heirs the sum of forty pounds current money of this province if it goes well with the woodland which I have conveyed to my five children; if not, my son Peter must pay to my aforenamed daughter Maria or her order the sum of sixty pounds current money as above.

Item. I give and bequeath to my two daughters Catharina and Maria and their heirs after my wife's death all my movables and household furniture except my sons' pictures, of which each shall have his own; furthermore I give to my daughter Cathariena or her heirs my negress named Alloon and to my daughter Maria or her heirs I give my negress named [305] Anne.

Item. I give and bequeath to my son Peter or his heirs my negro named Lott.

Item. I give and bequeath to my five above-named children, William, Lambarth, Peter, Cathariena and Maria, and to their heirs all my silver work, nothing excepted, to be equally divided among them, to the one no more than to the other.

Item. I give and bequeath to my son William and his heirs my brew kettle for which he is to pay three milch cows, one to my son Lambarth, one to my daughter Cathariena and one to my daughter Maria.

Item. I give and bequeath to my three sons, William, Lambarth and Peter Van Alstyn, to them and their heirs, my whole interest in the sawmill.

Item. I desire and order that if my aforenamed children or any of them be not content with what I have above bequeathed and given to them, but make further claims or pretensions on any part of my estate or on anything that I have heretofore sold or made over or conveyed, here or elsewhere, of whatsoever nature it may be, he who undertakes to do so shall be completely cut off from his inheritance or share herein bequeathed to him and my executors shall retain control of the same in order [306] to resist him according to my desire until the matter is settled, when they shall equally divide the remainder of the same among my other contented children and their heirs.

Item. I give and bequeath to my son Peter van Alstyn after my death all that lies within my fence, house, orchard and meadowland, which is now in possession of my son Lambarth, and it is my will and order that Lambarth shall turn over the same to my aforesaid son Peter.

Item. I give and bequeath to my son Peter van Alstyn and his heirs a parcel of hickory wood to the west of the high hill; also a piece of ground lying upon the west side of the Batten vly, between the ridge and said vly.

Item. Furthermore it is my will that my youngest daughter Maria shall remain at home with my son Peter until she marries.

Lastly, I nominate my worthy wife Maria van Alystyne and my son William van Alstyn and my friend Casparis Conyn, jun^r. executors of this my last will and testament and desire that in due time they shall pay my just debts which I may leave behind.

In witness of the truth hereof I have subscribed and sealed this and declared it to be my last will and testament, the day and year above written.

THOMAS VAN ALSTEN (L. S.)

Signed, sealed and declared by Thomas van Alstyn to be his last will and testament in presence of us as witnesses (the words " or their heirs," on the first page, were interlined before the signing and sealing hereof)

Petrus R $\overset{\text{his}}{\text{X}}$ *Coll, jun*^r.
mark

Seybout $\overset{\text{his}}{\text{X}}$ *Kranckheyt*
mark

Gerrit C. van Den Bergh

Albany } ss [307] Be it Remembered that on the 7 day of September 1765 Personally came and appeared before me John Depeyster Surrogate of the said County Petrus Cool Jur of Kinderhook in said County of Albany and Gerret Van Den Bergh of the manner of Renselaer in s^d County farmer and being duly Sworn on their Oaths Declared that they and Each of them did see Thomas Van Alsten sign & seal the within written Instrument proporting to be the will of the said Thom^s. Van Alsten bearing date the 15 day of November one thousand Seven Hundred and sixty four and hear^d. him publish & Declare the same as and for his Last will and testament that att the time thereof he the said Thomas Van Alsten was of Sound Disposing mind and memory to the best of their Knowledge and belief of them the deponents and that there names Subscribed to the said will are of there Respective hand writing which they subscrib^d. as witnesses to the said will in the Testators presence and that they also saw the other witness Sybout Krankheyt sygn his name as witness to said will in the Testators presence

Joⁿ. DE PEYSTER *Surrogate*

I do hereby certify the preceding to be a truly Copy of the Original ex^d. & Compared the 6th day of October 1781

P^r MAT: VISSCHER *Clk*

Will of Pieter van Woert

[324] In the name of God. Know all men by these presents that on this 26th day of March one thousand seven hundred and sixty-three, I, Pieter van Woort,[86] of the manor of Renselaerswyck, in the county of Albany, in the province of New York, being sick in body but having my senses, memory and understanding perfect, considering the shortness and frailty of human life, the certainty of death and the uncertain hour and time thereof, and being desirous to put my affairs in [325] good order, make this my last will and testament, hereby annulling, canceling and revoking all such will, testament or testaments as have heretofore been made or declared by me, whether orally or in writing, and [holding] this present instrument to be my last will and testament and none other.

Imprimis. I commend my soul to God my Creator and Savior and my body to the earth whence it came, to be buried in a proper and Christian manner. And as regards such temporal property as houses, grounds, lands, money and goods, being my whole estate, real and personal, nothing excepted, which the Lord far above my deserts has been pleased to grant me, I provide and dispose thereof in manner following:

Item. I give and bequeath to my wife Ariantie my whole estate, movable and immovable, that is, real and personal, wherever or whatever it may be, for the use and possession of my aforesaid wife during her widowhood.

Item. I give and devise to my nephew Jacob van Woort, son of my brother Jacob van Woort (after the death or remarriage of my aforesaid wife) my house and lot where I now dwell, lying in the manor of Renselarswyck, to the west of the path that goes to the patroon's or manor house, as the same now lies in its fence, together with my land on the east side of the aforesaid path that goes to the patroon's, as the same was devised to me by will of my father and mother, deceased; furthermore, I devise to my aforesaid nephew my part of a parcel of land held in company with my brother Jacob van Woort, known by the name of the Kloof,[87] lying to the west of the aforesaid path that goes to the patroon's, to him, my aforesaid nephew Jacob van Woort, his heirs and assigns [326] forever, excepting herefrom what I have devised to my nephew Lewis van Woort.

---

[86] One of the sons of Jacob Teunissen van Woert and a grandson of Teunis Jacobsen van Woert, or van Schoonderwoert.
[87] The same as the local term " Clove," meaning a cleft, or ravine.

Item. I devise to my nephew Lewis van Woort, son of my brother Jacob van Woort, a piece of ground lying in the Kloof, where Ryckert van Vranke has had a tannery, fifty feet square, Rhineland measure, with a path leading thereto, to him, my aforesaid nephew Lewis van Woort, his heirs and assigns, forever.

Item. It is my will and desire that my nephew Jacob van Woort shall always keep the burial plot for a burying place for the family, that it shall never be sold or alienated and that he shall also leave a path there to reach it; the said burial plot must be sixty feet long and thirty feet wide, Rhineland measure; furthermore he must maintain a fence around it so as to keep cattle out.

Item. I bequeath to my aforesaid nephew Jacob van Woort all my personal estate (after the death or remarriage of my said wife), of whatever nature it may be, to him, the said nephew Jacob van Woort, his heirs and assigns, forever, except the linen and woolen goods and household furniture of whatever description it may be, which I bequeath to my beloved wife Arriantie, to dispose thereof as she may see fit.

Lastly, I nominate as executors of this my last will and testament my friend Casparus Pruyn and Cornelis C. van den Bergh, son of my brother-in-law Claas van den Bergh.

In witness of the truth hereof I have signed, sealed and declared this to be my last will and testament, the day and year above written.

his
Pieter P W van Woort (L.S.)
mark

[327] Signed, sealed and declared by the testator Pieter van Woort to be his last will and testament, in presence of us,

Ryckert van Vranken
Theunis van Woort
Jn°. De Peyster

Albany } ss Be it Remembered that on the 17 day of November
County } one thousand seven Hundred and sixty six Personally Came and appeared before me John DePeyster Surrogate for the said County Richerd Van Franke & Thunis Van Woert Both of the manner of Renselaer In said County Yeoman and being duly sworn on their Oaths declared that they and each of them did see Peter Van Woort sign & seal the within written Instrument proporting to be [the] will of the said Peter Van Woert bearing date

the 26 day of march 1763 and hear him Publish & declare the same to be his last will and Testament That at the time thereof he the said Peter Van Woort was of sound disposing mind and memory to the best of their Knowledge & Belief and that their names subscribed to the said will are of their Respective proper handwriting which they subscribed as witnesses to the said will In the Testators Presence and that they also saw the other witness sign his name as Witness to the said will In the testators presence

JN^o. DE PEYSTER *Surrogate*

I do hereby Certify that the aforegoing will is a true Copy of the Originall Examined and Compared this 8th September 1767

P^r me STEP^n. DE LANCEY *Clerk*

Will of Casparus Conyn

[362] In the name of God, Amen. On this thirtieth day of October, in the sixth year of the reign of our King George the third, of Great Britain, France and Ireland, defender of the faith, etc., and in the year of our Lord and Savior Jesus Christ one thousand seven hundred and sixty-five, I, Casparus Knyn, of Claverack, in the county of Albany and province of New York, husbandman, being advanced in years but of sound mind and perfect memory (God be thanked therefor), considering the uncertain state of this life and that all flesh must yield unto death whenever it shall please the Lord to call, and being desirous of putting my affairs in order, make this my last will and testament in manner and form following (annulling, canceling and revoking all other testament or testaments heretofore by me made, and declaring this to be my last and only will and testament).

First. I commend my soul to the Almighty God my Creator and to Jesus Christ my Savior and to the Holy Ghost my Sanctifier, and my body to the earth from whence it came there to be buried in a Christian and proper manner, to rest until my soul and body be reunited on the day of general resurrection to become partaker of the insatiable joy of immortality, which God of His grace through the merits of Jesus Christ has promised and prepared for all such as . . . [88] temporal goods which the Lord far above my deserts has been pleased to bestow upon me, I give and dispose of the same in manner and form following:

---

[88] Line omitted in the record.

First. I give to my son Casparus C. Konyn my clock (*Klock*) for his right of primogeniture as being my eldest son, that he may not have any further claim upon my estate.

2^d. I give to my wife Eva Konyn all the goods which after my death shall remain of what she had when I married her, to dispose thereof as she pleases.

3^d. I give to my said son Casparus as follows, Beginning at a great hickory tree (*Noortsneuten Boom*) standing on the east side of Claverak kill and marked with the letter K and running thence with a straight course to a great pine tree standing on the hin- [363] dermost high land and also marked with the letter K and with the same course further to the Mill kill (*Meulen kill*), that is to say, all the land that I have or claim to the north of said course with buildings, orchard and all thereupon standing, to my said son Casparus, his heirs and assigns forever.

4th. I give to my son Laurans Konyn all the land that I have or claim to the south of the aforesaid course, for him, his heirs and assigns forever, and my son Casparus shall help him to build a house, forty feet long and twenty-five feet wide, if I in my lifetime do not do the same.

5th. It is my will and desire that my aforesaid two sons (after my death) shall pay four hundred pounds current money of New York, that is to say, one hundred and fifty pounds to my daughter Maria, one hundred and fifty pounds to my daughter Jannietje, and the remaining one hundred pounds to Maria, the daughter of my daughter Alida, deceased, whereof my said two sons must each pay a like half part within four years after my decease, a fourth part each year till paid.

6th. I will and desire that my said two sons shall give as good an outfit to my daughter Jannitie as each of my other daughters have had, if I in my lifetime do not give it myself.

7th. I give to my said wife one of my negresses to have for her use and service so long as she shall dwell with one of my children.

8th. I give to my daughter Maria my negress Dian and to my daughter Jannetie my negress named Bet, for them and their heirs and assigns. Furthermore I give to my said daughter Jannetie three milch cows and two young animals, for her and her heirs and assigns.

9th. I give to my son Casparus my young negro named Symen and to my son Laurens I give my negro named Philip, for them, their heirs and assigns, and the remainder of my blacks who are not herein bequeathed are to be divided between them, to each a just half, provided that they pay my debts if there be any after my wife's death.

10th. It is my express will and desire that if my said wife dwell with one of my [364] sons, my other son shall pay her yearly eight pounds, and if she come to dwell anywhere else, then must each of my sons pay her eight pounds yearly during her widowhood.

11th. I give to my said two sons, Casparus and Laurans all the farm utensils belonging to my house, barn and land, to each a like half, also to each a like half of all my horses, cattle and other animals, (hereinbefore not bequeathed) for them, their heirs and assigns.

12th. I give all the rest of my personal or movable household goods or [effects] belonging to the house to my said two daughters Maria and Jannetie to be divided between them in equal parts, to the one no more than to the other.

13th. I give to my son Lawrens twenty-five apple trees in my orchard to have for his use, and the fruit thereof for ten years and no longer.

14th. I will and desire that all sums of money that may be due me at my death, be divided equally among my said four children now living.

15th. It is my will and desire that if either of my aforenamed sons comes to die without lawful heirs of his body, his portion of land herein bequeathed shall go to my other son, for him, his heirs and assigns. I appoint as guardians, executors and administrators of this my last will and testament my said two sons Casparus C. Kenyn and Lawrens Kenyn and my friend Henry Van Renselaer, Esqr.

In acknowledgment of the truth of which I hereto set my hand and seal, the day and year first above written.

CASPARUS CONYN (L. S.)

Was signed, sealed and published in presence of us,
Nicklas Brissie

      his
Peter X *Muller*
    mark

Steph^n. V: Dyck

Albany }ss Be it Remembred that on the 2nd. Day of October County } One Thousand Seven Hundred & Seventy one Personally Came & appeared before me John De Peyster Surrogate of the said County of Albany Nicklas Brissie farmer & Peter muller Farmer both of Claverack in the County of Albany [365] And being Duly sworn on their Oaths Declared that they saw Casparus Conyn Sign & Seal the within written Instrument perporting to be the Will of the said Casparus Conyn bearing Date the 30th day of October one thousand Seven Hundred & Sixty five & heard him publish & Declare the same as and for his Last will & Testament that at the same Time thereof he the said Casparus Conyn was of Sound Disposing mind & memory to the best of their Knowledge & belief of them the Deponants & that their names Subscribed to the said will are of their Respective proper handwriting which they subscribed as witnesses to the said will in the Testators presence & Also further Declared that they saw the Other witness sign his name as a witness to the said will in the Testators Presence

Jn°. De Peyster Surrogate

I do hereby Certify the foregoing Record is a True Copy of the Original Ex^d. & Compared the same with the Original will this 4th Day of October 1771

Pr Stepⁿ De Lancey *Clerk*

[END OF DUTCH INSTRUMENTS IN PART I OF WILLS, 1691–1835]

BOOK OF WILLS No. 2
BEGAN THE 8TH DAY OF JUNE 1773
BY: STEPN. DE LANCEY CLERK

Will of Dirck van Vechten of Lonenburg

[30] In the name of God, Amen. On this tenth day of May in the year of our Lord and Savior Jesus Christ seventeen hundred and sixty-four, Dirck Van Vegte, dwelling upon the flat in the district of Lonenburg in the county of Albany in the government of New York, being sound of body, after considering with deliberate and mature counsel the certainty of death and the uncertain hour thereof, without the inducement, persuasion or misleading of any person, declared to have made, ordered and determined this his last will and testament in form and manner following:

First and foremost commending his immortal soul whenever it departs from his body to the gracious and merciful hands of God, his Creator and Savior, and his body to a Christian burial at the discretion of his executors hereinbelow named, he disposes of his effects left behind as follows:

First. It is my will and desire that all my just debts be paid out of my personal estate.

Item. I give to my eldest son Teunis Van Veghte and to his heirs forever the choice of my horses for his birthright.

Item. I give to my worthy wife Helena Van Veghte my whole estate, real and personal, nothing whatever excepted, during her life and no longer.

Item. I give to my son Teunis V. Veghten and to the heirs of his body my farm on which he now dwells, being on the map made by Chers Clinton[89] lot no. seventy-seven and failing of heirs of his body, after his death [31] I give said farm to my grandson Dirick Van Veghten, son of my son Albartus, and to his heirs forever.

Item. I give to my son Teunis Van Veghte and to the heirs of his body the half of a lot in the *Bougat,* being on the aforesaid map no. seventy-two (72).

Item. I give to my son Hubartis Van Veghte and to his heirs forever the other half of the lot in the *Bougat,* being on the said map the lot no. seventy-two, and in case my son Teunis has no heirs of his body, it is my will and desire that the half hereinbefore devised to my son Teunis Van Veghte shall go to my son Hubartus Van Veghte, or to his heirs, forever.

Item. I give the farm on which I now dwell, as the same is now in use by me, after the death of my worthy wife Helena Van Veghte, to my daughter Jannetie and to her heirs or assigns, upon the following conditions, that she, my daughter Jannetie, or her heirs, pay to my daughter Sara Van Veghte, wife of Isaac Kalier, or to [her heirs] and to my daughter Eva Van Veghte, wife of Abraham Van Valkenburg, or to her heirs, to each of my aforenamed daughters a sum of fifty pounds current money of New York, to each the half, one year after the death of the survivor of me or my worthy wife, and the other half two years after our death, that is of the survivor of me and my worthy wife Helena Van Vechte, each payment a like half to my aforenamed daughters, to the one no more than to the other.

Item. I give to my daughter Maria Van Veghte, wife of Nicolas

---

[89] Charles Clinton, the father of Governor George Clinton.

Spoor, and to her heirs forever my five acres in the [32] *Bougat vley,* marked on the map made of the patent of Lonenburgh by Cherls Clinton, and being part of lot no. twenty-four.

Item. I give to my sons Teunis Van Vechte, Hubartis Van Veghte, and to my daughters Catariena Van Veghte, wife of Lambert Van Valkenburgh, Maria Van Veghte, wife of Nicolaus Spoor, and to my daughter Janetie Van Veghte, and to their respective heirs, all my portion in the wood that lies in common between the Halenbecks and Isaac Kalier and myself in the patent of Lonenburgh, likewise my part in the new patent of Stigkock,[90] or the hills to the west of the patent of Lonenburgh, for each of them a share in proportion to their land, so that they may make such use thereof as they shall need without being hindered by the others, till such time as they shall have reason each to take his own.

Item. I give after the death of my beloved wife Helena Van Vechte to my sons Teunis Van Vechte and Hubartis Van Vechte and to my daughters Catariena Van Vechte, wife of Lambert Van Valkenburgh, Sara Van Veghte, wife of Isaac Kalier, Maria Van Veghte, wife of Nicolas Spoor, and to my daughter Jannatie Van Vechten and to Even Van Veghte, wife of Abraham V. Valkenburgh, or to their respective heirs or assigns my entire personal estate, to be divided equally among them, to the one no more than to the other, it being understood that the blacks which they have received of me and divided among my son Teunis and daughters, Catariena, Sara and Eva Van Vechten shall be accounted [33] in their portions according to the value they have received for them; and in speaking here of my entire personal estate, it is to be understood that out of it shall be paid my just debts and to my son Teunis a portion for his birthright; and furthermore it is my desire and will that my sons Teunis and Hubartis Van Vechte shall divide between them equally my woolen and linen clothing and that my daughters Catariena, Sara, Maria, Eva and Janetie Van Vechte shall divide the clothing of their mother equally among them, both linen and woolen; and it is my desire that my two sons Teunis and Albartis shall divide my tools among them equally.

Lastly. I nominate and appoint as executors of this my last will and testament, my son Hubartis Van Vechte, my son-in-law Lambert Van Valkenburgh and my son-in-law Nicolaus Spoor, on the day and year above written.

DIRK V. VEGHTEN

---

[90] Stighcook, a tract of land in Greene county, granted to Casparus Brunk and others in 1743. E. M. Ruttenber, *Indian Geographical Names,* p. 176.

Signed, sealed and declared by the aforenamed Dirck V. Veghten to be his last will and testament, in the presence of the undersigned witnesses.

John Ten Broeck
Martin Lydious
Jacob Roseboom
John H. Lydious

May 30th, 1764

Item. It is my further will and desire that if it happen that my daughter Jannatie Van Veghte die without heirs of her body before the hund- [34] red pounds be paid out as I herein have ordered, it is my will and desire that the inheritance from the farm which I now dwell upon shall go to my son Huba[r]tus Van Veghte and to his heirs forever, on condition of the same obligation to make payment to my daughters Sara and Eva Van Vechte, as heretofore my daughter Jannatie was obliged to do.

Item. It is my will and desire that all my house furniture after the death of my worthy wife Helena Van Vechte shall be divided equally among my five daughters or their heirs forever, to wit, Catariena, Sara, Maria, Eva and Janetie Van Veghten, to the one no more than to the other.

DIRICK V. VECHTEN

Signed, sealed and declared by the testator Dirick Van Veghte to be a supplement to and a part of the within written will, in presence of us:

John Ten Broeck
Martin Lydious
Jacob Roseboom
John H. Lydious

Be it Remembred that on the eight day of February in the Year of Our Lord One thousand seven hundred & eighty two personally appeared before me Robert Yates Esquire one of the Judges of the supreme Court of Judicature of the State of New York the above named Martin Lydious and Jacob Rosebom, who being severally sworn on the Holy Evangelist of Almighty God deposed and say that they severally have seen the above named Dirick Van Vechten sign seal publish and declare the within Instrument as and for his last will [35] and Testament and have also seen him sign seàl publish and declare the above Instrument, as a Codocil to the said last will and Testament that they respectively subscribed their names to the said Instruments as Witness To the execution thereof, Thay [sic] they severally have seen John Ten Broeck and John H. Lydious respectively subscribed their names as witness to the Execution of the said Instruments, and I have Inspected the said Instrument do allow the same to be recorded.

ROBERT YATES

[*The remainder of part 2 of Wills, 1691–1835, is in English*]

INDEX

Abeel, John, 149
Abeel, Stoffel Jansen, house and lot, 8, 59; sureties for, 59; surety, 61; attorney, 106; mentioned, 8
Abrahams, Maria, 32
Adams, Tannetje, 127
Adriaensen, Jacob, buys house and lot, 62
Adriaensen, Pieter, *see* Van Woggelum, Pieter Adriaensen
Alberts, Eva, 44
Alberts, Femmetie, bond and mortgage, 39, 42, 63; husband, 39
Albertsen, Barent, *see* Bratt, Barent Albertsen
Albertsen, Reyer, *see* Elbertsen, Reyer
Albertsen, Wouter, *see* Van den Uythoff, Wouter Albertsen
Andriessen, Albert, *see* Bratt, Albert Andriessen
Andriessen, Arent, special attorney, 34
Andriessen, Hendrick, 11
Andriessen, Jan, from Dublin, deed from, 103
Andros, Sir Edmund, 162
Anthony, Allart, bond of Jan Labatie to, 114
Appel, Adriaen Jansen, farming of burghers' excise to, 85, 86, 115; farming of tapsters' excise to, 88, 114; bond of, 107; witness, 121
Arents, Cornelia, 122
Auction sales, account of, 53

Backer, Jan Claessen, *see* Van Oossanen, Jan Claessen
Bancker, Evert, 123, 166; witness, 137
Bancker, Gerardus, witness, 188
Bancker, Gerritt, house and lot, 72; surety, 109; mentioned, 33, 54

Barents, Geertruy, 32
Barentsen, Frans, 105
Barentsen, Jan, *see* Wemp, Jan Barentsen
Barheyt, Jeronimus, will, 170
Barheyt, Rebecka, 170
Barheyt, Wouter, 170
Bastiaensen, Harmen, *see* Visscher, Harmen Bastiaensen
Becker, Hendrick, 188
Becker, Jan Juriaensen, will, 135; wills executed before him as notary public, 121, 126, 142, 145; signs his name Johannes Becker, senior, 169; referred to as John Becker, 137
Becker, Jannetie, 188
Becker, Johannes, junior, son of Jan Juriaensen, 135; witness, 126, 169
Becker, Martina, 136, 137
Becker, Martynus, 188
Becker, Nicholas, 188
Becker, Victor, wife, 186, 187
Beeckman, Hendrick, witness, 179
Belding (Beldins), widow, 182
Bembo, Jan, power of attorney from, 19
Bensingh (Bensem), Dirck, sale of house, 32; widow, 32; bond and mortgage of, 83
Bensingh (Bensing), Samson, 138
Bever, Claes, 53, 78
Bevers kill, 134
Bleecker, Rutger, witness, 165
Bogaerdt, Teunis Gysbertsen, special attorney, 87
Bogardus, Anneke Jans, son, 10, 100
Bonvou, Daniel, 73
Boon, François, wife, 27; special attorney, 71, 76; mentioned, 8, 27; witness, 30, 31, 39, 41, 47, 50, 64, 66, 69, 75, 83, 84, 92, 98, 99, 105, 106
Borghard, Coenraed, 173

[207]

Borsboom, Pieter Jacobsen, bondsmen for, 23; mentioned, 18, 22, 54
Bos, Cornelis Teunissen, *see* Van Westbroeck, Cornelis Teunissen Bos
Bout, Evert, witness, 176
Bout, Willem Fredericksen, sells house and lot, 11, 61; deed from referred to, 20; bond of Dirck Bensingh to, 83; buys garden, 95; deed of garden to, 95; deed of lot to, 98; deed from, 99; mentioned, 54, 78
Bouts, Cors, 53
Bouts, Geertie, 79, 80
Bratt, Albert Andriessen, sale of sloop, 25; daughter, 44
Bratt, Andries Arentsen, 123
Bratt, Anthony, 145
Bratt, Barent Albertsen, power of attorney from, 45; mentioned, 48; witness, 23
Bratt, Dirk, witness, 126
Brissie, Nicklas, witness, 201
Bronck (Brunk), Casparus, 204
Bronck (Bronk), Jan, 130, 131, 134; deeds from, 134
Bronck, Pieter, house and lot, 12; surety, 82; mentioned, 11, 57, 109
Brouwer, Hendrick, 190
Brouwer, Willem, 192; garden, 41; bond of, 84; surety, 91
Bruyn, Jan Hendricksen, 157
Butt, James (Jems), 29

Canaan, 182
Carstensen, Carsten, power of attorney from, 50
Carstensen (Castense), Warner, witness, 137
Castle (Casteels) island, 131, 134
Catskill, 100, 101, 103, 131, 134, 140
Chambers, Thomas, house and lot, 96; deed from, 97
Claes, Neeltie, inventory of estate, 123
Claessen, Carsten, bond of Slingerlant to, 66
Claessen, Cornelis, 123
Claessen, Hendrick, 54

Claessen, Tierck, *see* De Witt, Tierck Claessen
Clarke, De Meyer, witness, 168
Claverack (Claverback), 173, 175, 182, 194, 202
Claverack kill, 200
Clinton, Charles, 203
Clinton, Governor George, 203
Clopper, Cornelis Jansen, deed of lot to, 34
Clute (Cloet), Johannes, garden lot, 91; deed from, 134; mentioned, 17; witness, 87
Cobes (Cobus, Cobussen), Ludovicus, witness, 10, 11, 13, 14, 15, 23, 26, 28, 33, 52, 59, 60, 61, 62, 76, 81, 82, 85, 90, 91, 95
Cock, Jan, inventory of estate, 137
Cook (Kock), Willem, 17
Coenraedtsen, Hendrick, 123
Coeymans, Andries, appointed guardian, 158; witness, 172
Coeymans, Barent Pietersen, 54, 78, 79, 80
Coeymans, Pieter, appointed guardian, 158
Colden, John, 179
Coll, Petrus, junior, witness, 196
Collier (Caljer), Elias, appointed guardian, 142
Collier (Caljer), Enoch, appointed guardian, 142
Collier (Kalier), Isaac, 204; wife, 203, 204
Coninck, Steven Jansen, sureties for, 107
Conyn, Alida, 200
Conyn, Allette, 128
Conyn, Casparus, will, 199
Conyn (Konyn), Casparus C., 195, 200, 201
Conyn, Casper Leendertsen, 128
Conyn (Konyn), Eva, 200
Conyn, Jannetje, 200
Conyn (Konyn), Laurens, 200, 201
Conyn, Maria, 200
Conyn, Philip, wife, 182, 183
Cool, Peter, 166
Cornelis, Elisabeth, 27

INDEX

Cornelissen, Broer, see Van Slyck, Cornelis Anthonissen
Cornelissen, Claes, death, 73
Cornelissen, Cornelis, see Van Sterrenvelt, Cornelis Cornelissen
Cornelissen, Gysbert, widow, 27
Cornelissen, Jacques, see Van Slyck, Jacques Cornelissen
Cornelissen, Pieter, special attorney, 75
Cornelissen, Poulus, 55
Cortelyou (Coutillau), Jacques, 34
Costers, Antony, 162; wife, 161
Coxsackie (Coxhachy, Koxhaghje), 130, 134
Cregier, Annatie, 186, 187, 188
Cregier, Elizabeth, 186, 187
Cregier, Geertruy, 186, 187
Cregier, Jannetje, will, 185
Cregier, Martin, widow, 185
Cregier, Martynus, son of Martin Cregier, 186, 188
Cregier, Samuel, 186, 187, 188
Crooked creek, 190
Croon, Dirck Jansen, house and lot, 7; power of attorney from, 110; mentioned, 52, 106; witness, 12, 66
Cruyff, Eldert Gerbertsen, 79; farm at Catskill, 100
Cuyler, Abraham, witness, 159
Cuyler, Johannes, justice, 139, 163; wife, 161; witness, 148, 149, 159, 172

Danielsen, Arent, 149; witness, 150
Dareth, Jan, buys lot, 39; purchase of cannon from, 67, 69; purchase of gun barrels from, 67; house and lot, 72; power of attorney from, 74; deed of garden to, 104; deed from, 105; mentioned, 92
Dareth, Joost, 74
Davids, Christopher (Kit), 55
De Boer, Cornelis Cornelissen, see Cornelissen, Cornelis
De Brouwer, Jacob, 96
Deep Valley creek, 175
De Forest (Foreest), Isaack, 29
De Graff, Jan Andriessen, bondsmen for, 23

De Groot, Jan, 53; sale of land, 90
De Hinse, Jacob, 7; house and lot, 65
De Hooges, Antony, 44
De Hoop (sloop), 24
De Hulter, Johanna, bond of Cornelis Vos to, 49; bond of Teunis Slingerlant to, 49; special attorney, 63; mentioned, 67, 81, 101
De Hulter, Johannes, widow, 49, 50; conditions of sale of land, 101
De Laet, Johanna, see De Hulter, Johanna
De Laet, Johannes, daughter, 49
De Lancey, Pieter Stephen, 199, 202
De Lanoy, Abraham, 53
De Maecker, Pieter, surety, 37; special attorney, 42; house and lot, 47, 52, 64; bond of, 59; sale of house and lot, 106; mentioned, 55
De More (D'More), Phillip, 123
De Peyster, John, 185, 196, 199, 202; witness, 188, 198
De Vos, Andries, power of attorney from, 34
De Vos, Cornelis, see Vos, Cornelis
De Vos, Mattheus, 111
De Wandelaer, Adriaen, 156
De Wandelaer, Alida, 155, 156
De Wandelaer, Andries, 155, 156
De Wandelaer, Anna, 155, 156
De Wandelaer, Catharina, 155, 156
De Wandelaer, Johannes, 155, 156; witness, 179
De Wandelaer, Johannes, senior, will, 154
De Wandelaer, Pieter, 156; witness, 179
De Wandelaer, Sara, 155, 156
De Winter, Bastiaen, public sale of personal property, 78
De Witt, Tierck Claessen, lease of house, 86; sale of horse and cart, 90
Dingeman, Adam, will, 165
Dircks, Susanna, 46
Dircksen, Dirck, power of attorney from, 48
Dircks, Susanna, 46
Dircksen, Jan, see Van Bremen, Jan Dircksen

Dircksen, Luycas, 112
Dircksen, Poulus, 54, 78, 79
Dongan, Gov. Thomas, 139, 162
Douw (Dow), Grietie Volkertsen, 147
Douw, Jonas Volkertsen, 131, 134, 148
Douw (Dow), Petrus, 148, 179
Douw, Volckert Jansen, surety, 109; mentioned, 38, 78, 79, 80
Dyckman, Johannes, 103

Ebbing (Ebbingh, Ebbinck), Jeronimus, bond of Willem Brouwer to, 84; mentioned, 50, 101
Ebbing, Johanna, 49, 50, 101. See also De Hulter, Johanna
Eerraets (Eerrats, Eerraerts, Eeraerts), Johannes, testimony of, 73; witness, 18, 19, 20, 74
Egberts, Egbertie, will, 117
Egbertsen, Barent, witness, 181
Elbertsen, Reyer, sells house and lot, 12; bondsman, 28; mentioned, 53, 54, 112
Engel, Robbert, 54
Esopus, 101, 128

Falckner (Valkenaer), Rev. Justus, wife, 175
Fonda, Hendrick, 180, 181
Fonda, Jellis, 146
Fox kill, 9
Fredericksen, Carsten, deed from, 91; garden lot, 91; release of property, 92; deed to Van Aecken referred to, 92; mentioned, 78, 79, 92
Fredericksen, Meyndert, garden lot, 91; release of patent to, 92; deed to Van Aecken referred to, 92; mentioned, 72
Fredericksen, Willem, see Bout, Willem Fredericksen
Fuyck, 7

Gansevoort, Harmen, 185.
Gardenier, Andries, 123; will, 157
Gardenier, Andries, junior, 157
Gardenier, Arye, 158
Gardenier, Eytje, 157

Gardenier, Hendrick, widow, 123
Gardenier, Jacob, 157
Gardenier, Jacob Jansen, 124
Gardenier, Samuel, appointed guardian, 158
Gauw, Jan, see Gouw, Jan
Gerard, Philip, widow of, 111
Gerardi, Jan, 111
Gerbertsen, Eldert, see Cruyff, Eldert Gerbertsen
Gerretsen, Adriaen, see Van Papendorp, Adriaen Gerritsen
Gerritse, Elisabeth, 150
Gerritsen, Albert, deed from, 34; power of attorney from, 35; deed of garden, 41; bond of, 46; proposed sale of house and lot, 94; account of, 94; witness, 46
Gerritsen, Barent, surety, 81
Gerritsen, Cornelis, see Van den Bergh, Cornelis Gerritsen
Gerritsen, Goosen, see Van Schaick, Goosen Gerritsen
Gerritsen, Gysbert, see Van Brakel, Gysbert Gerritsen
Gerritsen, Hendrick, see Vermeulen, Hendrick Gerritsen
Gerritsen, Luykas, 145
Gerritsen, Marten, see Van Bergen, Marten Gerritsen
Gevick, Jacob, see Hevick, Jacob
Gilbert (Gilbertsen), Jan, 122
Glen (Glenn), Antje Sanders, 124, 126
Glen (Glenn), Jacob, 125, 187; major, 192
Glen (Glenn), Johannes, appointed guardian, 120; mentioned, 125, 126
Glen (Glenn), Sander, son of Johannes Glen, 125, 126
Glen (Glenn), Captain Sander, will, 124
Glen, Sander Leendertsen, deposition of, 26; deed from, 98; mentioned, 65; witness, 114
Goes, Anna, 173
Goes, Dirck, will, 172
Goes, Elizabeth, 172
Goes, Jan Tysen, 151; witness, 174
Goes, Johannes, 173

INDEX

Goes, Luyckas, 173
Gouw (Gauw), Jan, witness, 77
Greenbush, 20, 100
Groenewout, Juriaen Jansen, *see* Van Groenewout, Juriaen Jansen
Groesbeeck, Claes Jacobsen, 112
Groodt, Symon, 53
Gysbertsen, Gerrit, 123; witness, 139

Halenbeck, Abram, land of, 182
Halenbeck, Dirk, witness, 166
Halenbeck, Willem, witness, 166
Halenbeck, family, land of, in Loonenburg patent, 204
Hanse, Gerritje, 118
Hansen, Andries, 118
Hansen, Hendrick, witness, 156
Hardenberg, Jan, money due estate of, 35
Hardick, Francis, will, 174
Hardick, Gerritje, 175
Hardick, Jan, 175
Hardick, Sarah, 175
Hardick, Volkje, 176
Hardick, Willem, 175, 176
Harmense, Dirkje, 118
Harmensen, Bastian, 118
Harmensen, Frederick, witness, 58
Harmensen, Jan, sells house and lot, 59; mentioned, 79, 80
Harmensen, Jan, junior, deed of lot to, 91
Harmensen, Myndert, witness, 119
Hartgers, Pieter, house and lot, 10, 40; debt of Femmetie Albers to, 42; special attorney, 50; deed of house to, 100; mentioned, 84; witness, 30, 31, 39, 43, 45, 47, 58, 63, 64, 67, 68, 99, 104, 105, 106
Helmsen, Jan, buys hops, 80
Hendricksen, Andries, will, 121
Hendricksen, Claes, 33, 70, 96, 97
Hendricksen, Hendrick, 31
Hendricksen, Jacob, bond of Van Twiller to, 73; power of attorney from, 77
Hendricksen, Jan, *see* Van Bael, Jan Hendricksen
Hendricksen, Marten, proposed sale of house and lot, 93

Hendricksen, Philip, surety, 52; bond of, 107; mentioned, 112
Herberdingh, Jan, appointed guardian, 144
Herbertsen, Andries, surety, 28, 61, 73, 85, 86, 89, 114; mentioned, 14, 54, 68; witness, 33, 113
Herder, Pieter Pietersen, 98
Hevick (Gevinck), Jacob, patent, 31; wife, 32
Hillebrant, Nicolaes Gregory, charges against, 69
Hoffman, Catharina, 194
Hoffman, Petrus, widow, 194
Hofmeyer (Hoffemeyer), Willem, deed from, 18; mentioned, 22
Hogen, William, wife, 137
Hoogeboom, Adriaentje (Arriantie), 183
Hoogeboom, Bartholomeus, 182, 183, 184
Hoogeboom, Catryntie, 182, 183
Hoogeboom, Cornelis, 182
Hoogeboom, Geertruy, 183, 184
Hoogeboom, Hilletie, 182, 183
Hoogeboom, Jeremias, 183, 184
Hoogeboom, Johannes, 183, 184
Hoogeboom, Marytie, 183, 184
Hoogeboom, Pieter, will, 182
Hoogeboom, Peter, grandson of Pieter Hoogeboom, 182
Hoogeboom, Rachel, 182
Hues, Willem Martensen, buys sloop, 25; sureties for, 26
Hun, Harmen Thomassen, wife, 32
Hunter, Governor Robert, 163

Jacobse, Catelnytie, 138
Jacobsen, Caspar, 78
Jacobsen, Claes, *see* Groesbeeck, Claes Jacobsen
Jacobsen, Cornelis, *see* Van Oossanen, Cornelis Jacobsen
Jacobsen, Harmen, sloop, 37
Jacobsen, Harpert, 138
Jacobsen, Jan, special attorney, 98
Jacobsen, Pieter, *see* Borsboom, Pieter Jacobsen
Jacobsen, Rutger, *see* Van Schoonderwoert, Rutger Jacobsen

Jacobsen, Teunis, *see* Van Schoonderwoert, Teunis Jacobsen
Jans, Anneke, *see* Bogardus, Anneke Jans
Jans, Antie, first wife of Gerrit Teunissen Van Vechten, 147
Jans, Maritien, special attorney, 45, 48
Jansen, Aasuerus, 169
Jansen, Annetie, 168; wife of Marcelis Jansen, 168
Jansen, Arent, power of attorney from, 24; witness, 48
Jansen, Carel, house and lot, 37, 47, 52, 64; power of attorney from, 42; mentioned, 55
Jansen, Cobus, 32, 54
Jansen, Dirck, 47
Jansen, Evert, witness, 156
Jansen, Gysbrecht, 169
Jansen, Harmen, 53, 54
Jansen, Helmer, 134; witness, 139
Jansen, Hendrick, *see* Van Bremen, Hendrick Janssen
Jansen, Huybert, deed of lot to, 30; deed from, 31
Jansen, Huybertje, 169
Jansen, Jacobus, buys house, 32
Jansen, Jan, the miller, 123. *See also,* Van Otterspoor, Jan Jansen
Jansen, Jonathan, *see* Witbeck, Jonathan Jansen
Jansen, Judith, 169
Jansen, Jurriaen, 78
Jansen, Lourens, garden lot, 91
Jansen, Marcelis, deed of house and lot to, 57; will, 168; mentioned, 15
Jansen, Michiel, ancestor of Vreeland family, 111; witness, 111
Jansen, Pieter, a soldier from Stockholm, power of attorney from, 87
Jansen, Rem, bond of, 23; sale of property, 36; deposition of, 67; power of attorney from, 87, 104; sale of house, etc., 108; mentioned, 54, 105
Jansen, Roelof, *see* Van Masterlant, Roelof Jansen
Jansen, Steven, *see* Coninck, Steven Jansen

Jansen, Stoffel, *see* Abeel, Stoffel Jansen
Jansen, Symon, *see* Romeyn, Symon Jansen
Jansen, Sytje, 169
Jansen, Thomas, *see* Mingael, Thomas Jansen
Jansen, Volckert, *see* Douw, Volckert Jansen
Jansen, Willem, special attorney, 24
Jochemsen, Hendrick, house, 17; bond of, 65; mentioned, 53, 69, 73, 79, 80; witness, 26, 65
Jochimsen, Tryn, 78
Joosten, Jan, deposition of, 67

Kalier, *see* Collier
Ketelhuyn (Keteluyn), Jochim, 18, 22, 69
Ketelheyn, Willem, 126
Keyser, Dirck Dircksen, power of attorney from, 70
Kieft, Director General Willem, 50
Kinderhook, 121, 152, 153, 157, 172, 194
Kinderhook kill, 162
Kip, Abraham, 123
Klein (Cleyn), Ulderick, sells house and lot, 51; bond of, 55
Knickerbacker, Cornelia, 167
Knickerbacker, Cornelis, 167
Knickerbacker, Elizabeth, 167
Knickerbacker, Evert, 167
Knickerbacker, Harmen, witness, 181
Knickerbacker, Harmen Jansen, will, 166
Knickerbacker, Johannes, 167, 168, 180
Knickerbacker, Lowrens, 167, 168
Knickerbacker, Pieter, 167
Knistageione, *see* Niskayuna
Konyn, *see* Conyn
Kranckheyt, Seybout, witness, 196

Labatie, Jan, house and lot, 65; bond and mortgage of, 114
Lambertsen, Jan, conditions of sale of house and lot, 110; witness, 25, 34
La Montagne, Johannes, 3, 79

INDEX

Lansing, Hendrick, junior, 167
Lansing, Jan, 137
Lansing, Jannetie, 167
Lasher (Lissjer), Johannes, wife, 161
Leendertsen, Casper, 130, 145, 146
Leendertsen, Gabriel, garden lot, 91
Leendertsen, Sander, *see* Glen, Sander Leendertsen
Legget, Christina, 163
Levi, Asser, deposition of, 71
Lewis (Lewisse), Livynes, appointed guardian, 181
Lievese, Maritje, 118
Lievesen, Harmen, 118
Lissjer, Johannes, *see* Lasher, Johannes
Livingston (Livingstone), Philip, junior, 174, 176
Livingston, Robert, 119, 129, 159, 161, 166
Livingston manor, 159, 166
Loockermans, Govert, attorney, 35, 40; debt of Femmetie Alberts to, 39; special attorney, 58; attorney for estate of Jan Van Hardenbergh, 62
Loockermans (Lokermans), Jacob, 138, 145
Loockermans, Jacob Jansen, garden, 60; conditions of public sale of house and lot, 68, 111; mentioned, 78
Loockermans, Pieter, mentioned, 30, 31, 94
Loonenburgh, 204
Lounhard, Pieter, witness, 185
Lourensen, Lourens, mentioned, 11
Lourensen, Pieter, sale of sloop, 24
Lucassen (Luykassen), Jan, 124, 126
Lydius (Lydious), John H., witness, 205
Lydius (Lydious), Martin, witness, 205

Maby, Abraham, 191
Marcelis (Marseles), Myndert, witness, 170
Martensen, Hendrick, 138
Martensen, Jacob, witness, 122

Martensen, Jan, sloop bought by, 24; bond and mortgage of, 76, 82; mentioned, 9
Martensen, Poulous, *see* Van Benthuysen, Poulous Martensen
Martensen, Willem, *see* Hues, Willem Martensen; Moore, Willem Martensen
Metselaer, Teunis Teunissen, *see* Teunissen, Teunis
Meyer, Jillis Pietersen, house and lot, 8; surety, 10; mentioned, 8, 22
Meyndersen, Barent, buys house, 33; mentioned, 33, 112
Michiels, Jannetie, 140
Mill creek, 20, 200
Mingael (Mingaal), Johannes, executor, 165; witness, 156, 165
Mingael, Maritien, 31
Mingael, Thomas Jansen, bond of, 26; to sell house, 27; deed of lot to, 31; widow, 31, 32; daughter, 32; surety, 60; mentioned, 53, 54, 93
Mohawk river, 190
Moore (Moer), Willem Martensen, 53
Moree, Pieter, 73
Mulder, Jan Pieters, witness, 98
Muller, Peter, witness, 201
Mutsjes kill, 157
Mynders, Neeltje, 131, 134
Myndertsen, Johannes, witness, 150

Niskayuna (Knistageione), 186

Oak Tree (sloop), 37
Obe, Hendrick Hendricksen, sale of sloop, 28
Osterhout, Gysbert, witness, 166

Pastoor, Frans Barentsen, sale of slaughter excise to, 82
Pels, Evert, sale of sawmills, 20; deed from Bout to, 20; house, 21; deed from referred to, 21; power of attorney from, 98; deed of house and lot to, 99

Pietersen, Claes, witness, 71
Pietersen, Jan, witness, 33, 42
Pietersen, Jillis, see Meyer, Jillis Pietersen
Pietersen, Nataniel, witness, 23, 33, 51, 74
Pietersen, Philip, surety, 10, 15
Pile, Pieter, witness, 168
Ploeg, Jan, witness, 168
Pollet, Marie, 111
Pootman (Pottmann), Johannes, 123
Potter, Cornelis Martensen, sale of negroes, 112
Poulussen, Michiel, surety for, 23; the carter, 54
Powell (Poulussen, Pouwel), Thomas, deed from, 56; mentioned, 54, 78, 79, 80, 112
Provoost, Johannes, 3, 4, 54, 80; witness, 10, 11, 13, 14, 15, 18, 20, 23, 24, 25, 26, 28, 52, 58, 60, 61, 62, 63, 65, 71, 72, 74, 76, 77, 81, 82, 85, 87, 88, 90, 91, 95, 98, 104, 107
Pruyn, Casparus, 198

Radcliff, Jochem, wife, 182, 183
Rees, Jonathan, wife, 175
Rees, Leendert, wife, 176
Reyndersen, Barent, mentioned, 33, 78, 79
Rinckhout, Daniel, power of attorney from, 27; assignment from Slingerlant to, 63
Ripsen, Claes, see Van Dam, Claes Ripsen
Robens (Robinson?), Samuel, 182
Roelofsen, Jan, buys house and lot, 10; conveys to Pieter Hartgers, 10; son of Anneke Jans, 10; garden, 41, 60; deed from, 100; mentioned, 58; witness, 35
Romeyn, Symon Jansen, 35; special attorney, 87
Roseboom, Jacob, witness, 205
Roseboom, Johannes, witness, 159
Rosevelt, Claes, 123
Rutsen, Jacob, 170
Rutsen, John, 170

Rutten kill, 7, 40
Rycken, Lysbet, 74
Rycken, Reynier, bond of Klein to, 55
Ryckman, Albert, inventory of estate of Jan Cock, 137; appointed guardian, 152; justice, 150, 153; witness, 130
Ryckman, Gerritje, 119
Ryverdinck, Pieter, surety, 115

Salisbury, Capt. Sylvester, patent, 134
Sanders, Annetje, see Glen, Antje Sanders
Sanders, Elisabeth, 144, 145
Sanders, John, witness, 192
Sandersen, Egbert, witness, 48
Sandersen, Robert, witness, 145
Saratoga (Sarachtoge), 161
Schaets (Scaets), Rev. Gideon, 38; wife, 79
Schaghticoke (Schagtekoek), 179
Schenectady (Schonhectade, Schoneetendy), 123, 137, 149, 189
Schermerhorn, Jacob, witness, 170
Schermerhorn, Jacob Jansen, 18, 21, 22, 79; witness, 73
Schermerhorn, Reyer Jacobsen, 53, 54
Schodack (Shotak), 123
Schoonmaker, Egbert, 170
Schutt, Willem Jansen, 78, 80, 111
Schuyler, Abraham, wife, 161, 171; will, 171
Schuyler, Abraham, junior, 171
Schuyler (Shuyler), Arent, 123
Schuyler, Christyna, 171
Schuyler, David, brother of Abraham Schuyler, 172; witness, 149
Schuyler, David, son of Abraham Schuyler, 171
Schuyler, Dirck, 171
Schuyler, Geertruy, 161, 171
Schuyler, Jacobus, 171
Schuyler, John, justice, 150, 153
Schuyler, Myndert, 166, 172, 176, 179, 181, 189, 193

Schuyler, Philip Pietersen, special attorney, 19, 70; receipt of, 71; surety, 73, 115; conditions of public sale of house, 109; mentioned, 18, 22; witness, 12, 150
Schuyler, Pieter, 161; appointed guardian, 120; witness, 133, 135
Scott, William, witness, 163
Servaes, Tys, testimony of, 73
Sickles (Seckels, Seeckels), Zacharias, account of, 24; witness, 24, 34, 42, 51, 111
Siversen, Claes, 132, 134, 135
Slingerlant, Albert, executor, 165; witness, 165
Slingerlant, Arent, will, 163
Slingerlant, Engeltie, 164
Slingerlant, Geertruy, 164
Slingerlant, Gerrit, 164, 165
Slingerlant, Sarah, 165
Slingerlant, Teunis, son of Arent Slingerlant, 164, 165
Slingerlant, Teunis Cornelissen, house and lot, 43, 96; house, proposed sale, 44; bond and mortgage of, 49, 66; bond of Femmetie Alberts to, 63
Soundhard, Pieter, witness, 184
Spoor, Jan, 123
Spoor, Nicolas, wife, 204; appointed executor, 204
Staets (Staas), Abraham, deposition of, 69; house and lot, 97; witness, 27, 36, 40, 43, 49, 58, 67, 68, 71, 93, 103
Staets, Surgeon Jacob, witness, 121
Steenwyck, Cornelis, attorney, 91; bond of Vermeulen to, 113
Stevensen, Abraham, 73
Stighcook, 204
Stol, Jacob Jansen, 63
Stol, Willem Jansen, deed from, 30; mentioned, 31
Stuyvesant, Director General Peter, 18, 87, 103
Swart, Cornelis, witness, 169, 170
Swartwout, Roelof, garden, 38; sale of lots, 38; bond and mortgage of, 62; mentioned, 44

Switts, Isaak, witness, 126
Symons, Marritien, 98
Symonsen, Adriaen, bond of Albert Gerritsen to, 46; deposition of, 67; mentioned, 53, 54; witness, 46
Symonsen, Pieter, power of attorney from, 71
Symonsen, Volkert, 150

Tadens (Tates), Michiel, witness, 35
Tappen, Jurriaen Teunissen, sells house and lot, 9; sale of hops, 80; proposed sale of land, 81; sale of land, 90; house brought of, 100; conditions of sale of house and lot, 107; mentioned, 54, 78
Teller (Teljer), Willem, 26, 80, 99, 125
Ten Broeck, Catalyntje, 161
Ten Broeck, Christyna, 160, 161, 163
Ten Broeck, Cornelia, 161
Ten Broeck, Dirck Wessels, appointed guardian, 120, 152, 181; grants certificate of probate, 143, 150, 153; will, 159; witness, 130, 135, 152, 176, 181
Ten Broeck, Elisabeth, 161
Ten Broeck, Elsje, 161
Ten Broeck, Geertruy, 161
Ten Broeck, Johannes, 160, 161, 162
Ten Broeck, John, witness, 205
Ten Broeck, Lidia, 161
Ten Broeck, Samuel, 160, 161, 172; witness, 176
Ten Broeck, Tobias, 160, 161
Ten Broeck, Wessel, 160, 161, 172; witness, 148, 149, 152
Ten Eyck, Johannes, witness, 184
Teunise, Anna, 118
Teunise, Willemtie, 118
Teunissen, Cobus, 112
Teunissen, Cornelis, *see* Van Westbroeck, Cornelis Teunissen Bos; Van Slyck, Cornelis Anthonissen
Teunissen, Egbert, 118
Teunissen, Gerrit, *see* Van Vechten, Gerrit Teunissen

Teunissen, Jan, inventory of property, 57; sells house and lot, 60; sells garden, 94; deed from, 95
Teunissen, Martyn, 118
Teunissen, Teunis (Metselaer), buys house, 27, 28; special attorney, 77; sale of hops, 80; proposed sale of land, 81; sale of land, 90; will, 117; mentioned, 53; witness, 74
Thomassen, Jan, *see* Witbeck, Jan Thomassen
Thomassen, Willem, skipper, delivery of beavers to, 26
Turck, Jacobus, witness, 154
Tymonsen, Pieter, 54
Tyssen, Jacques, mortgage of house, 35
Tyssen, Jan, *see* Goes, Jan Tysen

Valkenaer, Domine Justus, *see* Falckner, Rev. Justus
Van Aecken, Jan Coster, surety, 52; bond of, 59; deed from referred to, 72; deed to referred to, 92; attorney, 106; mentioned, 53, 54, 55, 78, 79, 80, 91, 92, 105
Van Alen, Johannes, wife, 161; witness, 154
Van Alen (Alle), Laurence, land at Kinderhook, 151; wife, 183; witness, 137
Van Alstyne, Catharina, 194, 195
Van Alstyne, Lambarth, 194, 195
Van Alstyne, Maria, 194, 195
Van Alstyne, Peter, 194, 195
Van Alstyne, Thomas, will, 193
Van Alstyne, William, 193, 194, 195
Van Bael, Jan Hendricksen, 51, 54, 56; witness, 109
Van Benthuysen, Poulus Martensen, power of attorney from, 63
Van Bergen, Gerrit, 131
Van Bergen, Marten Gerritsen, appointed administrator of Pieter Winne's estate, 128; will, 130; inventory of estate, 134; appointed guardian, 142; witness, 129
Van Bergen, Myndert, 131
Van Bergen, Neeltje, 133, 134

Van Bockhoven, Claes, 54; buys land, 90
Van Bommel, Hendrick, deed of house and lot to, 29
Van Brakel, Elisabeth, 150
Van Brakel, Gerrit Gysbertsen, 149
Van Brakel, Gysbert, 149
Van Brakel, Gysbert Gerritsen, will, 149
Van Bremen, Hendrick Janssen, 88, 104, 146
Van Bremen, Jan Dircksen, deed from, 100; account of, 101; deed of land to, 103; mentioned, 58
Van Bruggen, Carel, 18, 19, 87
Van Brugh, Pieter, 139, 166, 170; witness, 172
Van Buren, Catelina Martense, 151
Van Buren, Cornelia Martense, 151
Van Buren, Magdalena Martense, 151
Van Buren, Maria Martense, 151
Van Buren, Marten Cornelissen, will, 151
Van Buren, Marten Martensen, 151, 153
Van Buren, Peter Martensen, 151, 153
Van Buren, Tobias Cornelissen, 151; wife, 173
Van Curler, Arent, fire in house of, 68
Van Dam, Claes Ripsen, buys house and lot, 10, 15
Van den Bergh (Van den Berch), Arent, power of attorney from, 19; mentioned, 16; witness, 104
Van den Bergh, Claas, 198
Van den Bergh, Cornelis C., 198
Van den Bergh, Cornelis Gerritsen, wife, 151
Van den Bergh, Gerrit C., 178, 179; witness, 196
Van den Bergh, Margrieta, 178
Van den Hoeck, Arent Isaacksen, house leased to, 86
Van den Uythoff, Wouter Albertsen, deed of house and lot to, 45; witness, 142

Van der Heyden, Jacob Tyssen, 22
Van der Volgen, Lawrence, 191
Van der Zee, Storm Albertsen, attorney for Teunis Slingerlant, 96
Van Deusen, Matheus Abrahamsen, 78, 79
Van Deusen, Robert, wife, 151
Van Dyck, Arent, witness, 174
Van Dyck, Cornelis, 134; appointed administrator of Pieter Winne's estate, 128; witness, 119, 129
Van Dyck, Stephen, witness, 201
Van Eeckelen, Jan, 46, 55, 78, 79, 94
Van Groenewout, Juriaen Jansen, 31
Van Gutsenhoven, Bastiaen Jansen, bond of Slingerlant to, 66
Van Hamel, Dirck, witness, 63
Van Hardenberch (Van Hardenbergh), Jan, money due estate of, 40, 62
Van Harstenhorst, Hendrick Hendricksen, 32
Van Hoesen, Casper, executor, 165; witness, 165
Van Ilpendam, Adriaen Jansen, patent to, 18; deed of lot and garden to, 22; mentioned, 4, 54, 80, 122, 127
Van Imborch, Surgeon Gysbert, witness, 76
Van Lingen, Jan Bembo, see Bembo, Jan
Van Marle, Barent, 54; debt of Cornelis Vos to, 39
Van Masterlant, Roelof Jansen, 10, 100
Van Neften (Nesten), Pieter Pietersen, attorney, 28
Van Ness, Gerrit, 145
Van Ness, Mayken, 53
Van Ness, Willem, wife, 183, 184
Van Nieukerck, Wouter Aertsen, 56
Van Noortstrant, Jacob Jansen, deed from, 43
Van Olinda, Daniel, wife, 186, 187
Van Olinda, Maritie, 187
Van Oossanen (Oostsanen), Cornelis Jacobsen, power of attorney from, 75; witness, 73

Van Oossanen, Jan Claessen Backer, power of attorney from, 76; public sale of hats and furniture, 112; witness, 72
Van Oossanen, Jan Harmsen Backer, 78, 79
Van Otterspoor, Jan Jansen, sale of hops on land of, 80; conditions of public sale of land, 81
Van Papendorp, Adriaen Gerritsen, mentioned, 77, 80, 94, 95; witness, 36, 41, 44, 48, 49, 55, 56, 57, 70, 75, 83, 84, 92, 99, 100
Van Petten, Frederick (Vredrhek), witness, 192
Van Rensselaer, Henry, 201
Van Rensselaer, Jeremias, payments to, 48; bond of Cornelis Vos to, 55; mentioned, 94, 96, 187
Van Rensselaer (Rencelaer), Johan Baptist, buys house and lot, 13; surety, 14; attorney for Jan Labatie and Jacob de Hinse, 65; special attorney, 74
Van Rensselaer, Killiaen, 138; witness, 135
Van Rensselaer, Stephanus, witness, 188
Van Schaick, Cornelis, witness, 174
Van Schaick, Goosen Gerritsen, buys house and lot, 11; surety, 13; deed of house and lot, 57; bond of, 107; mentioned, 75, 94
Van Schaick, Livinus, 136; witness, 133
Van Schoonderwoert, Rutger Jacobsen, surety, 10, 32, 85, 86, 89, 114; house built by, 32; sale of sloop, 37; deposition of, 69; deed from, 75; deed of garden to, 105; mentioned, 33, 70, 105
Van Schoonderwoert, Teunis Jacobsen, see Van Woert, Teunis Jacobsen
Van Slichtenhorst (Slechtenhorst), Gerrit, buys house and lot, 14
Van Slyck, Cornelis Anthonissen, 79, 120
Van Slyck, Fytie, 120

Van Slyck, Geertruyt, 120
Van Slyck, Grietje, 120
Van Slyck, Helena, 120
Van Slyck, Herman, 119, 120
Van Slyck, Jacques Cornelissen, will, 119
Van Slyck, Lidia, 120
Van Slyck, Marte, 120
Van Slyck, Susanna, 120
Van Sterrenvelt, Cornelis Cornelissen, surety, 15; bond of, 23; deed from, 56; buys house and lot, 106; mentioned, 23
Van Twiller, Aert Goosen, bond of, 73
Van Twiller, Jan, 21
Van Valckenburg, Abraham, wife, 203, 204
Van Valckenburg (Valckenburgh), Jochem, wife, 183, 184
Van Valckenburg (Valckenborch), Lambert, power of attorney from, 58; wife, 204; appointed executor, 204; mentioned, 18, 22
Van Vechten, Abraham, 140
Van Vechten (Van Veghten), Albertus, 203, 204
Van Vechten, Angenietje, 178
Van Vechten, Anna, 180, 181
Van Vechten, Annetie, 140
Van Vechten, Benjamin, 181
Van Vechten (Van Veghte), Catarina, 204, 205
Van Vechten (of Lonenburg), Dirck, will, 202
Van Vechten (of Schaghticoke), Dirck, 177, 179; will, 179
Van Vechten (Van Veghten), Dirck, son of Albertus Van Vechten, 203
Van Vechten, Dirck Teunissen, will, 139
Van Vechten, Ephraim, 178
Van Vechten (Van Veghte), Eva, 203, 204, 205
Van Vechten, Fytie, 140
Van Vechten, Gerrit Teunissen, 131, 132, 134, 135, 177, 178; appointed guardian, 142; will, 146; witness, 152

Van Vechten, Harmen, 180, 181
Van Vechten (Van Veghte), Helena, 203, 204, 205
Van Vechten (Van Veghte), Hubertus, 203, 204, 205
Van Vechten, Jannetie, daughter of Dirck Teunissen Van Vechten, 140
Van Vechten, Jannetie, daughter of Dirck Van Vechten of Lonenburg, 203, 204, 205
Van Vechten, Jannetie Michiels, 140
Van Vechten, Johannes, son of Dirck Teunissen Van Vechten, 140
Van Vechten, Johannes, son of Gerrit Teunissen Van Vechten, 147
Van Vechten, Johannes, son of Volckert Van Vechten, 177, 178
Van Vechten, Leendert, 181
Van Vechten, Lidia, wife of Volckert Van Vechten, 161, 177
Van Vechten, Lidia, daughter of Ephraim Van Vechten, 178
Van Vechten, Margarita, 180, 181
Van Vechten (Van Veghte), Maria, 203, 204, 205
Van Vechten, Michiel, 140
Van Vechten, Neeltie, 140
Van Vechten, Philip, 181
Van Vechten, Samuel, 140
Van Vechten, Sara, daughter of Dirck Teunissen Van Vechten, 140
Van Vechten (Van Veghte), Sara, daughter of Dirck Van Vechten of Lonenburg, 203, 204, 205
Van Vechten (Van Veghte), Teunis, son of Dirck Van Vechten of Lonenburg, 203, 204
Van Vechten, Teunis, son of Dirck Van Vechten of Schaghticoke, 180, 181
Van Vechten, Teunis, son of Dirck Teunissen Van Vechten, 140
Van Vechten, Teunis Dircksen, house and lot, 16
Van Vechten, Volkert, 147; wife, 161; will, 177
Van Vechten, Volkert, grandson of testator, 177, 178
Van Vechten, Weyntie, 140

Van Velthuysen, Gysbert Philipsen, 11
Van Vleck, Tielman, special attorney, 110
Van Voorhout, Cornelis Cornelissen, 57
Van Voorhout, Cornelis Segersen, sells house and lot, 13; lot owned by, 14
Van Vranken, Ryckert, 198; witness, 198
Van Vranken (Francke), Ulderick, wife, 186, 187
Van Werckhoven, Cornelis, 34
Van Westbroeck, Cornelis Teunissen Bos, surety, 13, 14, 82; special attorney, 17; bond of, 26; buys house and lot, 61; mentioned, 81; witness, 86
Van Wie, Hendrick, will, 139; witness, 170
Van Wie (Wye), Jan, 157, 158
Van Woert, Ariaentie, 197
Van Woert, Jacob, brother of Pieter Van Woert, 197, 198
Van Woert, Jacob, nephew of Pieter Van Woert, 197, 198
Van Woert, Jacob Teunissen, 197
Van Woert, Lewis, 197, 198
Van Woert, Pieter, will, 197
Van Woert, Teunis, witness, 198
Van Woert, Teunis Jacobsen, surety, 11; power of attorney from, 17; mentioned, 53, 80, 197
Van Woggelum (Gemackelyck), Pieter Adriaensen, 53, 69
Van Wye, see Van Wie
Van Ysselsteyn, Marten Cornelissen, 151
Vedder, Albert, junior, 190, 191; witness, 192
Vedder, Angenietje, 191
Vedder, Antje, 191
Vedder, Arent, will, 189
Vedder, Corset, 191
Vedder, Elizabeth, 191
Vedder, Harmen, 189, 190, 191
Vedder, Harmen Albertsen, deed of house and lot to, 75; witness, 109
Vedder, Maria, 191
Vedder, Rebecca, 191
Vedder, Sarah, 189, 191
Vedder, Susanna, 191
Vedder, Symon, 190, 191, 192
Veeder, Myndert, 190
Verbeeck, Jan, 70; witness, 113, 114
Vermeulen, Hendrick Gerritsen, deed of lot to, 43; deed from, 43, 104; bond and mortgage, 113
Verveelen, Daniel, bond of Jan Martensen to, 76, 82; buys house and lot, 106; mentioned, 78, 80
Vinhaeghen (Vinhagel), Jan, sells house, 33; mentioned, 75
Visbeek, Gerrit, witness, 142
Visch (Vis), Jacob, bond of Jochemsen to, 65; special attorney, 104
Visscher, Harmen Bastiaensen, sells house and lot, 61
Visscher, Matthew, 196
Volkertsen, Jonas, see Douw, Jonas Volkertsen
Volckertsen, Symon, 35
Vonda, Jelles, see Fonda, Jellis
Vos, Cornelis, house and lot, 36; bond and mortgage, 39, 55; house, 42; deed from, 47; bond of, 49; mentioned, 7, 52, 64, 106
Vosburgh (Vosborgh), Abraham, 78, 96, 97
Vosburgh, Abraham Pietersen, daughter, 32
Vosburgh, Abram, junior, witness, 184
Vosburgh, Jan, witness, 163
Vosburgh, Pieter, 151; witness, 154, 163
Vreeland family, 111
Vreelandt, Enoch, 186, 187, 188
Vreelandt, Maria, 186, 187, 188
Vrooman, Adam, 123
Vrooman, Jan, 149
Vrooman, Pieter Meessen, house and lot, 16; bond of, 23
Wemp, Jan, 190
Wemp, Jan Barentsen, deed to referred to, 21; deed of lots to, 56; witness, 88

Wendel, Ephraim, 144
Wendel, Evert, junior, will, 143; witness, 122
Wendel, Evert Jansen, deed from, 29; wife, 32; witness, 145
Wendel, Johannes, appointed guardian, 144
Wendel, Robert, 144
Wendel, Susanna, 144
Wessels, Dirck, *see* Ten Broeck, Dirck Wessels
Wessels, Jochem, deed of lot to, 18; deed from, 22, 45; surety, 81; conditions of sale of house and lot, 108; mentioned, 8, 18
Westerkamp, Hendrick Jansen, widow, 39
Westerlo island, 134
Willemsen, Gerrit, witness, 19
Willemsen, Jan, witness, 86
Williams, Thomas, 156
Winding creek, 190
Winne, Adam, 128, 146
Winne, Daniel, 128, 145, 146
Winne, Eva, 128, 145
Winne, Frans, 128, 146
Winne, Jacob, 128, 146
Winne, Kiliaen, 128
Winne, Livinus, 128, 145, 146
Winne, Lyntje, 128
Winne, Marten, 128, 146
Winne, Pieter, will, 127; release of heirs of, for respective portions of their father's estate, 145; witness, 139

Winne, Pieter, junior, bequest to, 128; release of his share of mother's estate, 129
Winne, Rachell, 128
Winne, Teuntie, 146
Winne, Thomas, 128
Wisselpenningh, Reynier, 96, 113
Witbeck, Jan Thomassen, special attorney, 19; buys property, 36, 109; mentioned, 77, 78, 79, 95; witness, 27, 40, 41, 43, 44, 45, 48, 50, 55, 56, 57, 63, 64, 67, 69, 70, 83, 93, 98, 99, 100
Witbeck, Jannetje, 177
Witbeck, Jonathan Jansen, wife, 151
Withart, Johannes, surety, 32; house and lot, 40; mentioned, 84
Wyncoop, Cornelis, sells house and lot, 10; deed for property, 11; account of, 11; sells lot, 15; surety, 91
Wyncoop (Wynkook), Johannes, wife, 161
Wyngaert, Anna, will, 153
Wyngaert, Gerrit, 153
Wyngaert, Lucas Gerritsen, will, 153
Wyngaert, Luycas, 153
Wyngaert, Luycas Gerritsen, grandson of testator, 154
Wyngaert, Marya, 154

Yates, Robert, 205

Ziversen, Claes, 130